Sustainable Media

Green Lies and SJW Agendas

Billy-Bob Thompson

ISBN: 978-1-77961-460-5
Imprint: Holy Fuck Shut The Fuck Up
Copyright © 2024 Billy-Bob Thompson.
All Rights Reserved.

Contents

Definition and Importance of Sustainable Media   1

Historical Perspective   15
Evolution of Media Industry   15

Media and Environmental Impacts   31
Energy Consumption in Media Production   31
E-Waste and Consumer Electronics   47
Water Consumption in Media Production   62

Greenwashing and Media Manipulation   79
Understanding Greenwashing   79
Media Bias and Agenda-Setting   93

Social Justice Warrior (SJW) Agendas in Media   109
Understanding Social Justice Warrior (SJW) Movement   109
Cultural Appropriation and Media Representation   121
Intersectionality and Environmental Justice   132

Sustainable Media Practices and Solutions   145
Green Production Certifications and Standards   145
Sustainable Consumption of Media   158
Collaboration between Media Industry and Environmental Organizations   174

Conclusion   189
Recap of Sustainable Media Principles and Practices   189

Index   201

Definition and Importance of Sustainable Media

Understanding the concept of sustainability

Sustainability is a crucial concept that lies at the heart of efforts to address pressing environmental challenges and ensure a better future for our planet. In the context of media, sustainability refers to the principles and practices aimed at minimizing the negative impact of media production and consumption on the environment, society, and economy. It involves adopting strategies that promote long-term viability and ensure that our media practices are compatible with the needs of future generations.

To fully grasp the concept of sustainability, it is necessary to delve into its underlying principles and explore its various dimensions. Let's examine some key aspects of sustainability and how they relate to the media industry.

Environmental sustainability

Environmental sustainability focuses on protecting the natural environment and preserving ecological balance. Within the media industry, this means minimizing the use of non-renewable resources, reducing carbon emissions, preventing pollution, and safeguarding biodiversity.

For instance, media production processes, such as filming, editing, and broadcasting, often require substantial amounts of energy. To ensure environmental sustainability, media organizations can adopt energy-efficient technologies, utilize renewable energy sources, and implement measures to offset carbon emissions. By doing so, they can significantly reduce their ecological footprint and contribute to the overall goal of environmental preservation.

Social sustainability

Social sustainability emphasizes creating fair and inclusive societies that meet the needs of all individuals. In the context of media, this involves promoting diversity, inclusivity, and social justice. Media organizations have a responsibility to represent various perspectives, cultures, and voices, avoiding stereotypes and promoting accurate and respectful portrayals.

For example, media content should avoid cultural appropriation and ensure that it represents minority communities in a sensitive and authentic manner. By doing so, media can contribute to fostering understanding, empathy, and social cohesion.

Economic sustainability

Economic sustainability focuses on ensuring the long-term viability and stability of the media industry. This involves balancing economic growth with social and environmental concerns. Media organizations should strive for financial stability, innovation, and ethical business practices to sustain their operations over time.

For instance, adopting sustainable production practices can often result in cost savings in the long run. Additionally, diversifying revenue streams, embracing new technologies, and fostering collaborations with other industries can enhance the economic sustainability of media organizations.

Systems thinking

An essential aspect of understanding sustainability is embracing systems thinking. This approach recognizes that all elements within a system are interconnected and influence one another. In the context of media, this means understanding the complex relationships between media production, consumption, and societal behaviors.

By adopting a systems thinking perspective, media professionals can recognize their role in shaping public opinion, influencing behavior, and contributing to cultural phenomena. This understanding enables them to make informed decisions that support sustainability goals and avoid unintended negative consequences.

The three pillars of sustainability

To fully understand the concept of sustainability, it is important to consider the three pillars on which it rests: environmental, social, and economic sustainability. These pillars are interdependent and reinforce one another. Neglecting one pillar can undermine the overall sustainability of media practices.

When aiming for sustainability in media, it is essential to strike a balance between these pillars, ensuring that environmental concerns are addressed, social justice is promoted, and economic viability is maintained. This holistic approach is key to creating a media industry that is truly sustainable and able to contribute positively to society.

Key principles of sustainability

While understanding the concept of sustainability is important, it is equally crucial to identify the key principles that guide sustainable media practices. Let's explore some of these principles:

Long-term perspective

Sustainability requires a shift from short-term thinking to long-term planning. Instead of focusing solely on immediate gains, media organizations need to consider the long-term consequences of their actions. This involves considering the impacts on the environment, society, and the economy, both now and in the future.

Collaboration and partnerships

Addressing sustainability challenges in the media industry cannot be achieved by individual efforts alone. Collaboration and partnerships between media organizations, environmental experts, social justice advocates, and other stakeholders are fundamental to finding sustainable solutions. By working together, different actors can pool resources, share knowledge, and implement more effective strategies.

Transparency and accountability

Transparency and accountability are vital for sustainable media practices. Media organizations should be transparent about their environmental and social impact, disclosing relevant information to the public and stakeholders. Moreover, they need to take responsibility for their actions, acknowledging any negative consequences and working towards improvement.

Continuous improvement

Sustainability is not a one-time achievement; it is an ongoing process. Media organizations need to commit to continuous improvement by implementing sustainable practices, embracing innovative technologies, and adapting to changing circumstances. By constantly striving for improvement, they can remain at the forefront of sustainable media production and consumption.

Education and awareness

Promoting sustainability in the media industry requires educating and raising awareness among media professionals, audiences, and the wider public. By providing information on the environmental and social impact of media practices, as well as highlighting successful sustainability initiatives, media organizations can inspire others to adopt sustainable behaviors and advocate for positive change.

Challenges and opportunities

While the concept of sustainability offers immense opportunities for positive change in the media industry, it does not come without challenges. Let's explore some of the challenges and opportunities associated with sustainable media:

Technological advancements

Technological advancements provide opportunities for more sustainable media practices. For example, the shift from physical to digital media reduces the environmental impact associated with printing, distribution, and disposal. Additionally, innovative technologies, such as virtual reality and augmented reality, can be harnessed to educate audiences about sustainability and promote behavioral change.

However, technological advancements also pose challenges. The production and disposal of electronic devices contribute to e-waste, which raises concerns about resource depletion and pollution. Media organizations need to embrace technologies responsibly and consider the environmental implications throughout the life cycle of their products.

Changing consumer behavior

Consumer behavior plays a crucial role in driving sustainable media practices. As audiences become more aware of environmental and social issues, there is an increasing demand for media content that aligns with their values. Media organizations have the opportunity to cater to this demand by producing content that educates, inspires, and promotes sustainable behaviors.

However, changing consumer behavior is not without challenges. Media organizations need to strike a balance between catering to audience preferences and ensuring that sustainable content reaches a wide audience. They must also address the consumption patterns that perpetuate unsustainable media practices, such as excessive screen time or the constant need for the latest electronic devices.

Policy and regulation

Policy and regulation play a vital role in promoting sustainability in the media industry. Governments can create frameworks and incentives that encourage media organizations to adopt sustainable practices. For example, tax incentives for renewable energy use or stricter regulations on e-waste disposal can drive positive change.

However, policymakers and regulators also face challenges in keeping pace with the rapidly evolving media landscape. They need to adapt regulations to address emerging issues, such as data privacy and online misinformation, to ensure that sustainability concerns are adequately addressed.

Conclusion

Understanding the concept of sustainability is paramount for anyone interested in the media industry's role in addressing environmental and social challenges. By comprehending the principles of sustainability and recognizing the interconnectedness of environmental, social, and economic aspects, media professionals can drive positive change towards a more sustainable future.

The challenges and opportunities associated with sustainable media present a complex landscape. However, by embracing technological advancements, harnessing changing consumer behavior, and implementing effective policy and regulation, media organizations can play a pivotal role in promoting sustainable practices and inspiring a more conscious and responsible society. It is crucial to remember that sustainability is an ongoing process, requiring continuous learning, collaboration, and innovation.

Media's role in shaping public opinion and behavior

The media plays a significant role in shaping public opinion and behavior, as it has the power to influence the way people think, feel, and act. Through various forms like news, television, movies, advertising, and social media, the media has the ability to shape narratives and create awareness about social, political, and environmental issues. In this section, we will explore the ways in which the media influences public opinion and behavior and its implications for sustainability.

The persuasive power of media

Media has the persuasive power to shape public opinion by presenting information, ideas, and values in a way that influences viewers. Through news media and documentaries, the media can present facts, evidence, and expert opinions to inform public understanding of complex issues such as climate change, deforestation, or pollution. It can raise awareness about the urgency and importance of sustainability by highlighting the consequences of unsustainable practices.

Additionally, the media can shape public opinion through the portrayal of certain social, economic, or political ideas. By highlighting certain perspectives and downplaying others, the media can influence how people perceive specific issues. For example, media coverage that focuses on the economic benefits of renewable energy can shape public support for clean energy policies.

Agenda-setting and framing

Media not only influences what people think about but also what they think is important. Through agenda-setting, the media has the power to decide which issues receive significant attention and coverage, and which ones are marginalized or ignored. By emphasizing certain topics over others, the media can shape public perceptions and priorities.

Framing is another way in which the media influences public opinion. The media's choice of words, images, and narratives can shape how people understand and interpret an issue. For example, framing climate change as an urgent crisis may generate a sense of immediacy and promote action, whereas framing it as a distant or uncertain problem may lead to complacency.

Both agenda-setting and framing are important considerations when discussing sustainability issues. The media's choice to highlight or downplay environmental concerns can significantly impact public support for sustainable practices and policies.

Media as an agent of change

In addition to shaping public opinion, the media can also inspire and mobilize people to take action. Through storytelling, journalism, and documentaries, the media can create empathy and emotional connections with audiences, motivating them to make changes in their own lives or participate in collective action.

For example, a documentary exposing the devastating impact of plastic pollution in our oceans can lead viewers to reduce their plastic consumption and support initiatives to address the issue. A news story highlighting successful sustainable businesses can inspire entrepreneurs to adopt eco-friendly practices. By showcasing positive examples and highlighting success stories, the media can encourage individuals and communities to embrace sustainability.

The responsibility of media in promoting sustainability

With great power comes great responsibility. The media has a crucial role to play in promoting sustainability by providing accurate, balanced, and comprehensive coverage of environmental issues. Journalists and media organizations have the responsibility to fact-check information, avoid sensationalism, and present diverse perspectives.

Media outlets should also prioritize education and awareness by incorporating sustainability into their programming. They can feature stories on innovative sustainable practices, highlight the work of environmental advocates and organizations, and provide practical tips for individuals to adopt more sustainable lifestyles.

Furthermore, media organizations should strive for inclusivity and diversity in their content. By representing diverse voices and perspectives, the media can ensure a fair, comprehensive, and accurate portrayal of sustainability issues.

Case study: The role of social media in environmental activism

Social media has emerged as a powerful tool for environmental activism, allowing individuals and communities to share information, organize campaigns, and advocate for change. Platforms like Twitter, Facebook, and Instagram have been instrumental in mobilizing climate strikes, raising awareness about environmental issues, and pressuring corporations and governments to take action.

For example, the global youth-led movement Fridays for Future, started by Greta Thunberg, gained tremendous momentum and international attention through social media. Thunberg's powerful speeches and calls for urgent action against climate change were widely shared, leading to an increase in public awareness and engagement.

The role of social media in environmental activism illustrates the transformative potential of media in shaping public opinion and behavior. It shows how individuals can leverage the power of media to challenge the status quo, influence policy decisions, and drive sustainability initiatives.

Conclusion

The media's role in shaping public opinion and behavior cannot be underestimated. Through agenda-setting, framing, and persuasive storytelling, the media has the power to raise awareness about sustainability, inspire action, and mobilize communities. However, with this power comes the responsibility to provide accurate and balanced information, promote diverse perspectives, and prioritize sustainability in programming. By harnessing the potential of media, we can create a more sustainable future for all.

The need for sustainability in media production and consumption

Media plays a crucial role in shaping public opinion and behavior, and therefore, it holds a significant responsibility in promoting sustainable practices. As the world faces pressing environmental challenges, such as climate change and resource depletion, the media industry has a unique opportunity to contribute to the solution by prioritizing sustainability in both production and consumption. In this section, we will explore the reasons why sustainability is imperative in media and how it can be achieved.

Understanding the urgency of sustainability

The need for sustainability in media production and consumption arises from the urgent global environmental concerns that we face today. Climate change, overconsumption, pollution, and resource depletion are pushing our planet to its limits. As an industry that has a significant impact on the environment, the media cannot afford to ignore these challenges. Sustainable media practices are essential for conserving resources, reducing greenhouse gas emissions, and minimizing waste.

The environmental impact of media production

Media production processes, such as film and television production, have significant energy requirements and generate substantial carbon emissions. The use of energy-intensive equipment, transportation, and set constructions contribute to the carbon footprint of media production. Additionally, the production of consumer electronics and digital media devices consumes resources and contributes to electronic waste.

The power of media consumption

The environmental impact of media is not limited to production alone. Media consumption contributes to energy consumption, particularly in the case of digital media. Streaming, downloading, and viewing content online requires energy, primarily from data centers that power the internet. The increasing popularity of video streaming platforms and social media has resulted in a significant rise in energy consumption.

Promoting sustainable media production

To achieve sustainability in media production, various strategies can be employed. Firstly, the adoption of energy-efficient technologies and practices can significantly reduce the environmental impact of production processes. This includes using energy-efficient equipment, optimizing lighting and sound setups, and implementing efficient transportation logistics.

Secondly, the integration of renewable energy sources, such as solar or wind power, can help reduce the carbon footprint of media production. Investing in renewable energy infrastructure for film studios, television production facilities, and data centers can result in substantial carbon emissions reduction.

Thirdly, responsible waste management practices are crucial in media production. Implementing recycling programs, reducing plastic and packaging waste, and encouraging reusability can minimize the environmental impact of media sets, workshops, and offices.

Fostering sustainable media consumption

To promote sustainability in media consumption, it is essential to raise awareness among audiences about the environmental impact of their media choices. Educating viewers about the carbon footprint of streaming and downloading media, and encouraging energy-saving practices can make a significant difference. Furthermore, promoting sustainable alternatives to consumer electronics can help reduce electronic waste and resource consumption.

Media platforms can also play a significant role in promoting sustainable content consumption. By optimizing streaming technologies, investing in energy-efficient data centers, and supporting sustainable media projects, platforms can reduce their energy consumption and environmental impact.

Balancing sustainability and quality content

While embracing sustainability in media production and consumption is crucial, it is essential to strike a balance between sustainability and quality content. The focus should be on integrating sustainable practices without compromising creativity, innovation, and the artistic integrity of media productions. Embracing sustainability should be seen as an opportunity to explore new avenues, collaborate with eco-conscious creators, and engage with audiences on pressing environmental issues.

The role of stakeholders in promoting sustainability

Achieving sustainability in media production and consumption requires the collective effort of various stakeholders involved in the industry. Media companies, content creators, technology providers, policymakers, and consumers all play a role in promoting sustainable practices.

Media companies should prioritize sustainability in their business models, integrating it into their production processes, supply chains, and corporate strategies. Content creators have the power to shape narratives that promote sustainability, raise awareness, and inspire action.

Technology providers play a crucial role in developing energy-efficient devices, optimizing data centers, and providing sustainable solutions for media production and consumption. Policymakers can support sustainability through regulations, incentives, and frameworks that encourage eco-friendly practices in the media industry.

Lastly, consumers have the power to demand sustainable content and support media platforms and productions that prioritize sustainability. By consciously choosing sustainable media options and advocating for change, consumers can drive the industry towards more sustainable practices.

Conclusion

The need for sustainability in media production and consumption is clear. As an influential industry, the media has the power to shape public opinion and behavior. By embracing sustainable practices, media can contribute positively to environmental conservation, resource preservation, and climate change mitigation. Achieving sustainability requires a collective effort from all stakeholders, and it is our collective responsibility to ensure a more sustainable future for media.

Challenges and Opportunities in Promoting Sustainable Media

Promoting sustainable media comes with its own set of challenges and opportunities. In this section, we will explore the key obstacles that need to be addressed and the potential for positive change in the media industry.

Challenges

1. **Resistance to Change:** One of the major challenges in promoting sustainable media is the resistance to change within the industry. Many traditional media companies are hesitant to adopt sustainable practices due to concerns about cost,

competition, and potential disruptions to their existing production workflows. Overcoming this resistance requires a shift in mindset and the recognition that sustainability is not only crucial for the environment but also for the long-term viability of the industry itself.

2. **Lack of Awareness and Education:** Another challenge is the lack of awareness and education about sustainable media practices among industry professionals. Many media practitioners are unaware of the environmental impact of their work or the available sustainable alternatives. Therefore, there is a need for comprehensive training programs and educational initiatives that can raise awareness and provide practical guidance on sustainable media production and consumption.

3. **Complex Supply Chains:** The media industry relies on complex global supply chains, making it difficult to track and reduce the environmental impacts throughout the entire lifecycle of media products. From raw material extraction to manufacturing, distribution, and disposal, each stage contributes to carbon emissions, waste generation, and resource depletion. Addressing these challenges requires collaboration and transparency among all stakeholders involved in the media production process.

4. **Technological Limitations:** While technology has the potential to enable sustainable media practices, there are also limitations that need to be overcome. For example, green technologies such as renewable energy sources and energy-efficient equipment may require significant upfront investments, making them less accessible for smaller production companies or independent filmmakers. Developing scalable, affordable, and eco-friendly technological solutions is crucial for the wider adoption of sustainable media practices.

Opportunities

1. **Growing Consumer Demand:** There is a growing consumer demand for sustainable products and services across various industries, including media. This presents an opportunity for media companies to tap into a new market by producing and promoting eco-friendly content. By aligning their values with those of environmentally conscious audiences, media organizations can gain a competitive advantage and boost their brand reputation.

2. **Innovation and Creativity:** Promoting sustainable media requires innovation and creative thinking. Media professionals have the opportunity to explore new storytelling techniques, formats, and distribution channels that align with the principles of sustainability. This can lead to the development of unique

and compelling content that not only entertains but also educates and inspires audiences to adopt sustainable practices in their own lives.

3. **Collaboration and Partnerships:** Collaboration and partnerships between media organizations, environmental NGOs, and government agencies can play a crucial role in promoting sustainable media. By working together, industry stakeholders can share knowledge, resources, and best practices, leading to the development of industry-wide initiatives and standards for sustainability. Such partnerships can also help amplify the impact of sustainable media campaigns by reaching wider audiences and engaging communities in environmental conservation.

4. **Policy Support:** Government policies and regulations can provide a supportive framework for promoting sustainable media practices. By incentivizing and rewarding environmentally friendly initiatives, governments can encourage media companies to adopt sustainable production and consumption methods. Additionally, policies that promote transparency, accountability, and responsible advertising practices can help combat greenwashing and ensure that sustainability claims made by media organizations are genuine.

5. **Public Awareness Campaigns:** Media has a powerful role in shaping public opinion and behavior. By leveraging their reach and influence, media organizations can play an active role in raising public awareness about sustainability issues and motivating individuals to take action. Engaging audiences through thought-provoking documentaries, informative news content, and entertaining storytelling can contribute to a shift in societal attitudes towards sustainability.

In summary, promoting sustainable media faces challenges such as resistance to change, lack of awareness, complex supply chains, and technological limitations. However, there are opportunities in growing consumer demand, innovation, collaboration, policy support, and public awareness campaigns. By addressing these challenges and seizing these opportunities, the media industry can contribute to a more sustainable future.

The Structure of the Book and Overview of Chapters

In this section, we will provide a comprehensive overview of the structure and content of the book "Sustainable Media: Green Lies and SJW Agendas". The book is divided into seven chapters, each focusing on a specific aspect of sustainable media and its relation to environmental impacts and social justice narratives. Let's take a closer look at each chapter and the topics covered:

Chapter 1: Definition and Importance of Sustainable Media

This chapter serves as an introduction to the concept of sustainable media and its significance in today's world. We begin by clarifying the notion of sustainability and why it matters in the context of media production and consumption. We examine the role of media in shaping public opinion and behavior, emphasizing the need for sustainable practices in the industry. Additionally, we explore the challenges and opportunities that arise when promoting sustainable media. This chapter also provides an overview of the book's structure, giving readers a preview of the topics discussed in subsequent chapters.

Chapter 2: Historical Perspective

In this chapter, we delve into the historical evolution of the media industry and its impact on the environment. We explore the early forms of media and their environmental consequences, particularly during the industrial revolution when mass media emerged. We examine the influence of technology on media production and consumption, highlighting the environmental implications of media consolidation. Furthermore, we discuss the role of media in social justice movements, acknowledging its power to shape narratives and initiate societal transformations.

Chapter 3: Media and Environmental Impacts

Chapter 3 focuses on the environmental impacts of media production and consumption. We analyze the energy consumption associated with various media forms, such as film, television, and digital media, while exploring energy-efficient technologies and renewable energy solutions. Additionally, we scrutinize the issue of e-waste generated by consumer electronics and discuss responsible disposal and sustainable alternatives. Furthermore, we delve into water consumption in media production, providing strategies for reducing it and addressing water scarcity issues.

Chapter 4: Greenwashing and Media Manipulation

This chapter sheds light on the deceptive practice of greenwashing in media. We define greenwashing, provide examples, and discuss the role of advertising and public relations in perpetuating it. We also explore the techniques used in greenwashing and how to identify and combat them effectively. Furthermore, we examine media bias and its impact on sustainability discourse, emphasizing the importance of unbiased and balanced media coverage.

Chapter 5: Social Justice Warrior (SJW) Agendas in Media

Chapter 5 delves into the influence of the social justice warrior (SJW) movement on media production and its implications for sustainability discourse. We define the SJW movement, trace its origins, and analyze its impact on media content. We also explore the intersectionality between social justice and environmental justice, highlighting the role of media in amplifying voices of marginalized communities. Additionally, we discuss cultural appropriation, media representation, and the need for inclusivity and diversity in media.

Chapter 6: Sustainable Media Practices and Solutions

In this chapter, we provide practical solutions and strategies for promoting sustainable practices in media production and consumption. We examine green production certifications and standards, discussing their benefits, limitations, and successful case studies. We also discuss sustainable media consumption, alternative media platforms with sustainable practices, and the importance of media literacy in making informed choices. Additionally, we highlight the significance of collaborations between the media industry and environmental organizations for promoting sustainable media.

Chapter 7: Conclusion

The final chapter of the book summarizes the key principles and practices of sustainable media discussed throughout the book. We provide a concise recap of the main points and takeaways from each chapter, reinforcing the importance of individual actions in promoting sustainable media. Furthermore, we address the future of sustainable media, emphasizing ongoing research and innovation in the field. Finally, we conclude with a call to action, urging readers to play an active role in advancing sustainable practices and promoting environmental stewardship.

By organizing the book according to these chapters, we aim to provide readers with a comprehensive understanding of sustainable media, its complexities, and its intersections with environmental impacts and social justice narratives. Through practical solutions, case studies, and thought-provoking discussions, readers will gain the necessary knowledge and tools to navigate the rapidly changing landscape of sustainable media.

Historical Perspective

Evolution of Media Industry

Early forms of media and their impact on the environment

In order to understand the evolution of sustainable media, it is crucial to explore the early forms of media and their impact on the environment. Before the advent of digital technologies, media relied on various physical resources and had profound consequences for the environment.

Print Media

One of the earliest forms of media is print media, which includes newspapers, books, and magazines. The manufacturing process of print media involves the use of paper, ink, and energy for printing and distribution. The extraction of raw materials for paper production, such as timber, contributes to deforestation and habitat loss. Additionally, the chemicals used in ink production can have adverse effects on ecosystems if not properly managed.

Moreover, the production and transportation of print media require significant amounts of energy, contributing to carbon emissions and air pollution. The disposal of print media also poses environmental challenges, as paper waste often ends up in landfills, where it decomposes and generates methane, a potent greenhouse gas.

Example: One example of the environmental impact of print media is the newspaper industry. Each year, millions of trees are cut down to produce newspapers, resulting in the loss of important carbon sinks and contributing to climate change.

Solution: The rise of digital media has provided a more sustainable alternative to print media. By transitioning to online platforms, the consumption and production of print media can be significantly reduced, leading to less resource extraction, energy consumption, and waste generation. However, it is important to consider the environmental impact of digital technologies as well, as discussed later in this book.

Radio and Television

Radio and television have been influential forms of media that have shaped public opinion and behavior. In the early days of these media forms, the manufacturing of radio receivers and television sets involved the extraction of raw materials, such as metals and plastics, which can have harmful environmental consequences.

Additionally, the operation of radio and television stations requires energy, including electricity for broadcasting and powering the electronic devices. This energy consumption contributes to carbon emissions and air pollution, especially if the sources of electricity are not renewable.

Example: The television industry has experienced significant technological advancements, leading to the disposal of older television sets. Many of these devices contain hazardous materials, such as lead, mercury, and brominated flame retardants, which can contaminate water and soil if not properly managed.

Solution: The adoption of energy-efficient technologies and practices in broadcasting can help reduce energy consumption. Transitioning to renewable energy sources, such as solar or wind power, for powering radio and television stations can significantly mitigate their environmental impact. Additionally, proper recycling and disposal strategies should be implemented to manage electronic waste generated from older devices.

Cinema and Motion Pictures

Cinema and motion pictures have long been a popular form of media entertainment. The production of films involves complex processes, including set construction, lighting, and special effects, which require significant amounts of energy and resources. The use of artificial lighting, for example, increases electricity consumption and contributes to greenhouse gas emissions.

Furthermore, the production of film stock, which was commonly used in the past, involved the extraction and processing of raw materials, including silver, petroleum-based chemicals, and water. These processes have significant environmental implications, such as water contamination and depletion of natural resources.

Example: The film industry has historically used large sets and elaborate productions, resulting in excessive waste generation. For instance, the construction of temporary sets often leads to the disposal of building materials, contributing to landfill waste.

Solution: The film industry has started adopting sustainable practices to minimize its environmental impact. This includes using energy-efficient lighting systems, implementing waste reduction strategies, and recycling materials whenever possible. Additionally, the shift towards digital filmmaking and distribution has reduced the reliance on physical film stock, resulting in significant resource savings.

Connecting the Past to the Present

Understanding the environmental impact of early forms of media helps us recognize the need for sustainable practices in the modern media landscape. The lessons learned from the history of media can guide the development of strategies and innovations to mitigate the environmental consequences of media production and consumption.

It is important to note that while digital media has the potential to reduce the physical footprint of media, it is not without its own environmental challenges. The next section will delve into the impact of technology on media production and consumption and explore ways to address these challenges sustainably.

Industrial revolution and the rise of mass media

During the Industrial Revolution, which took place in the late 18th and early 19th centuries, there were significant advancements in technology, manufacturing, and transportation. This period marked a shift from an agrarian society to an industrialized one, as new machines and processes revolutionized production and led to the rise of mass media.

Early forms of media and their impact on the environment

Before the Industrial Revolution, media was primarily limited to handwritten manuscripts, paintings, and oral storytelling. The production and dissemination of these early forms of media had minimal environmental impact, as they were typically created using natural materials and did not require large-scale industrial processes.

However, as the Industrial Revolution gained momentum, new media technologies emerged, such as the printing press and the telegraph. These innovations enabled the mass production and distribution of printed materials, including newspapers, books, and magazines.

The advent of the printing press brought about a surge in paper production, which had significant environmental consequences. Wood pulp, derived from trees, became the primary raw material for paper production. As demand increased, vast areas of forests were cleared to meet the growing needs of the printing industry. This deforestation led to habitat loss, soil erosion, and increased carbon dioxide emissions.

Furthermore, the use of coal-powered steam engines to power printing presses and other machinery resulted in air pollution and contributed to the greenhouse effect. The burning of coal released large amounts of carbon dioxide, sulfur dioxide, and other pollutants into the atmosphere, exacerbating the environmental impacts of mass media production.

The impact of technology on media production and consumption

The Industrial Revolution not only transformed the means of media production but also revolutionized the way people consumed and accessed media. With the development of railroads and telegraph systems, media could be transported rapidly over long distances, enabling the dissemination of information and news on a scale previously unimaginable.

The invention of the telegraph, in particular, revolutionized communication by allowing almost instant transmission of messages across vast distances. This facilitated the emergence of wire services and news agencies, which played a crucial role in the dissemination of information to the public.

The rise of mass media during the Industrial Revolution also led to the development of new forms of entertainment, such as novels, theater, and music. The availability of printed materials and the growth of urban centers created a demand for leisure activities, which contributed to the rise of the entertainment industry.

However, the mass production and consumption of media during this period also had environmental and social consequences. The widespread use of coal for energy generation, along with the increased production of paper and other materials, contributed to the depletion of natural resources and the emission of greenhouse gases.

Media consolidation and its environmental consequences

As the Industrial Revolution progressed, there was a consolidation of media ownership, with a few powerful individuals and companies controlling the production and distribution of media. This consolidation had both economic and environmental implications.

Economically, media consolidation resulted in a smaller number of players dominating the industry, leading to less diversity and competition. This concentration of power allowed media owners to influence public opinion and control the information disseminated to the masses.

From an environmental perspective, media consolidation increased the pressure on natural resources. Large media conglomerates required massive amounts of raw materials, such as paper and chemicals, for their printing and production processes. This demand further exacerbated deforestation, pollution, and resource depletion.

The role of media in social justice movements

During the Industrial Revolution, mass media played a significant role in shaping social justice movements. The rise of newspapers and other print media provided a platform for individuals and organizations to voice their concerns and advocate for change.

Journalists and writers used their platforms to expose social inequalities, labor exploitation, and environmental degradation. The media's coverage of these issues helped raise public awareness and galvanize support for social justice causes.

For example, publications like "The Jungle" by Upton Sinclair exposed the unsanitary working conditions in the meatpacking industry and led to the passage of the Pure Food and Drug Act in the United States, which aimed to protect consumers from adulterated and mislabeled food.

The role of media in social justice movements during this period laid the foundation for the intersection between media and sustainability, as it highlighted the importance of media in advocating for positive social and environmental change.

Summary

The Industrial Revolution marked a significant turning point in the history of media, as advancements in technology and mass production revolutionized media production and consumption. However, these developments also had adverse environmental impacts, including deforestation, air pollution, and resource depletion.

The consolidation of media ownership further exacerbated these environmental consequences, as large media conglomerates required substantial amounts of natural resources for their operations. Additionally, during this period, media played a crucial role in raising awareness about social justice issues and advocating for change.

Understanding the historical context of the Industrial Revolution and the rise of mass media is essential in comprehending the origins of the sustainability challenges that exist in the contemporary media landscape. By examining the past, we can learn lessons and make informed decisions to promote sustainable media practices in the present and future.

The impact of technology on media production and consumption

The advent of technology has revolutionized the media industry, transforming the way media is produced, consumed, and distributed. In this section, we will explore the various impacts that technology has had on media production and consumption, and how these changes have influenced the sustainability of the industry.

Evolution of Media Production

The evolution of technology has opened up new possibilities in media production. With the introduction of digital cameras, editing software, and other high-tech tools, media producers now have access to powerful tools that enhance creativity, efficiency, and cost-effectiveness.

One major impact of technology on media production is the democratization of content creation. In the past, producing high-quality media required expensive equipment and professional expertise. However, with the advancement of technology, anyone with a smartphone and access to the internet can now create and distribute their own media content. This has led to a proliferation of user-generated content on platforms such as YouTube, TikTok, and Instagram.

Additionally, technology has enabled media producers to streamline their workflows and reduce production costs. Digital editing software allows for faster and more precise editing, eliminating the need for costly and time-consuming manual editing processes. Furthermore, the use of cloud storage and online collaboration tools has simplified the production process by enabling teams to work remotely and share files in real-time.

Implications for Media Consumption

Alongside the changes in media production, technology has also greatly influenced media consumption patterns. The rise of the internet and digital platforms has provided consumers with unprecedented access to a wide range of media content, anytime and anywhere.

One significant impact of technology on media consumption is the shift from traditional broadcast television to streaming services. Platforms such as Netflix, Amazon Prime Video, and Disney+ allow viewers to access a vast library of content on-demand, without the limitations of scheduled broadcasts. This has led to a decline in traditional television viewership and an increase in cord-cutting, where consumers opt to discontinue their cable or satellite subscriptions in favor of streaming services.

Furthermore, technology has facilitated the personalization of media consumption. Algorithms and recommendation systems enable platforms to tailor content suggestions to individual users based on their preferences and viewing history. This has the potential to create echo chambers and filter bubbles, where users are only exposed to content that aligns with their existing beliefs and interests. As a result, there is a growing concern about the impact of technology on media diversity and the potential for the reinforcement of biased viewpoints.

Sustainability Implications

The impact of technology on media production and consumption has both positive and negative implications for sustainability.

From a production standpoint, the proliferation of digital media has reduced the need for physical materials such as tapes, film reels, and DVDs. This has resulted in a significant reduction in the use of resources and the generation of waste. Digital distribution also eliminates the need for physical transportation, further reducing carbon emissions associated with the distribution process.

However, the increasing reliance on digital technology also has its environmental drawbacks. The energy consumption of data centers, which store and serve digital media, is a significant contributor to carbon emissions. Additionally, the constant upgrading and replacement of electronic devices, such as cameras and smartphones, leads to electronic waste accumulation.

In terms of consumption, the shift from traditional broadcasting to streaming services has reduced the energy consumption associated with broadcasting infrastructure. However, the increased demand for data streaming has led to a surge in energy consumption by data centers and network infrastructure.

To mitigate the environmental impact of technology on media production and consumption, various strategies can be implemented. Media producers can adopt energy-efficient technologies in their production processes and invest in renewable energy sources. They can also implement sustainable practices such as reducing paper waste, promoting recycling initiatives, and extending the lifespan of electronic devices.

Consumers, on the other hand, can practice conscious media consumption by being mindful of their energy use when streaming content, supporting sustainable media platforms, and engaging in collective actions such as digital detoxes and reducing screen time.

Overall, while technology has brought significant advancements to the media industry, its sustainability implications should not be overlooked. It is crucial for media producers, consumers, and technology companies to work together to ensure that the benefits of technology are harnessed in an environmentally responsible manner.

Case Study: The Impact of Video Streaming on Carbon Footprint

To better understand the sustainability implications of technology on media consumption, let's consider the specific case of video streaming and its carbon footprint.

Video streaming has become increasingly popular, and platforms such as Netflix and YouTube account for a significant portion of internet traffic. However, the energy consumption associated with streaming videos has raised concerns about its environmental impact.

Research conducted by the Shift Project in 2019 estimated that the carbon footprint of video streaming is responsible for about 300 million tons of CO_2 emissions annually, which is equivalent to the carbon emissions of Spain. This includes the energy consumption of data centers, network transmission, and end-user devices.

To put this into perspective, streaming one hour of high-definition video is estimated to produce between 150 and 1,000 grams of CO_2 emissions, depending on the video quality and device used. This is comparable to the carbon emissions produced by driving a car for 1 to 7 miles.

The high energy consumption of video streaming is primarily due to data centers, which store and process the vast amounts of data required for streaming. These data centers require massive amounts of electricity to power their servers and cool the equipment.

To reduce the environmental impact of video streaming, several strategies can be implemented. First, data centers can improve their energy efficiency by adopting advanced cooling technologies, optimizing server utilization, and investing in renewable energy sources. Second, media companies can educate consumers about the energy consumption associated with streaming and provide tools to help users make more sustainable choices, such as enabling lower resolution options and promoting offline viewing. Finally, consumers can reduce their carbon footprint by being mindful of their streaming habits, such as watching videos in lower resolutions, sharing accounts to minimize the number of devices streaming simultaneously, and downloading content for offline viewing whenever possible.

By implementing these strategies, the media industry can work towards reducing the carbon footprint of video streaming and promoting a more sustainable approach to media consumption.

Key Takeaways

- Technology has revolutionized media production, making it more accessible, efficient, and cost-effective. - The shift towards streaming services has transformed media consumption patterns, providing consumers with on-demand access to a wide range of content. - The environmental impact of technology on media production and consumption includes both positive and negative implications. - Strategies such as adopting energy-efficient technologies, promoting renewable energy sources, and practicing conscious media consumption can help mitigate the sustainability challenges posed by technology. - Video streaming, in particular, has a significant carbon footprint, highlighting the need for industry-wide efforts to reduce energy consumption and educate consumers about sustainable viewing habits.

Further Reading

- Balancing Green: When to Embrace Sustainability in a Business (and When Not To) by Yossi Sheffi. - Sustainable Media: Critical Approaches to Media and Environment by Nicole Starosielski and Janet Walker. - Sustainable Media Production by Carolyn S. Maher and David Leigey. - "Energy consumption in the wired and wireless access networks" by Andrea Bianco, et al. (2013) in Sustainable Internet and ICT for Sustainability.

Exercises

1. Research and compare the carbon footprint of different streaming platforms. What factors contribute to the variation in their environmental impact?

2. Conduct a media consumption audit by tracking your media consumption habits for a week. Calculate the estimated carbon footprint of your media consumption during that period. Identify areas where you can reduce your environmental impact.

3. Investigate energy-efficient technologies and practices used in media production. Choose a specific area within media production (e.g., film production, advertising) and propose sustainable solutions to reduce energy consumption.

4. Engage in a digital detox challenge by reducing your screen time for a week. Reflect on this experience and discuss the challenges and benefits of disconnecting from digital media.

5. Research and summarize the sustainability initiatives undertaken by a major media company or platform. How do these initiatives address the environmental impact of technology on media production and consumption?

Remember, these exercises are designed to deepen your understanding of the topic and encourage critical thinking about sustainable media practices.

Media consolidation and its environmental consequences

Media consolidation refers to the process of a few large corporations or companies acquiring and controlling a significant portion of the media industry. This trend of consolidation has become increasingly common in recent years, leading to fewer independent media outlets and a concentration of power in the hands of a few major players.

The environmental consequences of media consolidation are multi-faceted and often overlooked. This section will explore the various ways in which media consolidation impacts the environment and sustainability.

Impact on energy consumption

One of the major consequences of media consolidation is the increase in energy consumption. Large media conglomerates often operate multiple television networks, radio stations, and print publications, which require vast amounts of energy to power their operations.

Moreover, the consolidation of media also results in the centralization of production facilities, leading to longer transmission distances and increased energy consumption in the distribution of media content.

As a solution to reduce energy consumption, media organizations can employ energy-efficient technologies and practices. For example, using LED lighting in studios, implementing power-saving modes on equipment, and optimizing cooling and ventilation systems can significantly reduce energy usage.

Excessive waste generation

Media consolidation also contributes to the generation of excessive waste. With the proliferation of media outlets, there is a demand for the production of a vast amount of content in various formats such as print, digital, and video.

The production of these materials, including print newspapers and magazines, DVDs, and other media consumables, leads to the generation of significant amounts of waste, including paper, plastic, and electronic waste.

To address this issue, media organizations can adopt sustainable practices such as reducing paper usage by encouraging digital subscriptions, using eco-friendly printing materials, and implementing recycling programs for electronic waste.

Limited diversity and local content

Another consequence of media consolidation is the limited diversity and local content. As a few dominant corporations control the majority of media outlets, there is a homogenization of content catering to mass audiences.

This consolidation can lead to a decline in the representation of local stories, cultural diversity, and independent voices, which are essential for fostering sustainable communities and promoting environmental stewardship.

To combat this, media organizations should make a deliberate effort to include diverse perspectives and local content in their programming. This could involve partnering with local community organizations, supporting independent filmmakers and journalists, and providing platforms for underrepresented voices.

Influence on sustainability discourse

Media consolidation can also impact the sustainability discourse by creating a dominant narrative that aligns with the interests of the consolidated corporations. This influence can result in the suppression or underreporting of certain sustainability-related issues, such as corporate environmental negligence or government policies favoring unsustainable practices.

To address this challenge, media organizations should uphold journalistic integrity and transparency. They should strive to provide balanced and unbiased coverage of sustainability issues, hold corporations and policymakers accountable, and give voice to grassroots environmental movements and initiatives.

Unconventional Example: Media consolidation and climate change denial

An unconventional yet relevant example of the consequences of media consolidation is the perpetuation of climate change denial. Some media conglomerates have been known to downplay or propagate misinformation about the realities of climate change, largely to protect the interests of their corporate allies in polluting industries.

This manipulation of information has significant environmental consequences, as it hinders public understanding and action on climate change. To address this, media organizations should prioritize responsible reporting on climate change, ensure accurate scientific representation, and disclose any potential conflicts of interest.

In conclusion, media consolidation poses significant environmental consequences as it impacts energy consumption, waste generation, diversity of content, sustainability discourse, and can perpetuate climate change denial. However, media organizations have the power to mitigate these consequences by adopting sustainable practices, promoting local and diverse content, upholding journalistic integrity, and prioritizing responsible reporting on environmental issues. It is crucial for media stakeholders to recognize and address these challenges, as the media plays a vital role in shaping public opinion and behavior towards sustainable practices and environmental stewardship.

The role of media in social justice movements

Media plays a vital role in shaping public opinion and influencing social justice movements. It has the power to create awareness, mobilize communities, and promote meaningful change. In this section, we will explore the significant role that media plays in social justice movements, highlighting its impact, challenges, and strategies for effective communication.

Understanding the power of media in social justice movements

Media has always been a powerful tool for social change, giving a voice to marginalized communities and shedding light on injustices. Whether through traditional media outlets like newspapers, radio, and television or through digital platforms such as social media and online news sites, media has the ability to reach a vast audience and spark conversations that lead to collective action.

One of the ways media facilitates social justice movements is by bringing attention to systemic issues and human rights violations. Through in-depth reporting, investigative journalism, documentaries, and opinion pieces, media outlets can expose injustice and hold those in power accountable. By amplifying the voices of those affected by social injustice, media can motivate action, inspire empathy, and encourage public support for the cause.

Challenges faced by media in social justice movements

While media has the potential to be a powerful force for social change, it also faces various challenges in effectively covering and supporting social justice movements. These challenges can include:

1. **Bias and sensationalism:** Media outlets sometimes prioritize sensationalism and profit over accurate and unbiased reporting. This can lead to the distortion of facts and an emphasis on sensational stories, diverting attention from the core issues of social justice movements.

2. **Underrepresentation and misrepresentation:** Media often fails to accurately represent the diversity of social justice movements, perpetuating stereotypes and reinforcing existing power imbalances. It is crucial for media to provide a platform for the voices of marginalized communities and ensure their narratives are accurately portrayed.

3. **Gatekeeping and corporate control:** The media landscape is often dominated by a few large corporations, which can influence the narratives and perspectives presented to the public. This concentration of power can limit the representation of alternative viewpoints and hinder the visibility of social justice movements.

Strategies for effective media communication in social justice movements

Despite these challenges, media can still play a significant role in social justice movements by adopting effective strategies for communication. Here are some key strategies to consider:

1. **Promoting inclusivity and diversity:** Media organizations need to prioritize diversity both in their teams and in the stories they cover. By actively seeking out and amplifying diverse voices, media can ensure a more comprehensive and accurate representation of social justice movements.

2. **Engaging with grassroots organizations:** Building strong relationships with grassroots organizations provides media outlets access to authentic and firsthand accounts of social justice issues. This can help in accurately reporting on the ground realities and fostering a deeper understanding of the challenges faced by marginalized communities.

3. **Fact-checking and ethical reporting:** Journalistic integrity is crucial in social justice reporting. Fact-checking information, verifying sources, and presenting unbiased narratives are essential for maintaining credibility and trust. Media organizations should prioritize fact-based reporting and avoid spreading misinformation or contributing to the spread of fake news.

4. **Leveraging digital platforms:** Social media platforms offer a powerful tool for promoting social justice movements. Through hashtags, online campaigns, and viral content, media can raise awareness, mobilize large audiences, and facilitate conversations around social justice issues. However, it is important to navigate the online space with caution, ensuring that information shared is accurate and sensitive to the experiences of those involved.

5. **Collaborating with social justice organizations:** Media outlets can collaborate with social justice organizations to create impactful campaigns and initiatives. By pooling resources and expertise, media and social justice organizations can amplify their reach, generate wider public engagement, and bring about meaningful change.

Real-world example: The role of media in the Black Lives Matter movement

The Black Lives Matter (BLM) movement serves as a powerful example of how media can amplify social justice causes. The movement, which originated in response to police brutality and racial inequality, gained significant traction in part due to media coverage.

Traditional media outlets like newspapers and television networks covered protests, shared stories of victims, and facilitated conversations about systemic racism. At the same time, social media played a crucial role in spreading the movement, with hashtags like #BlackLivesMatter trending globally and facilitating conversations on a massive scale.

Through their coverage, media outlets brought attention to the urgent need for police reform and raised awareness about the experiences of marginalized communities. The sustained media attention on the movement led to increased public support, policy changes, and a broader discourse on racial justice.

However, the media's role in the BLM movement was not without challenges. Critics argue that media sometimes focused on sensational aspects of protests, leading to misrepresentation and diverting attention from the underlying issues of racial inequality. Additionally, biases within the media industry and limited representation of Black voices highlighted the need for increased diversity and inclusion.

Conclusion

Media plays a crucial role in social justice movements by raising awareness, mobilizing communities, and fostering public support for change. While it faces challenges such as bias and underrepresentation, media organizations can overcome these obstacles by prioritizing inclusivity, engaging with grassroots organizations, adopting ethical reporting practices, leveraging digital platforms, and collaborating with social justice organizations.

By recognizing the power of media and utilizing effective communication strategies, social justice movements can harness the media's potential to drive meaningful and lasting change.

Media and Environmental Impacts

Energy Consumption in Media Production

Energy-intensive processes in film and television production

Film and television production is an essential part of the media industry, but it also has significant environmental impacts, particularly in terms of energy consumption. In this section, we will explore the energy-intensive processes involved in film and television production and discuss the challenges and opportunities for reducing energy consumption in these processes.

Understanding the energy-intensive processes

Film and television production involves various energy-intensive processes that contribute to its overall carbon footprint. Some of the key processes that require substantial energy inputs include:

1. Lighting: Film and television sets require extensive lighting setups to ensure proper illumination for capturing scenes. Traditional lighting methods, such as incandescent bulbs, consume large amounts of energy and produce significant heat. While there is a shift towards more energy-efficient LED lighting, the industry still relies on conventional lighting techniques, especially for certain scenes or effects.

2. Equipment operation: Cameras, sound systems, editing equipment, and other production tools require a substantial amount of electrical energy to function. These devices often run for extended periods during shoots, consuming significant amounts of power. Additionally, portable power generators are frequently used on location, further increasing energy consumption.

3. Studio operations: Studios provide controlled environments for shooting and post-production activities. These facilities demand energy for heating, cooling,

ventilation, and overall maintenance. The size and complexity of studio operations contribute to their substantial energy consumption.

4. Special effects and visual effects: Film and television productions often employ special effects and visual effects to enhance storytelling and create captivating visuals. These effects rely heavily on computer-generated imagery (CGI), which requires powerful computing resources and energy-intensive rendering processes.

5. Set construction and transportation: Building sets and transporting production equipment and crew to different locations contribute to the energy footprint of film and television production. Construction materials, transportation vehicles, and logistics operations require energy inputs throughout the production cycle.

Challenges and opportunities for energy reduction

Reducing energy consumption in film and television production poses several challenges due to the industry's unique characteristics and requirements. However, there are also significant opportunities for implementing energy-saving measures. Let's explore some challenges and opportunities:

1. Balancing lighting requirements and energy efficiency: While lighting is essential for capturing high-quality footage, it is crucial to balance lighting needs with energy efficiency. By adopting energy-efficient lighting technologies like LED bulbs, studios can significantly reduce energy consumption without compromising the lighting quality.

2. Equipment efficiency and management: The industry can promote the use of energy-efficient equipment and proper equipment management practices. This includes implementing power-saving modes, regular maintenance, and upgrading to more energy-efficient models. Adopting sustainable procurement practices can also help in selecting energy-efficient equipment.

3. Sustainable set construction and transportation: Implementing sustainable construction practices for sets, such as using recycled or eco-friendly materials, can reduce the energy footprint. Additionally, optimizing transportation logistics and using fuel-efficient vehicles can minimize energy consumption during location shoots.

4. Harnessing renewable energy sources: Embracing renewable energy solutions, such as solar panels or wind turbines, can power film and television productions while reducing reliance on fossil fuels. By generating clean energy on-site or utilizing renewable energy from the grid, the industry can significantly decrease its carbon footprint.

5. Efficient post-production processes: Post-production involves extensive rendering and data processing, which consume substantial energy. Adopting energy-efficient hardware and software solutions, optimizing workflows, and utilizing cloud computing or data centers powered by renewable energy can help reduce energy consumption in post-production.

Example: The use of solar-powered film studios

To illustrate the potential of renewable energy solutions in film and television production, let's consider the example of solar-powered film studios. Some production companies have started to embrace solar energy by installing solar panels on studio rooftops. These solar panels can generate clean and sustainable electricity to power the production activities, including lighting, equipment operation, and studio operations.

Solar-powered film studios not only reduce the carbon footprint but also showcase the industry's commitment to sustainability. They serve as inspiring examples for other production companies to adopt renewable energy solutions and spur innovation in the field.

Resources and further reading

1. Green Production Guide: A comprehensive resource for sustainable practices in film and television production, including energy efficiency tips and case studies. Available at: https://www.greenproductionguide.com/

2. Sustainable Film and Television Alliance: An organization focused on promoting sustainability in film and television production, offering resources and support for eco-friendly practices. Visit their website at: https://www.sustainablefilmtv.com/

3. Sustainable Filmmaking Toolkit: A collection of guides, case studies, and resources to help filmmakers incorporate sustainability into their productions. Access the toolkit at: https://www.sustainablefilmmaking.org/

4. Renewable Energy in Film Production: A research paper exploring the potential of renewable energy in film production, discussing practical implementations and associated benefits. Available at: https://www.researchgate.net/publication/345678689_Renewable_Energy_in_Film_Production

Exercises

1. Conduct a research project on the energy consumption of a specific film or television production. Identify the energy-intensive processes involved and suggest sustainable alternatives to reduce energy consumption.
2. Create a storyboard or visual presentation showcasing the benefits and challenges of implementing renewable energy solutions in film and television production.
3. Interview a professional in the film or television industry and ask them about their experiences with energy-saving practices and their thoughts on the industry's responsibility towards environmental sustainability.

Remember to think critically while engaging in these exercises and consider the context and unique requirements of the film and television industry in your solutions.

Energy-efficient technologies and practices in media production

In today's world, where climate change and environmental sustainability are major concerns, it is crucial for the media industry to adopt energy-efficient technologies and practices. Media production, including the filming of movies and television shows, consumes a significant amount of energy, contributing to greenhouse gas emissions and other environmental impacts. By implementing energy-efficient measures, the media industry can reduce its carbon footprint and promote sustainability. In this section, we will explore various energy-efficient technologies and practices that can be adopted in media production.

Understanding energy efficiency

Before delving into specific technologies and practices, it is important to understand the concept of energy efficiency. Energy efficiency refers to the ability to accomplish a desired task or achieve a specific output while using less energy. In the context of media production, energy efficiency involves finding ways to reduce the energy consumption associated with various processes, without compromising the quality or effectiveness of the production.

Energy-efficient lighting

Lighting plays a crucial role in media production, especially in the filming of movies and television shows. Traditional lighting systems, such as incandescent light bulbs, consume a significant amount of energy and generate heat, which can lead to increased cooling requirements. To address these energy challenges, energy-efficient lighting technologies have emerged as viable alternatives.

One such technology is Light Emitting Diodes (LEDs). LEDs have gained popularity in recent years due to their energy efficiency and longer lifespan compared to traditional lighting sources. LEDs use up to 80

Another energy-efficient lighting technology is Compact Fluorescent Lamps (CFLs). CFLs are more energy-efficient than incandescent bulbs and have a longer lifespan. Though not as versatile as LEDs, CFLs are still a viable option for media production, especially in areas where color accuracy is not a primary concern.

To further optimize energy efficiency in lighting, it is essential to implement efficient lighting control systems. These systems allow for precise control of lighting levels and enable automatic dimming or turning off of lights when not in use. Motion sensors and timers can be incorporated into lighting control systems to ensure lights are only active when necessary, reducing energy waste.

Energy-efficient equipment

Apart from lighting, various types of equipment are used in media production that contribute to energy consumption. By selecting energy-efficient equipment and implementing best practices, significant energy savings can be achieved.

Cameras are one of the most critical components in media production. Traditional film cameras consume a considerable amount of energy, and the film development process is energy-intensive. However, technological advancements have led to the rise of digital cameras, which are more energy-efficient. Digital cameras eliminate the need for film processing, reducing energy consumption. Additionally, modern digital cameras have advanced power management features, allowing precise control over energy usage. By leveraging these energy-efficient cameras, media producers can reduce their carbon footprint.

In addition to cameras, other equipment such as computers, servers, and storage devices are used extensively in media production. Selecting energy-efficient models and properly managing power settings can contribute to significant energy savings. Energy-saving features such as sleep mode, power management software, and efficient cooling systems should be utilized to minimize energy consumption during idle periods.

Renewable energy solutions

In addition to adopting energy-efficient technologies and practices, media production can further reduce its environmental impact by utilizing renewable energy sources. Renewable energy, such as solar power and wind energy, offers a sustainable alternative to conventional fossil fuels.

Installing solar panels on production facilities can provide a reliable source of clean energy. Solar power can be used to generate electricity for lighting, equipment, and other energy needs. By generating sustainable energy on-site, media production companies can reduce their reliance on grid-supplied electricity, resulting in lower carbon emissions.

Similarly, wind turbines can also be utilized in areas with a favorable wind resource. Wind energy can be harnessed to power various aspects of media production, including lighting, equipment, and heating or cooling systems. Collaboration with local wind energy projects or purchasing renewable energy credits can provide additional avenues for supporting renewable energy.

Awareness and education

Promoting energy-efficient technologies and practices in media production requires awareness and education among industry professionals. Training programs and workshops can be organized to educate filmmakers, production crews, and other stakeholders about the importance of energy efficiency and the available technologies and practices.

Additionally, providing resources and guidelines, such as energy-saving checklists and case studies showcasing successful energy-efficient productions, can inspire and encourage media professionals to adopt eco-friendly practices. Industry associations and organizations can play a vital role in disseminating information and facilitating knowledge sharing.

It is also essential to involve the audience and viewers in promoting energy-efficient media. Including sustainability messages in media content can raise awareness among the general public and encourage them to make energy-conscious choices in their own lives.

Case study: Energy-efficient film production

To exemplify the implementation of energy-efficient technologies and practices in media production, let's consider a case study of a film production company. This company aims to reduce its energy consumption and minimize its environmental impact.

The company starts by retrofitting its lighting systems with LED fixtures, replacing outdated incandescent bulbs. This upgrade significantly reduces energy consumption without compromising the quality of lighting in film sets.

Next, the company invests in energy-efficient cameras, which not only consume less power but also eliminate the need for film processing. This transition to digital cameras reduces energy consumption and eliminates the associated environmental impacts of film development.

To further optimize energy efficiency, the company adopts energy-saving practices for its equipment, such as enabling power-saving features and implementing efficient cooling systems. It also ensures that computers and servers are turned off or put into sleep mode when not in use.

In addition to these measures, the company explores opportunities for utilizing renewable energy. It installs solar panels on its production facilities, harnessing the power of the sun to meet a portion of its energy needs. By generating clean energy on-site, the company reduces its reliance on fossil fuel-derived electricity and decreases its carbon footprint.

Throughout the film production process, the company educates its staff about the importance of energy efficiency and encourages sustainable practices. It also incorporates sustainability messages in its films, promoting environmental awareness among the audience.

By implementing these energy-efficient technologies and practices, the film production company successfully reduces its energy consumption and environmental impact. The case study showcases the potential for large-scale energy savings and demonstrates the feasibility of adopting sustainable practices in media production.

Conclusion

In this section, we explored energy-efficient technologies and practices that can be adopted in media production. By embracing energy-efficient lighting, equipment, and renewable energy solutions, the media industry can significantly reduce its carbon footprint and contribute to environmental sustainability. Additionally, raising awareness, educating industry professionals, and involving the audience in promoting energy-efficient media are essential steps towards a greener and more sustainable media industry. It is crucial for media professionals to embrace these energy-efficient technologies and practices and play an active role in creating a more sustainable future.

The Carbon Footprint of Digital Media

One of the key considerations when discussing sustainable media is the carbon footprint of digital media. As society becomes increasingly reliant on technology and digital media, it is important to understand the environmental impact associated with its production and consumption.

Definition of Carbon Footprint

The term "carbon footprint" refers to the total amount of greenhouse gas emissions, measured in carbon dioxide equivalent (CO_2e), that are directly or indirectly caused by an individual, organization, event, or product throughout its lifecycle. In the context of digital media, the carbon footprint is a measure of the environmental impact resulting from the production, distribution, and use of digital media content.

Environmental Impact Factors

The carbon footprint of digital media can be attributed to various factors, including:

1. **Energy Consumption:** The production and operation of digital media requires a significant amount of energy, particularly in data centers, networks, and device manufacturing. This energy is often derived from fossil fuels, leading to greenhouse gas emissions.

2. **Electronic Waste:** The disposal of electronic waste (e-waste) from outdated or discarded digital devices contributes to the carbon footprint. E-waste contains harmful substances and requires energy-intensive processes for recycling or disposal.

3. **Internet Infrastructure:** The internet infrastructure, including servers, routers, and data centers, consumes substantial energy to handle the increasing data traffic associated with digital media consumption. This energy consumption results in greenhouse gas emissions.

4. **Cloud Computing:** The storage and processing of digital media content rely on cloud computing, which requires a network of data centers. These data centers consume a significant amount of energy and contribute to the carbon footprint.

5. **Device Manufacturing:** The production of digital devices, such as smartphones, tablets, and computers, requires raw materials, energy-intensive manufacturing processes, and transportation. These activities generate greenhouse gas emissions throughout the supply chain.

Calculating the Carbon Footprint

Calculating the exact carbon footprint of digital media can be complex due to the interconnected nature of various components and stages involved. However, there are some key factors to consider when estimating the carbon footprint:

1. **Energy Consumption:** The amount of energy consumed during the production, distribution, and use of digital media content can be measured. Factors such as energy sources and efficiency of devices and infrastructure play a significant role in determining the carbon footprint.

2. **Emissions Factors:** Different energy sources have different carbon intensities, meaning they emit varying amounts of CO_2e per unit of energy produced. By considering the emissions factor of the energy sources used in digital media production and consumption, it is possible to estimate the carbon footprint more accurately.

3. **Lifecycle Assessment:** To calculate the carbon footprint comprehensively, a lifecycle assessment approach can be employed. This involves considering the environmental impact of all stages, including raw material extraction, manufacturing, distribution, use, and end-of-life disposal or recycling.

Reducing the Carbon Footprint

Reducing the carbon footprint of digital media is crucial for promoting sustainability. Here are some strategies that can be implemented:

1. **Energy Efficiency:** Improving the energy efficiency of digital devices, data centers, and network infrastructure can significantly reduce energy consumption and emissions. This can be achieved through the use of energy-efficient hardware, software optimization, and adopting renewable energy sources.

2. **E-waste Management:** Implementing responsible e-waste management practices, such as recycling and proper disposal, can minimize the environmental impact associated with electronic devices. Encouraging device longevity and repairability can also reduce the need for frequent device upgrades.

3. **Data Center Optimization:** Optimizing data center operations, such as cooling mechanisms and server virtualization, can reduce energy consumption. Additionally, locating data centers in areas with access to renewable energy sources can further minimize the carbon footprint.

4. **Cloud Computing Efficiency:** Enhancing the energy efficiency of cloud computing infrastructure and optimizing data storage and processing can lead to reduced energy consumption and emissions.

5. **Awareness and Behavior Change:** Promoting awareness among digital media users about the environmental impact of their consumption habits can encourage more sustainable behaviors. This can include actions such as streaming content in lower resolutions, enabling power-saving features on devices, and conscious media consumption choices.

By implementing these strategies and raising awareness, the digital media industry can significantly reduce its carbon footprint and contribute to a more sustainable future.

Concluding Thoughts

Understanding and addressing the carbon footprint of digital media is essential for achieving sustainability in the media industry. By taking proactive measures to reduce energy consumption, manage e-waste, optimize infrastructure, and promote sustainable behaviors, we can mitigate the environmental impact without compromising the accessibility and convenience offered by digital media.

It is important for media organizations, technology companies, and consumers to collaborate and adopt sustainable practices to ensure the long-term viability of digital media while minimizing its carbon footprint. Continued research and innovation in energy-efficient technologies and practices can further drive the sustainability agenda in the digital media industry.

Let us strive towards a future where digital media is not only entertaining and informative but also environmentally friendly and sustainable. Together, we can create a media landscape that aligns with our commitment to a greener and more sustainable world.

Renewable energy solutions for media productions

Media production, especially film and television, is known to be energy-intensive. The traditional methods of media production often rely on fossil fuels, leading to a significant carbon footprint. However, with increasing concerns about climate change and the need for sustainable practices, renewable energy solutions have emerged as a viable option for reducing the environmental impact of media production.

The Benefits of Renewable Energy for Media Productions

Renewable energy sources, such as solar and wind power, offer several advantages for media productions:

- **Reduced greenhouse gas emissions:** Unlike traditional fossil fuel-based energy sources, renewable energy generates electricity without releasing greenhouse gases. This helps to mitigate the carbon footprint of media production and contributes to global efforts in combating climate change.

- **Cost savings:** While the upfront costs of installing renewable energy systems may be higher, media production companies can benefit from long-term cost savings. Once installed, renewable energy systems have lower operational and maintenance costs compared to traditional energy sources, reducing the overall production expenses.

- **Energy independence:** Renewable energy sources offer greater energy independence, allowing media production companies to produce their own energy on-site. This reduces dependence on the grid and decreases the vulnerability to power interruptions.

- **Positive image and reputation:** Adopting renewable energy solutions can enhance the reputation of media production companies. As consumers become more aware of environmental issues, supporting sustainable practices can attract a broader audience and create a positive brand image.

Implementing Renewable Energy Solutions

Integrating renewable energy solutions in media productions requires careful planning and investment. Here are some strategies for adopting renewable energy in the media industry:

1. **Solar power systems:** Installing solar panels on production facilities, soundstages, and other structures can generate clean and renewable energy. Solar power is especially advantageous for media productions since they often require significant amounts of energy during daylight hours. Additionally, solar panels can be used to charge batteries that can power equipment and lighting during nighttime shoots or in remote locations.

2. **Wind turbines:** For media production companies located in windy regions, wind turbines can be a viable option for generating renewable energy. These turbines can be placed on production sites or in nearby areas to harness wind power.

3. **Hydroelectric power:** In certain locations with access to flowing water, small-scale hydroelectric power systems can be installed to generate renewable energy for media productions. This can be a sustainable option, provided that environmental impact assessments are conducted to ensure the preservation of water ecosystems.

4. **Energy-efficient equipment:** In addition to generating renewable energy, media production companies can also invest in energy-efficient equipment. This includes using LED lighting, energy-efficient cameras and computers, and optimizing the energy consumption of production processes.

5. **Energy management and monitoring systems:** Implementing robust energy management systems can help media production companies monitor and optimize their energy usage. These systems can track energy consumption patterns, identify areas of improvement, and provide real-time data on energy efficiency.

Case Study: Warner Bros. Entertainment

Warner Bros. Entertainment, a prominent Hollywood production company, has embraced renewable energy solutions to reduce its environmental impact. In 2010, Warner Bros. set a target to reduce greenhouse gas emissions by 20

- **Solar array installation:** Warner Bros. installed a massive solar array on the roof of its Studio Lot in Burbank, California. With over 3,000 solar panels, this installation generates approximately 1.9 million kilowatt-hours of clean energy annually, reducing the company's reliance on fossil fuels.

- **LED lighting retrofit:** Warner Bros. upgraded its lighting systems to energy-efficient LED technology across its studio facilities and soundstages. This retrofit resulted in significant energy savings and reduced maintenance costs.

- **Renewable energy purchases:** In addition to on-site renewable energy generation, Warner Bros. participates in renewable energy purchasing programs. By procuring renewable energy from local utilities and third-party providers, the company supports the growth of the renewable energy market.

Warner Bros. Entertainment's commitment to renewable energy solutions exemplifies how media production companies can contribute to sustainability efforts while maintaining high production standards.

Challenges and Considerations

While renewable energy solutions offer numerous benefits for media productions, there are some challenges and considerations that need to be addressed:

- **Initial costs:** The upfront investment required for installing renewable energy systems can be a significant barrier for media production companies, particularly smaller-scale productions with limited budgets. Organizations may need to seek financial incentives, grants, or partnerships to make the initial investment more feasible.

- **Intermittency:** Solar and wind power, the most common renewable energy sources, are subject to intermittency. Fluctuations in weather conditions can affect the availability and reliability of these energy sources. Backup energy storage systems, such as batteries, can help mitigate this issue and ensure uninterrupted power supply.

- **Space constraints:** Media production facilities, especially those located in urban areas, may have limited space for installing renewable energy systems. In such cases, companies can explore innovative solutions like solar panels on rooftops, parking structures, or adjacent vacant land.

- **Regulatory and permitting issues:** Each jurisdiction has its own regulations and permitting processes for renewable energy installations. Media production companies must navigate these legal requirements to ensure compliance and streamline the implementation of renewable energy solutions.

Conclusion

Renewable energy solutions offer a promising pathway for reducing the environmental impact of media productions. By adopting solar, wind, and hydroelectric power, media production companies can significantly reduce their carbon footprint, save costs, and enhance their brand image. However, overcoming challenges such as initial costs, intermittency, space constraints, and regulatory issues is crucial for successful implementation. Through innovative solutions and partnerships, the media industry can play a significant role in driving the transition towards a more sustainable and eco-friendly future.

Impact of media consumption on energy consumption

As we delve into the topic of sustainable media, it is crucial to examine the impact of media consumption on energy consumption. Media consumption refers to the act of using and engaging with various forms of media, such as television, film, video streaming, and social media platforms. This section explores how our media consumption habits contribute to energy consumption and the subsequent environmental consequences.

Understanding the relationship between media and energy

Media consumption has become an integral part of our daily lives, with digital media platforms enabling us to access a wide range of content anywhere, anytime. However, what often goes unnoticed is the energy required to power these media services. Energy consumption in media production and distribution is a substantial contributor to the overall environmental footprint of the media industry.

The energy consumed in media consumption can be divided into two main categories: the energy used for media production and the energy used for media consumption.

Energy consumed in media production

Media production involves various energy-intensive processes, particularly in the creation of films and television shows. Production studios require extensive lighting setups, equipment operation, and specialized facilities, all of which rely on significant amounts of energy. Additionally, the use of high-definition cameras, computer graphics, and post-production editing software further amplifies the energy demand.

To address the energy consumption in media production, industry professionals are increasingly adopting energy-efficient technologies and practices. For instance, LED lighting is being widely used as a more energy-efficient alternative to traditional lighting setups. Moreover, studios are investing in renewable energy solutions, such as solar panels, to decrease their reliance on conventional grid electricity.

It is important for media consumers to be aware that the energy consumed during the production phase contributes to the overall carbon footprint of the media content they consume. By supporting media produced using sustainable practices, consumers can indirectly reduce the environmental impact of their media consumption habits.

Energy consumed in media consumption

The energy consumed during media consumption largely depends on the medium through which it is accessed. Traditional television broadcasting relies on a centralized infrastructure that uses a significant amount of energy for transmission and distribution. However, with the advent of digital media platforms and online streaming services, the energy consumption has shifted towards the consumers' end.

Streaming media, whether it is video, music, or podcasts, requires substantial energy for data transmission and processing. The servers and data centers that host these platforms consume vast amounts of electricity to ensure fast and reliable content delivery to end-users. Additionally, the devices used for media consumption, such as smartphones, tablets, and smart TVs, also contribute to energy consumption.

To understand the environmental impact of our media consumption, it is crucial to consider the entire lifecycle of the media content, including the infrastructure and devices involved in its delivery. Increased demand for streaming services has led to the proliferation of data centers, which are notorious for their high energy consumption. Therefore, minimizing energy consumption during media consumption requires a multi-faceted approach that includes both the industry and individual consumers.

Reducing energy consumption in media consumption

While media consumption tends to be energy-intensive, there are several steps individuals can take to minimize their energy footprint:

1. Optimize streaming settings: Adjusting video quality settings to lower resolutions and reducing screen brightness can significantly reduce the energy consumption of streaming services.

2. Power management: Enable power-saving features on devices and ensure they are properly shut down when not in use. This simple practice can save significant amounts of energy over time.

3. Choose energy-efficient devices: When purchasing new devices for media consumption, consider energy-efficient models that have low standby power consumption and are certified with energy efficiency labels.

4. Device usage habits: Encourage responsible device usage by consciously limiting screen time and avoiding unnecessary media consumption. This not only reduces energy consumption but also promotes a healthier digital lifestyle.

5. Support sustainable media: As media consumers, we have the power to influence the industry by supporting content that is produced using sustainable practices. Choose media platforms and providers that prioritize energy efficiency and environmental sustainability.

By adopting these practices, we can collectively reduce the energy consumption associated with our media consumption habits and contribute to a more sustainable media landscape.

Real-world example: Netflix's energy-saving efforts

Netflix, one of the world's leading video streaming platforms, has been actively working to minimize the energy consumed during media consumption. In 2021, Netflix committed to achieving net-zero greenhouse gas emissions by the end of 2022. As part of its efforts, the company has implemented various strategies to reduce energy consumption in its content delivery system.

One notable example is the development of a new video encoding algorithm called AV1. This algorithm enables more efficient video compression without compromising video quality. By using AV1 for video playback, Netflix can significantly reduce the amount of data transmitted, leading to lower energy consumption in data centers and devices.

Furthermore, Netflix is collaborating with device manufacturers to improve energy efficiency in streaming devices. By optimizing power management features and promoting energy-saving practices, they aim to minimize the energy footprint of streaming devices.

Netflix's initiatives demonstrate the importance of industry-wide efforts to address the energy consumption associated with media consumption. Such examples serve as inspiration for other media providers and consumers to prioritize energy efficiency and contribute to a more sustainable media ecosystem.

Summary

In summary, media consumption has a significant impact on energy consumption and subsequently contributes to environmental consequences. The energy consumed in media production and consumption has wide-ranging implications for the sustainability of the media industry.

To minimize the energy consumption associated with media consumption, it is essential to consider both the production phase and the consumption phase. Encouraging energy-efficient practices in media production, such as using LED lighting and renewable energy sources, can reduce the environmental footprint of media content.

Additionally, as media consumers, we can optimize our media consumption habits by adjusting streaming settings, managing device power usage, supporting energy-efficient devices, and promoting responsible device usage. By embracing these practices, we can collectively reduce the energy consumption of media consumption and contribute to a more sustainable media landscape.

Real-world examples, such as Netflix's energy-saving endeavors, highlight the potential for positive change within the media industry. It is important for stakeholders to continue collaborating and innovating to create a more sustainable future for media consumption.

E-Waste and Consumer Electronics

Toxic materials in consumer electronics

The production and disposal of consumer electronics pose significant environmental challenges due to the presence of toxic materials. These materials can cause harm to both human health and the environment if not handled properly. In this section, we will explore the various toxic materials commonly found in consumer electronics, their impact, and the importance of responsible disposal.

Toxic materials commonly found in consumer electronics

Consumer electronics such as smartphones, laptops, and televisions contain a variety of toxic materials. Some of the most common ones include:

1. **Lead (Pb)**: Lead is often found in older electronic devices, especially in solder used for circuit boards. It is harmful to humans, especially children, and can cause developmental issues, neurological damage, and other health problems.

2. **Mercury (Hg)**: Mercury is commonly used in flat-screen displays and compact fluorescent lamps (CFLs) found in electronics. It is a potent neurotoxin and can contaminate water sources and fish, posing a risk to both humans and wildlife.

3. **Cadmium (Cd)**: Cadmium is present in rechargeable batteries, such as nickel-cadmium (NiCd) batteries found in older electronic devices. It is toxic to humans and can cause kidney and lung damage. Improper disposal of cadmium-containing batteries can also contaminate soil and water.

4. **Brominated flame retardants (BFRs)**: BFRs are used to reduce the flammability of electronic devices. However, they are persistent organic pollutants and have been linked to hormone disruption and neurological effects. BFRs can also pose risks during the recycling and disposal of electronic waste.

5. **Polyvinyl Chloride (PVC)**: PVC is commonly used in cables, wires, and casings of electronic devices. During its production and disposal, PVC can

release toxic chemicals, including dioxins, which are known carcinogens and can harm the environment.

6. **Arsenic (As):** Arsenic is often used in the production of glass screens for electronics. It can pose health risks to both humans and animals if ingested or inhaled and is classified as a carcinogen.

It is essential to understand the presence of these toxic materials in consumer electronics to address the environmental and health risks associated with their production and disposal.

Impact of toxic materials

The improper handling and disposal of electronic waste can have various negative impacts on the environment and human health. Here are some key impacts of toxic materials:

- **Pollution of air, soil, and water:** When electronic waste is incinerated or landfilled, toxic substances such as lead, mercury, and brominated flame retardants can leach into the environment, contaminating air, soil, and water. This contamination poses risks to ecosystems, wildlife, and human populations.

- **Health risks to workers:** Electronic waste recycling and disposal often take place in informal settings, exposing workers to hazardous materials without proper safety measures. Workers involved in these processes can suffer from respiratory issues, skin diseases, and other health problems due to their exposure to toxic substances.

- **Resource depletion and energy consumption:** The extraction and processing of raw materials for electronic devices contribute to resource depletion and energy consumption. Proper recycling and recovery of materials from electronic waste can help reduce the need for new resource extraction and save energy.

To mitigate these impacts, it is crucial to adopt responsible practices throughout the lifecycle of consumer electronics, from production to disposal.

Responsible disposal and recycling

Responsible disposal and recycling of electronic waste are essential to minimize the environmental and health impacts of toxic materials. Here are some key strategies for ensuring responsible disposal:

- **E-waste collection systems:** Governments, manufacturers, and recycling organizations should establish convenient and accessible e-waste collection systems that enable consumers to recycle their electronic devices easily. These systems should be properly regulated to ensure that the collected waste is handled and processed safely.

- **Safe recycling practices:** Electronic waste recycling facilities should adhere to strict guidelines and regulations to protect workers and the environment. This includes proper handling and treatment of hazardous materials, as well as the safe extraction and recovery of valuable components.

- **Extended producer responsibility:** Manufacturers should take responsibility for the entire lifecycle of their products, including the safe disposal and recycling of electronic waste. Implementing extended producer responsibility programs encourages manufacturers to design products with fewer toxic materials, improve recyclability, and provide incentives for eco-friendly disposal practices.

Promoting awareness among consumers about the importance of responsible disposal and recycling is also crucial. Educational campaigns, eco-labeling schemes, and partnerships with electronics retailers can help raise awareness and encourage sustainable practices.

Case study: Apple's recycling program

Apple, a leading consumer electronics company, has implemented a comprehensive recycling program to address the issue of toxic materials in electronic waste. The program includes the following initiatives:

- **Product design:** Apple strives to eliminate or reduce toxic materials in its products. For example, they have eliminated the use of mercury in their displays and reduced the amount of lead in their devices.

- **Recycling infrastructure:** Apple has established recycling programs in various countries, allowing customers to return their old devices for proper recycling. They have also invested in recycling technologies to recover valuable materials from electronic waste.

- **Material recovery:** Apple's recycling facilities utilize advanced techniques to recover precious metals like gold and copper from recycled devices. This reduces the dependence on mining for these resources.

- **Renewable energy:** Apple aims to power all its facilities, including recycling centers, with renewable energy, minimizing the carbon footprint of the recycling process.

Apple's recycling program serves as a model for other manufacturers, showcasing the importance of responsible disposal and recycling to minimize the impact of toxic materials.

Conclusion

Toxic materials in consumer electronics present significant challenges for both the environment and human health. Understanding the presence of these materials and their impact is crucial for promoting responsible production, consumption, and disposal practices.

By adopting strategies such as responsible recycling, extended producer responsibility, and eco-design, we can mitigate the environmental and health risks associated with toxic materials in consumer electronics. It is the collective responsibility of individuals, manufacturers, and policymakers to prioritize sustainability and ensure a safer future for both electronic devices and the planet.

Planned obsolescence and its impact on e-waste

Planned obsolescence is a strategy employed by manufacturers to intentionally design products with a limited lifespan. The goal is to encourage consumers to purchase new products, creating a continuous cycle of consumption. While this may seem like a smart business strategy, planned obsolescence has significant implications for e-waste generation and environmental sustainability.

Background

The concept of planned obsolescence emerged in the early 20th century with the rise of mass production. Manufacturers realized that by intentionally making products prone to failure or becoming outdated quickly, they could stimulate demand and boost sales. This strategy was initially applied to light bulbs, but it soon extended to a wide range of consumer goods, including electronics.

Principles of Planned Obsolescence

There are different types of planned obsolescence, each targeting a specific aspect of a product's lifespan:

1. **Functional obsolescence:** Products are intentionally designed with components that are likely to fail or become obsolete after a certain period. This makes repairs difficult or costly, encouraging consumers to replace the entire product rather than fixing it.

2. **Technological obsolescence:** Products are purposely designed to become outdated quickly due to rapid advancements in technology. This creates a constant desire for the latest version or model, even if the current one is still functional.

3. **Style obsolescence:** Products are designed to go out of style or become aesthetically undesirable within a short period. This encourages consumers to purchase new products to keep up with changing trends.

Impact on E-Waste

Planned obsolescence contributes significantly to the generation of electronic waste, or e-waste. As consumers are compelled to replace their electronic devices more frequently, the discarded products end up in landfills or improperly disposed of, posing environmental and health risks. Here are some key impacts of planned obsolescence on e-waste generation:

1. **Increasing e-waste volumes:** With shorter product lifecycles, the rate of e-waste generation has skyrocketed. The United Nations estimates that around 50 million metric tons of e-waste were generated globally in 2019 alone. This rapid increase in e-waste poses challenges for waste management and recycling systems.

2. **Toxic components in e-waste:** Electronic devices contain various hazardous substances such as lead, mercury, cadmium, and brominated flame retardants. When improperly disposed of, these toxic substances can leach into the soil and water, polluting ecosystems and posing risks to human health.

3. **Limited recycling options:** E-waste recycling is complex due to the diverse range of materials used in electronic devices. Many components, such as circuit boards and batteries, require specialized processes to extract valuable materials. However, due to the high costs and technical challenges, a significant portion of e-waste still goes unrecycled.

4. **Energy and resource consumption:** The manufacturing of electronic devices consumes substantial amounts of energy and resources. When these products are replaced frequently due to planned obsolescence, it leads to unnecessary resource depletion and increased carbon emissions.

Addressing the Impact

Combatting the impact of planned obsolescence on e-waste requires a multi-faceted approach involving various stakeholders, including manufacturers, consumers, and policymakers. Here are some strategies and solutions that can help mitigate the problem:

1. **Design for longevity and repairability:** Manufacturers can prioritize product durability and easy repairability by using modular designs, standardized components, and accessible repair manuals. This would extend the lifespan of products and reduce the need for frequent replacements.

2. **Promote sustainable consumption:** Consumers can make informed choices by considering the environmental impact of products before purchasing. Supporting companies that prioritize sustainability and longevity can incentivize manufacturers to adopt more responsible practices.

3. **Implement extended producer responsibility (EPR):** Governments can enforce regulations that hold manufacturers responsible for the end-of-life disposal of their products. EPR programs can incentivize manufacturers to design products with recyclability in mind and ensure proper recycling and disposal mechanisms are in place.

4. **Encourage recycling and proper disposal:** Improving e-waste recycling infrastructure and accessibility can help reduce the environmental impact. Governments, NGOs, and electronics manufacturers should collaborate to establish convenient recycling programs and educate the public about the importance of proper disposal methods.

5. **Advocate for policy changes:** Policymakers play a crucial role in incentivizing sustainable practices and discouraging planned obsolescence. They can introduce legislation, such as mandatory labeling indicating a product's repairability and durability, or tax incentives for manufacturers that adopt sustainable production and design practices.

Case Study: Fairphone

Fairphone, a Dutch social enterprise, provides a remarkable example of addressing planned obsolescence and promoting sustainability in electronics. They have developed modular smartphones designed for repairability and longevity. The modular design allows users to replace individual components, such as the camera or battery, instead of replacing the entire phone. Fairphone also prioritizes ethically sourced materials and supports fair working conditions throughout the supply chain. Their approach demonstrates that it is possible to create electronic devices that have a reduced environmental and social impact.

Conclusion

Planned obsolescence poses a significant challenge to environmental sustainability, particularly in the context of e-waste generation. The intentional design of products with limited lifespans exploits consumer behavior and contributes to the rapid accumulation of toxic electronic waste. Mitigating the impact of planned obsolescence requires a collaborative effort involving manufacturers, consumers, and policymakers. By focusing on design for longevity, responsible consumption, recycling, and policy changes, we can work towards a more sustainable and circular economy, reducing the environmental impact of electronic devices. Let us take a step towards a future where products are built to last, promoting a healthier planet for generations to come.

Recycling and Responsible Disposal of Electronic Devices

In today's digital age, electronic devices have become an integral part of our lives. From smartphones to laptops to televisions, these devices not only provide us with entertainment and convenience but also contribute to various environmental challenges. The improper disposal and lack of recycling of electronic devices have resulted in the accumulation of electronic waste or e-waste, which poses significant environmental and health risks. In this section, we will explore the importance of recycling and responsible disposal of electronic devices, along with strategies and initiatives that promote sustainable practices.

Understanding Electronic Waste

Electronic waste, commonly referred to as e-waste, includes discarded electronic devices such as computers, mobile phones, televisions, and other consumer electronics. These devices contain hazardous materials like lead, mercury, cadmium, and brominated flame retardants, which can contaminate the environment if not disposed of properly.

The rapid advancement of technology and the increasing demand for newer devices have led to a significant rise in e-waste generation. According to a report by the United Nations, approximately 53.6 million metric tons of e-waste was generated globally in 2019, with only 17.4

The Environmental Impact of Improper Disposal

When electronic devices are improperly disposed of, they often end up in landfills or incinerators. This has severe consequences for both the environment and human health. Here are some of the key environmental impacts of improper e-waste disposal:

- **Toxic Chemical Leaching:** The hazardous materials present in electronic devices can seep into the soil and groundwater, contaminating water sources and posing a risk to ecosystems and human health.

- **Air Pollution:** Improper incineration of e-waste releases toxic fumes, including heavy metals and dioxins, contributing to air pollution and exacerbating respiratory problems.

- **Resource Depletion:** Electronic devices contain valuable resources such as gold, silver, copper, and rare earth metals. Improper disposal results in the loss of these resources, leading to increased mining activities and further environmental degradation.

Importance of Recycling Electronic Devices

Recycling electronic devices is vital to minimize the environmental and health risks associated with e-waste. Here are some reasons why recycling electronic devices is of utmost importance:

- **Conservation of Natural Resources:** Recycling electronic devices allows for the extraction of valuable resources from old devices, reducing the need for raw material extraction through mining.

- **Reduction of Hazardous Waste:** Proper recycling ensures the safe disposal of hazardous materials present in electronic devices, preventing their release into the environment and minimizing health risks.

- **Energy Conservation:** Recycling requires less energy compared to the extraction and refining of raw materials. By recycling electronic devices, we can conserve energy and reduce carbon emissions associated with manufacturing processes.

- **Promoting Circular Economy:** Recycling electronic devices promotes the concept of a circular economy by extending the lifespan of products and keeping valuable materials in the production cycle.

Strategies for Responsible Disposal and Recycling

To promote responsible disposal and recycling of electronic devices, various strategies and initiatives have been implemented at different levels. Here are some key strategies:

- **Collection Programs:** Governments, manufacturers, and environmental organizations have established collection programs where individuals can drop off their old electronic devices for proper recycling. These programs aim to make the process convenient and easily accessible for consumers.

- **E-Recycling Facilities:** Dedicated e-recycling facilities ensure the safe handling and recycling of electronic devices. These facilities employ specialized techniques to extract valuable materials while minimizing the release of hazardous substances.

- **Extended Producer Responsibility (EPR):** EPR is a regulatory approach that holds manufacturers accountable for the entire lifecycle of their products, including responsible disposal and recycling. By implementing EPR policies, manufacturers are encouraged to design products that are more easily recyclable and environmentally friendly.

- **Awareness and Education:** Raising awareness among individuals and educating them about the importance of e-waste recycling is crucial. Informative campaigns can be conducted through media, schools, and community programs to encourage responsible disposal practices.

Case Study: Dell's Recycling Initiatives

Dell Technologies, a leading computer manufacturer, has implemented innovative recycling initiatives that promote responsible disposal of electronic devices. One such initiative is the Dell Reconnect Program, which partners with Goodwill Industries to provide a convenient drop-off location for consumers to recycle their old computers and accessories. Dell also operates a take-back program that allows customers to return Dell products for recycling at no cost.

Through these initiatives, Dell has successfully diverted millions of pounds of e-waste from landfills, conserving valuable resources and reducing environmental impacts. Such successful case studies can inspire other companies and individuals to adopt sustainable practices in electronic device disposal.

Exercise

Consider a scenario where you own a smartphone that is no longer in use. How would you ensure its responsible disposal? Outline the steps you would take to recycle the device and minimize its environmental impact.

Conclusion

The responsible disposal and recycling of electronic devices are critical for mitigating the environmental and health risks associated with e-waste. By implementing proper recycling practices and raising awareness about the importance of responsible disposal, we can contribute to a more sustainable and circular economy. It is our collective responsibility to ensure that electronic devices are recycled responsibly, preserving valuable resources and protecting our planet for future generations.

Sustainable Alternatives to Consumer Electronics

In today's digital age, consumer electronics play a significant role in our lives. However, the rapid advancement and obsolescence of these devices contribute to a significant amount of electronic waste (e-waste) and environmental impacts. To address this issue, it is crucial to explore sustainable alternatives to consumer electronics. In this section, we will discuss various sustainable options that can help reduce the environmental footprint of electronic devices.

Repair and Refurbishment

One sustainable alternative to consumer electronics is repairing and refurbishing devices instead of replacing them. Often, when electronic devices encounter minor issues or malfunctions, people tend to discard them and purchase new ones. However, by promoting repair services and refurbishment programs, we can extend the lifespan of electronic devices and reduce e-waste.

Repair cafes and specialized repair shops are becoming more common, offering services to repair smartphones, laptops, and other electronic devices. By fixing broken components or upgrading outdated hardware, these repair services not only reduce e-waste but also save consumers money.

Some manufacturers have also begun offering official repair programs, providing spare parts, and manuals to assist consumers in fixing their devices. By supporting these repair initiatives, we can encourage a shift towards a more sustainable approach to consumer electronics.

Modular Design

Another sustainable alternative is the adoption of modular design in electronic devices. Traditional electronic products are often manufactured as a single unit, making it difficult to repair or upgrade individual components. However, modular design allows for the replacement of specific modules or parts, making repairs and upgrades easier.

By designing electronic devices with modules that can be easily replaced or upgraded, we can reduce the need for replacing entire devices. For example, modular smartphones have emerged in recent years, enabling users to replace components like the camera, battery, or display, instead of buying an entirely new phone.

Modular design not only helps extend the lifespan of electronic devices but also reduces the overall environmental impact by minimizing e-waste generation. It promotes a more sustainable approach by allowing users to adapt their devices to changing needs, enhancing their longevity.

Open-Source Hardware and Software

Open-source hardware and software are gaining popularity as sustainable alternatives in the realm of consumer electronics. Open-source hardware refers to the release of hardware designs and specifications to the public, allowing individuals and communities to build, modify, and upgrade electronic devices using readily available information.

Similarly, open-source software provides access to the source code, enabling users to modify and customize the software to suit their specific requirements. By embracing open-source solutions, consumers have more control over their devices, reducing dependence on manufacturers and promoting a culture of reusability and repairability.

Open-source initiatives also foster communities of knowledge-sharing, encouraging collaboration and innovation in sustainable electronic solutions. They provide platforms for individuals to document their repair experiences, share troubleshooting techniques, and collectively work towards improving the lifespan and sustainability of consumer electronics.

Ethical and Sustainable Brands

When considering sustainable alternatives to consumer electronics, it is essential to support ethical and sustainable brands. Some manufacturers prioritize sustainability in their production and supply chain practices, offering electronics with lower environmental footprints.

These brands may focus on using responsibly sourced materials, reducing energy consumption in production, implementing waste reduction measures, or supporting recycling programs. By consciously choosing products from these brands, consumers can contribute to creating a demand for sustainable electronics while encouraging other manufacturers to adopt environmentally friendly practices.

Take ethical considerations into account when purchasing consumer electronics. Look for certifications like the Electronic Product Environmental Assessment Tool (EPEAT) or certifications related to responsible mineral sourcing, such as the Conflict-Free Sourcing Initiative (CFSI) for minerals like tantalum, tin, tungsten, and gold.

Consumer Awareness and Education

Education and awareness play a vital role in promoting sustainable alternatives to consumer electronics. By informing consumers about the environmental impacts of electronic devices and the availability of sustainable options, we can empower individuals to make informed choices.

Educational campaigns, workshops, and online resources can help spread awareness about the importance of responsible consumption and the available alternatives in the market. Governments, non-profit organizations, and educational institutions can collaborate to develop materials and initiatives aimed at educating consumers on sustainable electronic practices.

Additionally, fostering media literacy and critical thinking skills among consumers can help identify and avoid greenwashing tactics employed by companies that falsely claim sustainability. Being able to distinguish between genuinely sustainable options and those that merely appear to be can guide consumers towards making more sustainable choices.

Conclusion

In conclusion, sustainable alternatives to consumer electronics are essential to address the environmental impacts associated with the production, consumption, and disposal of electronic devices. Repair and refurbishment, modular design, open-source hardware and software, supporting ethical brands, and consumer awareness and education are all important strategies to reduce e-waste and promote sustainable practices.

By embracing these alternatives, we can contribute to a more sustainable future and minimize the negative environmental consequences of consumer electronics. It is crucial for individuals, manufacturers, and policymakers to work together towards the adoption and implementation of sustainable practices in the realm of consumer electronics.

The role of media in promoting sustainable electronic choices

In today's digital age, electronic devices have become an integral part of our lives. From smartphones and laptops to televisions and gaming consoles, these devices have revolutionized the way we communicate, work, and entertain ourselves. However, the rapid advancement of technology has led to a concerning issue—electronic waste, also known as e-waste. As media plays a significant role in shaping public opinion and behavior, it has a crucial role to play in promoting sustainable electronic choices.

Understanding the impact of electronic consumption

Before we delve into the role of media in promoting sustainable electronic choices, let's first understand the impact of electronic consumption on the environment. Electronic devices are composed of various components, including toxic materials such as lead, mercury, and cadmium. Improper disposal of these devices can lead to serious environmental pollution and health hazards.

Additionally, the production of electronic devices also has substantial environmental consequences. Energy-intensive processes, extraction of raw materials, and the disposal of hazardous substances during manufacturing contribute to greenhouse gas emissions and the depletion of natural resources.

Media's responsibility in raising awareness

Media has a powerful influence in shaping public opinion and behavior. As such, it has a responsibility to raise awareness about the environmental impact of electronic consumption and the importance of sustainable choices. Through various channels such as news articles, documentaries, and social media campaigns, media can educate the general public about the detrimental effects of e-waste and the need for sustainable electronic practices.

Furthermore, media can highlight success stories and initiatives of companies that prioritize sustainability in their electronic products. By showcasing innovative designs, responsible manufacturing practices, and recycling programs, media can inspire individuals and businesses to adopt sustainable electronic choices.

Promoting eco-friendly alternatives

In addition to raising awareness, media can play a crucial role in promoting eco-friendly alternatives to traditional electronic devices. For instance, media can showcase the benefits of energy-efficient appliances, such as laptops and televisions, which consume less electricity compared to their conventional counterparts. By emphasizing the long-term cost savings and environmental benefits of such devices, media can encourage consumers to make sustainable choices.

Media outlets can also feature emerging technologies, such as renewable energy-powered devices and solar-powered chargers, to demonstrate the potential for a greener future. Moreover, media can educate consumers about the importance of extending the lifespan of electronic devices through repair and upgrade programs, reducing the demand for new products.

Collaboration with electronic manufacturers

To have a transformative impact, media must collaborate with electronic manufacturers to promote sustainable practices. By highlighting sustainable brands and companies that prioritize ethical sourcing, responsible manufacturing, and take-back programs, media can shape consumer preferences towards environmentally conscious products.

Media can also provide a platform for open discussions between manufacturers, consumers, and policymakers to address the challenges and opportunities for sustainable electronic choices. Through interviews, debates, and forums, media can foster dialogue and encourage transparency in the electronics industry.

Empowerment through media literacy

To truly make a difference in promoting sustainable electronic choices, media literacy is essential. Media outlets should focus on educating the public about critical thinking, fact-checking, and understanding biased information. By empowering individuals with media literacy skills, people can discern greenwashing tactics used by companies and make informed decisions about sustainable electronic choices.

Moreover, media can collaborate with educational institutions to introduce sustainability-focused curriculum and programs. By integrating sustainability into media studies, students can develop a deeper understanding of the environmental impact of electronic devices and the role of media in promoting sustainable practices.

Unconventional approach: Gamification for sustainable electronic choices

To engage and educate the public on sustainable electronic choices, an unconventional yet effective approach is gamification. Media can develop interactive games or apps that simulate the impact of electronic consumption on the environment. By allowing players to make choices and witness the consequences of their actions, these games can raise awareness and encourage sustainable electronic behaviors in a fun and engaging way.

Conclusion

The role of media in promoting sustainable electronic choices is instrumental in addressing the environmental impact of electronic consumption. Through raising awareness, promoting eco-friendly alternatives, collaborating with electronic manufacturers, empowering individuals through media literacy, and exploring unconventional approaches such as gamification, media can drive change and steer society towards a more sustainable future. It is through collective efforts that we can create meaningful change and ensure a greener and more responsible electronic ecosystem.

Water Consumption in Media Production

Water-intensive processes in media production

In the production of media, such as film and television, there are several processes that require significant water consumption. This section will explore these water-intensive processes and discuss strategies for reducing water consumption in the media industry.

Water is an essential resource in various stages of media production. From location scouting and set design to on-set activities and post-production, water plays a crucial role in ensuring the smooth execution of these processes. However, the excessive use of water can have harmful effects on the environment and contribute to water scarcity.

Water-intensive processes in media production

Media production involves several water-intensive processes. Let's explore some of the key areas where water consumption is significant:

1. **Set design and construction:** When creating sets for film and television productions, water is often required for various purposes such as mixing paints, creating artificial landscapes, or constructing water features. The use of water-based materials and techniques can result in substantial water consumption during the production phase.

2. **Special effects and stunts:** Many films and TV shows incorporate water-driven special effects and stunts. These may involve creating rain scenes, water explosions, or water-based action sequences. These effects require significant amounts of water and can contribute to excessive water consumption.

3. **Location scouting and production activities:** The selection of filming locations can also have implications for water consumption. Some locations may have limited water resources, and the production team may need to rely on external water supply or filtration systems. Additionally, on-set activities such as washing equipment, catering, and sanitation facilities also contribute to water usage.

4. **Post-production and visual effects:** In post-production, water-related effects and visual effects may be added to enhance the final product. This process may involve compositing water elements, creating virtual water bodies, or adding rain effects. These activities may not directly consume physical water but still contribute to the overall water footprint of media production.

Strategies for reducing water consumption in film and television production

To address the water-intensive nature of media production, the industry can adopt various strategies to reduce water consumption. These strategies aim to promote sustainable water practices and minimize the environmental impact of media production. Here are some examples:

   1. **Water-efficient technologies and practices:** The use of water-efficient equipment and technologies can significantly reduce water consumption in media production. For example, employing low-flow plumbing fixtures, water-saving washing machines, and efficient irrigation systems can help conserve water without compromising the quality of the final product.

   2. **Recycling and reuse of water:** Implementing water recycling systems can significantly reduce the need for freshwater intake. Techniques such as greywater recycling, which involves treating and reusing water from sinks, showers, and other non-sewage sources, can be employed on sets to minimize water demand. Additionally, rainwater harvesting systems can provide an alternative source of water for non-potable uses.

   3. **Educating production teams and crew:** Raising awareness among production teams and crew members about sustainable water practices is crucial. Providing training and education on water conservation techniques, such as turning off taps when not in use, using water-efficient cleaning methods, and promoting overall responsible water behavior, can help reduce water consumption on sets.

   4. **Selecting water-conscious locations:** Considering the water availability and limitations of potential shoot locations can minimize the need for excessive water usage. Choosing locations with access to ample water resources or implementing techniques like waterless filming can contribute to water conservation.

   5. **Collaboration with water conservation organizations:** Collaborating with water conservation organizations can provide valuable insights and guidance on promoting sustainable water practices in media production. Such partnerships can help develop industry-specific guidelines and best practices that align with global water conservation efforts.

Example: Water conservation in a film production

To illustrate the implementation of water conservation practices, let's consider the production of a film set in a desert location. The production team can take several steps to minimize water consumption:

First, the team can use water-efficient construction techniques for creating artificial water features. By using materials that require less water to maintain the desired visual effects, the production can reduce water consumption during set construction.

Second, during location scouting, the team can prioritize areas with access to water resources or implement waterless filming techniques where water usage is minimal or eliminated.

Third, on-set, the crew can be educated about the importance of water conservation and encouraged to adopt practices such as reusing water bottles, minimizing water usage during catering, and using water-efficient equipment for cleaning and sanitation.

Additionally, the production team can collaborate with local water conservation organizations to develop sustainable water management plans specific to the desert environment. This partnership can help identify opportunities for water recycling and implement water-wise practices throughout the production process.

By implementing these strategies, the film production can significantly reduce its water footprint and contribute to sustainable water practices in the media industry.

Conclusion

Water-intensive processes in media production have implications for both the environment and water resources. To promote sustainability, the industry needs to prioritize water-saving strategies and adopt water-efficient technologies.

By minimizing water consumption in set design, special effects, location scouting, and post-production, the media industry can make significant progress towards reducing its water footprint. Collaboration with water conservation organizations and educating production teams about water conservation practices are also essential steps in achieving sustainable water practices.

The importance of water conservation extends beyond the media industry. It is a responsibility shared by individuals, organizations, and governments alike to ensure the availability and responsible use of this vital resource. By adopting sustainable water practices, media production can play a role in raising awareness and inspiring positive change for a more sustainable future.

Strategies for reducing water consumption in film and television production

Water conservation is a crucial aspect of sustainable media production. Film and television production processes often require significant amounts of water, from set construction and maintenance to catering and special effects. In this section, we will explore various strategies that can be implemented to reduce water consumption in the film and television industry.

Understanding the Water-Intensive Processes

Before we delve into the strategies, it is essential to understand the water-intensive processes involved in film and television production. These processes include:

- Set construction and maintenance: Water is often used for cleaning sets, watering plants, and creating artificial water bodies such as pools and ponds.

- Catering: Production sets require catering services that use water for food preparation, dishwashing, and cleaning.

- Special effects: Water is frequently used in special effects, such as rain scenes or simulated waterfalls.

- On-location shooting: Filming on location may require access to water for various purposes, including makeup and hygiene, equipment cleaning, and providing water for crew members.

By identifying these water-intensive processes, we can develop strategies to minimize water consumption without compromising the quality of the production.

Implementing Water Conservation Techniques

1. Use water-efficient equipment and fixtures: In film and television production, using water-efficient equipment and fixtures can go a long way in reducing water consumption. For example, using low-flow faucets and low-flush toilets in production facilities and portable restrooms can significantly reduce water usage.

2. Implement proper water management practices: Training production crew members on proper water management is crucial. This includes educating them on the importance of turning off faucets, fixing leaks promptly, and using water responsibly during shoots.

3. Optimize water use during set construction and maintenance: Set construction and maintenance practices can be modified to minimize water usage. By incorporating techniques such as drip irrigation, using mulch to retain moisture in plants, and employing water-efficient cleaning methods, substantial water savings can be achieved.

4. Utilize recycled or alternative water sources: Exploring alternative water sources can help reduce the strain on freshwater supplies. Consider using recycled or treated wastewater for non-potable purposes like cleaning sets or watering plants. Additionally, rainwater harvesting systems can be implemented to provide water for various on-site needs.

5. Plan shooting schedules strategically: Proper scheduling of shoots can minimize water usage. For example, shooting scenes that require water-intensive special effects consecutively can reduce the need for repeated setup and water usage.

6. Encourage sustainable practices among crew and cast: Promote awareness among crew members and cast about the importance of water conservation. Encourage them to adopt sustainable practices in their personal habits, such as taking shorter showers and using water-saving techniques in their daily routines.

Real-World Examples

Several film and television productions have already adopted water conservation measures successfully. Some notable examples include:

1. The film industry in India: Bollywood films have implemented practical measures to reduce water consumption during shoots. They have adopted practices like using recycled water for sets, rainwater harvesting, and employing eco-friendly artificial rain techniques.

2. BBC Earth documentary "Blue Planet II": The production team behind this documentary implemented various water conservation strategies during filming. For instance, they used a closed-loop system to capture and recycle water for tanks and aquariums used to film marine life.

Additional Resources

In addition to the strategies mentioned above, various resources can assist the film and television industry in reducing water consumption. Some of these resources include:

1. Green Production Guide: This comprehensive guide provides filmmakers with practical advice and resources for adopting sustainable practices in all aspects of production, including water conservation.

2. Sustainable Production Certification Programs: Organizations like the Environmental Media Association and the Green Seal Certification offer certification programs that recognize sustainable production practices. These programs provide guidelines and resources for reducing water consumption.

3. Film-specific water conservation consultants: Hiring water conservation consultants who specialize in the film and television industry can provide valuable insights and customized solutions to minimize water usage during production.

Exercises

1. Conduct a water audit: Choose a film or television production and conduct a water audit to identify areas of water consumption and potential water-saving measures.
2. Develop a water management plan: Create a comprehensive water management plan for a fictional film production. Include strategies to reduce, reuse, and recycle water throughout the production process.

Caveats

While implementing strategies for reducing water consumption in film and television production is crucial, it is essential to consider potential challenges. Some caveats to keep in mind include:
1. Balancing water conservation with production requirements: It is essential to strike a balance between water conservation and the specific needs of the production. The strategies implemented should not compromise the quality or vision of the project.
2. Compliance with local regulations: Ensure that any water conservation measures align with local regulations and permits. Some areas may have specific guidelines in place that need to be followed.

Conclusion

Incorporating strategies for reducing water consumption in film and television production is crucial for achieving sustainable media practices. By understanding water-intensive processes, implementing water conservation techniques, learning from real-world examples, and utilizing available resources, the industry can make significant strides in water conservation. Through collective efforts, the film and television industry can contribute to the larger goal of achieving a sustainable and environment-friendly media landscape.

Water scarcity and its impact on media production

Water scarcity is a serious issue that affects various industries, including the media production sector. In this section, we will explore the concept of water scarcity, its causes, and its implications for media production. We will also discuss strategies and techniques that can help mitigate the impact of water scarcity on this industry.

Understanding water scarcity

Water scarcity refers to the lack of sufficient access to clean water for various purposes, including human consumption, agriculture, and industrial activities. It arises when the demand for water exceeds the available supply in a particular region or during a specific period.

There are several factors that contribute to water scarcity. One major factor is the growing global population, which increases the demand for water resources. Additionally, climate change and erratic weather patterns can exacerbate water scarcity, leading to droughts, reduced precipitation, and decreased water availability. Poor water management practices, inefficient irrigation methods, and pollution of water sources also contribute to this issue.

Water scarcity and media production

Media production, particularly film and television production, requires a significant amount of water for various processes such as set construction, prop creation, and cleaning. Water scarcity can have several implications for this industry:

1. Increased costs: When water scarcity occurs, the demand for water increases, which can lead to higher water prices. The increased water costs can significantly impact the budget of media production projects, making them financially challenging to undertake.

2. Production delays: Water scarcity can result in water rationing and restrictions imposed by local authorities. These restrictions can affect the regular functioning of media productions, leading to delays in shooting schedules and overall project timelines.

3. Environmental impact: The media production industry's water consumption contributes to the depletion of local water sources. This can have adverse effects on the environment, including the destruction of wildlife habitats, ecosystem imbalance, and reduced availability of water for local communities.

4. Reputation and public image: With increasing awareness of sustainable practices, media production companies are under scrutiny to adopt environmentally responsible approaches. Any perceived wastage or mismanagement of water resources can damage the reputation and public image of media projects and companies involved.

Mitigating the impact of water scarcity

To address the impact of water scarcity on media production, several strategies and techniques can be employed:

1. Water-efficient practices: Media production companies can adopt water-efficient technologies and practices to minimize their water consumption. This includes using low-flow water fixtures, recycling and reusing water, and implementing water-efficient production processes.

2. Location scouting: Choosing filming locations in regions with abundant water resources or areas that employ sustainable water management practices can reduce the impact of water scarcity on media production. This requires careful consideration during the pre-production phase.

3. Water conservation awareness: Educating the cast, crew, and production staff about the importance of water conservation can promote responsible water usage on set. This can include training on water-saving techniques, encouraging the use of alternative water sources, and regularly reminding everyone about the environmental impact of water scarcity.

4. Collaboration with water conservation organizations: Media production companies can partner with environmental organizations and water conservation initiatives to gain access to expertise, resources, and guidance on sustainable water practices. These partnerships can help ensure that production processes align with water conservation goals.

5. Innovation and technology: Embracing innovative solutions and technologies can also contribute to reducing water consumption during media production. For example, using computer-generated imagery (CGI) instead of building elaborate physical sets can minimize the need for water-intensive construction and reduce overall water usage.

Case study: sustainable water practices in film production

One notable example of sustainable water practices in film production is the production of the movie "Mad Max: Fury Road" directed by George Miller. The film was shot in the arid desert landscapes of Namibia, where water scarcity is a pressing issue.

The production team employed various water-saving techniques such as minimizing water usage on set, implementing efficient irrigation methods for vegetation, and utilizing water treatment and recycling systems. The crew also worked closely with local communities to ensure responsible water usage and conservation during the filming process.

By adopting these sustainable water practices, the production of "Mad Max: Fury Road" minimized its impact on the already water-stressed region, showcasing how media production can be accomplished while being mindful of water scarcity concerns.

Conclusion

Water scarcity poses significant challenges for the media production industry. However, by implementing water-efficient practices, raising awareness of water conservation, and collaborating with water conservation organizations, media production companies can mitigate the impacts of water scarcity on their projects.

The case study of "Mad Max: Fury Road" serves as an inspiration for sustainable water practices in the industry. It highlights the importance of considering the environmental impact of media production and demonstrates how responsible water management can be integrated into filmmaking processes.

In the face of increasing water scarcity, it is crucial for the media production industry to embrace sustainable approaches and contribute to the conservation of this precious resource. By doing so, media professionals can not only minimize their environmental footprint but also inspire positive change and set an example for other industries to follow.

Water Conservation Techniques for Media Industry

Water consumption is a significant concern in the media production industry. From film and television production to broadcasting and streaming platforms, the media industry relies on water-intensive processes that can contribute to water scarcity and environmental degradation. Therefore, implementing water conservation techniques is essential to promote sustainability in the media industry.

Understanding Water-Intensive Processes in Media Production

Media production involves various processes that consume considerable amounts of water. Some of these processes include:

- Set construction and design: The creation of elaborate sets often requires the use of water for painting, wetting materials, and cleaning.

- Wardrobe and makeup: Water is used for cleaning costumes and makeup brushes, as well as providing water supply for actors and crew members.

- Location shooting: Outdoor shoots may require water for various purposes like wetting the ground, creating rain effects, and providing drinking water on-site.

- Equipment cooling: Many production equipment, such as cameras and lighting fixtures, require cooling systems that use water.

- Post-production: Water is used in editing facilities for cooling equipment and maintaining optimal working conditions.

These water-intensive processes can result in significant water consumption, which can be alleviated through the implementation of conservation techniques.

Strategies for Reducing Water Consumption in Film and Television Production

1. Water-efficient equipment: Using water-efficient equipment, such as low-flow nozzles for hoses, can significantly reduce water consumption during set construction, cleaning, and location shooting. Additionally, utilizing energy-efficient cooling systems for equipment can indirectly contribute to water conservation by reducing the energy demand for cooling, which in turn reduces water consumption at power plants.
2. Reusing and recycling water: Implementing systems to collect and treat wastewater on set can enable its reuse for non-potable purposes. For example, treated wastewater can be used for irrigation, washing vehicles, or providing temporary water supplies to crew members. Moreover, capturing rainwater during location shooting can help offset water demand and provide a sustainable water source.
3. Efficient scheduling and planning: Proper planning and scheduling of shoots can minimize water consumption. Shooting scenes that require water-intensive processes on the same day or consecutive days can reduce water wastage due to setup and cleanup. Additionally, optimizing the order of shoots based on their water requirements can help ensure efficient water usage.
4. Education and awareness: Raising awareness among production teams about the importance of water conservation and providing training on water-efficient practices can encourage responsible water usage. This can include educating crew members about the impact of their actions on water resources and providing guidelines for minimizing water consumption during production.
5. Monitoring and measurement: Implementing water monitoring systems can help production teams track and assess their water usage. By understanding water

consumption patterns, it becomes easier to identify areas of excessive usage and implement targeted water-saving measures. Regularly monitoring water consumption also allows for continuous improvement and the identification of opportunities for further conservation.

Water Scarcity and Its Impact on Media Production

Water scarcity is an increasing concern globally, and the media industry is not exempt from its consequences. Filming in areas experiencing water scarcity can lead to conflicts with local communities and strain already limited water resources. This can result in production delays, increased costs, and damage to the reputation of media projects. Therefore, media production companies should consider the following strategies to address water scarcity:

1. Water footprint assessment: Conducting a water footprint assessment helps identify the water-intensive stages in the production process and evaluate the overall water consumption. This assessment allows companies to develop specific water conservation measures tailored to their unique operations and prioritize areas where water-saving efforts will have the most significant impact.

2. Collaboration with local communities: Engaging and collaborating with local communities and water management authorities is crucial to ensure responsible water usage. This can involve obtaining permits, adhering to water restrictions, and involving local communities in water conservation initiatives. Open communication and cooperation can help mitigate conflicts and build sustainable relationships.

3. Offsetting water consumption: Supporting water conservation projects or investing in water restoration initiatives can help offset the water consumption associated with media production. This can include funding local water infrastructure upgrades, supporting watershed restoration projects, or partnering with organizations working towards water conservation.

4. Alternative water sources: In areas with limited water resources, exploring alternative water sources can be an effective solution. This can involve implementing rainwater harvesting systems, utilizing treated or recycled water, or exploring innovative water sourcing technologies like atmospheric water generators. Leveraging new technologies and strategies can help reduce reliance on traditional water sources and ensure a more sustainable water supply.

The Responsibility of Media in Addressing Water-Related Issues

The media industry holds a unique position in influencing public opinion and behavior. Therefore, media organizations have a responsibility to raise awareness about water-related issues and promote sustainable water practices. Here are some ways in which the media can contribute to addressing water-related issues:

1. Reporting on water scarcity: Media outlets can play a vital role in informing the public about water scarcity concerns worldwide and highlighting the impact of water consumption in various industries, including the media sector. By shedding light on these issues, media organizations can encourage the adoption of sustainable practices by individuals, businesses, and governments.

2. Promoting water conservation practices: Through documentaries, news features, and entertainment media, the industry can portray water conservation techniques used in media production. This can inspire individuals and organizations to adopt similar practices and create a ripple effect of sustainable water usage.

3. Collaboration with environmental organizations: Media organizations can collaborate with environmental NGOs and water conservation groups to create awareness campaigns and educational initiatives. This collaboration can include producing content that showcases the importance of sustainable water usage and the role of individuals in conserving water resources.

4. Advocacy for policy changes: Media outlets have the power to advocate for policy changes and regulations that encourage sustainable water practices across industries. By highlighting success stories and sharing data-driven evidence, media organizations can influence policymakers to prioritize water conservation and support initiatives that address water scarcity.

5. Engaging the audience: Utilizing digital platforms and social media, media organizations can engage their audience in online campaigns that promote water conservation. This can include interactive quizzes, sharing tips for water-saving practices, and encouraging individuals to pledge their commitment to reduce water consumption.

In conclusion, water conservation is a crucial aspect of sustainable media production. By implementing water-saving techniques, addressing water scarcity, and using their influence, media organizations can contribute to a more sustainable and responsible industry. It is vital for the media industry to take proactive measures to minimize its water footprint and promote sustainable water practices for a more environmentally conscious future.

Key Takeaways:

- Media production involves water-intensive processes such as set construction, wardrobe, and location shooting.

- Water conservation techniques include using water-efficient equipment, reusing and recycling water, efficient scheduling, and education and awareness.

- Water scarcity impacts media production and can be mitigated through water footprint assessment, collaboration with local communities, offsetting water consumption, and exploring alternative water sources.

- The media has a responsibility to address water-related issues by reporting, promoting water conservation practices, collaborating with environmental organizations, advocating for policy changes, and engaging the audience.

Resources:

- Sustainable Production Guide: Water Conservation (Produced By MediaGreenhouse)

- Water Efficiency in the Entertainment Industry (Green Production Guide)

- Sustainable Filmmaking Toolkit (Sustainable Production Alliance)

- Water Footprint Assessment Guidelines (Water Footprint Network)

- Alliance for Water Efficiency (Non-profit organization focused on water conservation)

Exercises:

1. Conduct research on a film or television production that successfully implemented water conservation techniques. Present your findings, highlighting the strategies used and the impact of these techniques on water consumption.

2. Imagine you are the director of a media production company. Design a comprehensive water conservation plan for the company, considering different stages of production and potential water-saving measures.

3. Create an awareness campaign targeting the general public about the importance of water conservation in the media industry. Outline the key messages, platforms, and strategies you would use to promote sustainable water practices.

The responsibility of media in addressing water-related issues

Water scarcity is a pressing global issue that requires the collective efforts of individuals, organizations, and industries to address. The media, with its powerful influence and reach, has a unique role to play in raising awareness, promoting conservation, and advocating for sustainable water practices. In this section, we will discuss the responsibility of the media in addressing water-related issues, the challenges they face, and the strategies they can employ to make a positive impact.

Understanding the water crisis

Before delving into the responsibility of the media, it is essential to understand the gravity of the global water crisis. Water scarcity affects millions of people worldwide, causing severe social, economic, and environmental consequences. Dwindling water resources, pollution, climate change, and inefficient water management practices exacerbate the problem. It is crucial for the media to educate the public about the severity of the crisis and its implications for both individuals and communities.

Informing and educating the public

One of the primary responsibilities of the media is to inform and educate the public about water-related issues. Through various media platforms such as television, radio, newspapers, and online content, the media can raise awareness and disseminate accurate and actionable information. This includes informing the public about water scarcity, the importance of water conservation, and sustainable water management practices.

Media organizations can feature news articles, documentaries, and interviews with experts to highlight the challenges faced by communities affected by water scarcity. By presenting real-life stories and experiences, the media can humanize the issue, making it more relatable and compelling for the audience.

Furthermore, the media can provide practical tips, guidelines, and resources to help individuals and households reduce water consumption. This can include information on water-saving technologies, behavior changes, and water-efficient appliances. By providing actionable steps, the media can empower individuals to contribute to solving the water crisis.

Promoting water-conscious behavior

In addition to raising awareness, the media should play an active role in promoting water-conscious behavior among its audience. This can be achieved through various strategies:

1. **Content integration:** The media can incorporate water conservation messages into popular TV shows, movies, and advertisements. For example, characters can be shown practicing water-saving habits or discussing the importance of water conservation in the context of the storyline. Advertisements can promote water-efficient products or services, encouraging viewers to make sustainable choices.

2. **Public service announcements (PSAs):** Media organizations can create and broadcast PSAs that highlight the significance of water conservation. These short video or audio clips can be aired during prime time or shared on social media platforms, reaching a wide audience. PSAs can deliver powerful messages, using compelling visuals and narratives to drive behavior change.

3. **Partnerships with water organizations:** The media can collaborate with water conservation organizations, NGOs, and governmental agencies to develop joint campaigns or initiatives. These partnerships can provide platforms for information sharing and amplification of water-saving messages. Media organizations can utilize their platforms to interview experts, share success stories, and promote the work of these organizations.

Investigating and exposing water-related issues

Media organizations have a vital role to play in investigating and exposing water-related issues, such as water pollution, mismanagement of water resources, and conflicts over water rights. Through in-depth investigative journalism and unbiased reporting, the media can uncover instances of corruption, illegal practices, and environmental harm, ensuring accountability and transparency.

Journalists can interview experts, conduct research, and analyze data to shed light on hidden water-related issues. By exposing these issues to the public, the media can put pressure on governments, industries, and other stakeholders to take corrective actions. This can range from stricter regulations and enforcement to corporate accountability and public pressure for change.

Challenges and considerations

While the media has a critical role in addressing water-related issues, there are several challenges and considerations they need to navigate carefully:

- **Balancing sensationalism and accuracy:** The media should strive for balanced and accurate reporting, avoiding sensationalism or exaggeration that could undermine the credibility of water-related issues. Journalists should fact-check their sources, verify information, and provide context to the audience.

- **Avoiding conflicts of interest:** Media organizations should maintain their independence and avoid conflicts of interest that may compromise the integrity of their coverage. They should disclose any affiliations or relationships that could influence their reporting on water-related issues.

- **Reaching diverse audiences:** The media should ensure that their coverage of water-related issues reaches diverse audiences across different socioeconomic backgrounds, age groups, and geographic locations. This can be achieved by utilizing multiple media platforms, languages, and localizing the content to make it relevant to specific regions or communities.

- **Engaging with stakeholders:** Media organizations should actively engage with experts, policymakers, and community members to gain diverse perspectives and insights. By including diverse voices in their coverage, the media can provide a comprehensive understanding of water-related issues and foster dialogue and collaboration.

Conclusion

The responsibility of the media in addressing water-related issues is crucial in tackling the global water crisis. By informing, educating, promoting behavior change, investigating, and exposing water-related issues, the media can leverage its influence to create awareness, inspire action, and drive positive change. Through accurate and engaging content, the media can empower individuals, communities, and decision-makers to prioritize water conservation and sustainable water management practices. It is through collective efforts and a sense of responsibility that we can overcome the water crisis and ensure a sustainable future.

Greenwashing and Media Manipulation

Understanding Greenwashing

Definition and Examples of Greenwashing in Media

Greenwashing refers to the practice of companies or organizations misleading the public about the environmental benefits of their products or practices. It is a form of deceptive marketing that aims to create a positive environmental image for a company, brand, or product, without actually implementing significant sustainable practices. Greenwashing can also be observed in media, where companies use various techniques to enhance their sustainability image and deceive consumers.

4.1.1 Defining Greenwashing

Greenwashing is essentially a form of disinformation, where companies strategically manipulate their marketing messages to appear environmentally responsible, even if their actual practices do not align with sustainability goals. This deceptive messaging can involve claims that are misleading, exaggerated, or simply false. Greenwashing not only misleads consumers but also undermines the efforts of genuinely sustainable companies and weakens the overall credibility of sustainability initiatives.

To identify greenwashing, it is important to understand the various tactics employed by advertisers and media companies. Some common techniques include:

1. Irrelevant or Vague Environmental Claims: Companies often make general statements about their environmental efforts without providing specific details or evidence to support their claims. For example, a company may claim its product is "green" or "eco-friendly" without clearly explaining how it reduces its environmental impact.

2. Hidden Trade-Offs: This involves highlighting a single environmental

benefit of a product or practice while ignoring other negative impacts. For instance, a company may advertise its use of recyclable packaging while not addressing the fact that the product itself is harmful to the environment.

3. Lack of Proof or Certification: Greenwashing may involve making unsubstantiated claims without providing any evidence or certifications to support them. Genuine sustainable companies often obtain certifications from recognized organizations to validate their claims, such as LEED (Leadership in Energy and Environmental Design) certification for buildings or Fair Trade certification for products.

4. Manipulative Imagery: Advertisements may use natural imagery, green colors, or images of plants and animals to create an association with nature and sustainability, even if the product or company has no genuine commitment to the environment.

5. Misleading Labels or Symbols: Companies may use misleading labels or symbols, such as deceptive recycling symbols, to create the impression that the product is environmentally friendly when it may not be.

4.1.2 Examples of Greenwashing in Media

To illustrate the concept of greenwashing in media, here are a few examples:

1. Energy Companies and "Clean Coal": Some energy companies promote the idea of "clean coal" as a sustainable energy source through advertisements and sponsored content. However, the term is misleading as there is no such thing as truly clean coal, and burning coal still contributes significantly to greenhouse gas emissions.

2. Fast Fashion Brands and Sustainable Collections: Certain fast fashion brands have introduced "sustainable" or "eco-friendly" clothing lines to improve their environmental image. However, the overall practices of these brands, such as fast production cycles and poor labor conditions, contradict the sustainability claims of these collections.

3. Cosmetic Companies and Natural Claims: Some cosmetic companies market their products as "natural" or "organic," creating the perception that their products are safer and more environmentally friendly. However, these claims are often unsupported, and the products may still contain harmful chemicals or use unsustainable sourcing methods.

4. Bottled Water Companies and Recycling Initiatives: Bottled water companies often highlight their recycling initiatives through advertising campaigns, suggesting that their products are environmentally responsible. However, the overall environmental impact of single-use plastic bottles remains high, and recycling rates for these products are often low.

It is crucial for media consumers to be vigilant and critically evaluate claims made by companies and organizations. By recognizing these examples of greenwashing, individuals can make informed choices and support genuinely sustainable practices.

Overall, greenwashing in media contributes to a climate of misinformation and prevents consumers from making truly sustainable choices. It is important for media organizations and regulatory bodies to ensure transparent and accurate reporting, hold companies accountable for their sustainability claims, and promote genuinely sustainable practices.

The role of advertising and public relations in greenwashing

Advertising and public relations play a significant role in the phenomenon of greenwashing. Companies often use these communication strategies to create a positive image of themselves and their products or services, particularly in relation to their environmental impact. Greenwashing refers to the practice of misleading consumers about the environmental benefits of a product, service, or company, leading them to believe that they are making a sustainable choice when, in reality, they are not.

1. Definition of greenwashing:

Greenwashing is the act of misleading consumers through advertising and PR campaigns to make a company or product appear more environmentally friendly than it actually is. It involves creating false or exaggerated claims about a product or company's environmental impact and sustainability practices. Greenwashing aims to capitalize on consumers' growing concern for the environment and their desire to make environmentally responsible choices.

2. Strategies used in greenwashing:

a. Deceptive language: Companies often use vague or misleading terms such as "eco-friendly," "green," or "natural" without providing any substantial evidence to support these claims. These terms do not have standardized definitions, allowing companies to use them flexibly. This lack of clarity makes it difficult for consumers to make informed decisions.

b. Irrelevant claims: Some companies may highlight a small environmentally friendly aspect of their product or operation while ignoring other significant negative environmental impacts. By focusing on a single green feature, they attempt to divert attention from larger sustainability issues.

c. False certifications and labels: Greenwashing can also involve using misleading certifications or labels that make a product appear more environmentally friendly than it actually is. These certifications might lack credibility or be self-awarded, without any independent verification.

d. Green imagery and symbolism: Companies may use images of nature, sustainability icons, or green colors in their advertising or packaging to create an association with environmental responsibility. However, these visual cues do not necessarily reflect the actual sustainability practices of the company or product.

e. Diverting attention: Greenwashing can involve diverting attention away from real environmental concerns by focusing on small, inconsequential changes or by highlighting charitable initiatives. This tactic gives the illusion of environmental responsibility without addressing core issues.

3. The impact of advertising and public relations in greenwashing:

a. Influence on consumer behavior: Advertising and PR campaigns play a crucial role in shaping consumers' perception of a company or product. By utilizing persuasive messaging and imagery, companies can influence consumer choices, leading them to believe that they are making sustainable or environmentally responsible decisions while purchasing products or services.

b. Reinforcement of consumer values: Advertising and PR campaigns often tap into consumers' desire for sustainability and environmental responsibility. By associating their products or services with these values, companies create a positive image that resonates with consumers and aligns with their beliefs.

c. Reputation management: Companies utilize advertising and PR strategies to manage their reputation and protect themselves against negative public perception. By highlighting their environmentally friendly initiatives, they attempt to offset criticism or concerns regarding their actual environmental impact.

d. Competitive advantage: Through greenwashing, companies may gain a competitive edge over their rivals by presenting themselves as environmentally responsible. This advantage can increase market share and profitability, as environmentally conscious consumers are more likely to choose products or services that they perceive as sustainable.

4. Examples of greenwashing in advertising and public relations:

a. A clothing company promotes its garments as sustainable, organic clothing, emphasizing the natural fibers used in their production. However, they fail to disclose the harmful chemicals used in the dyeing process or the exploitative labor conditions in their supply chain.

b. An automobile manufacturer presents its new electric vehicle (EV) as a green alternative to traditional fuel-powered cars. However, they fail to mention that a majority of their energy-intensive manufacturing processes still heavily rely on fossil fuels. The company's messaging creates an illusion of environmental friendliness while downplaying the carbon emissions associated with the production and disposal of the EV.

c. A fast-food chain showcases its commitment to reducing plastic waste by introducing compostable packaging for some of its products. However, it fails to address the larger issue of excessive packaging or the environmental impacts associated with its meat sourcing practices.

5. Combating greenwashing:

a. Increased transparency: Companies should provide accurate and transparent information about their sustainability practices and environmental impact. Clear and standardized definitions of eco-friendly terms can help consumers make informed choices.

b. Independent verification: Third-party certifications and labels should carry credibility and strict standards to ensure that they accurately reflect a product or company's environmental claims. Independent audits can help prevent self-awarded certifications.

c. Regulatory oversight: Government regulations can play a significant role in curbing greenwashing practices. Strict guidelines and penalties can discourage companies from making false or exaggerated environmental claims.

d. Consumer education: Improved media literacy and consumer education can empower individuals to identify greenwashing tactics and make informed decisions. By increasing awareness about greenwashing practices, consumers can demand genuine sustainability from companies.

e. Media watchdogs: Journalism, investigative reporting, and media watchdog organizations can play a crucial role in exposing greenwashing practices. By bringing attention to misleading claims, these organizations help hold companies accountable for their environmental impact.

6. Caveats and challenges:

a. Lack of standardized definitions: The use of terms such as "eco-friendly" and "green" without standardized definitions makes it challenging for consumers to discern genuine environmentally responsible products or companies.

b. Complex supply chains and hidden impacts: Companies often have complex supply chains with multiple stakeholders, making it difficult to track and measure their overall environmental impact accurately. Greenwashing can occur when companies focus on one aspect of their operations while ignoring more significant sustainability challenges.

c. Insufficient regulation and enforcement: In some jurisdictions, regulations regarding greenwashing can be limited or inadequate. Lack of enforcement mechanisms can allow companies to continue making false or exaggerated environmental claims without repercussions.

In conclusion, advertising and public relations play a crucial role in greenwashing by creating a positive image of products or companies, often through misleading strategies. Understanding these tactics and fostering transparency, independent verification, regulation, consumer education, and media watchdog efforts are crucial in combating greenwashing and promoting genuine sustainability. It is essential for consumers to be critical and informed to make responsible choices that align with their environmental values.

Greenwashing techniques and their implications

Greenwashing is a deceptive marketing and PR strategy that is used by organizations to portray themselves as environmentally friendly and sustainable, while in reality, their practices may be harmful to the environment. This section will explore some common greenwashing techniques and the implications they have.

Vague or misleading claims

One of the most common greenwashing techniques is the use of vague or misleading claims in marketing materials. For example, a company may use terms like "eco-friendly," "green," or "sustainable" without any clear definition or evidence to support these claims. This can make it difficult for consumers to understand the actual environmental impact of a product or service.

Implication: Vague or misleading claims can lead consumers to believe that they are making environmentally friendly choices when they are not. This can undermine efforts to promote genuine sustainability and can make it challenging for consumers to make informed decisions.

Irrelevant or exaggerated certifications

Another common greenwashing technique is the use of irrelevant or exaggerated certifications. Some organizations may display labels or logos that imply their products or services meet certain environmental standards, even if those standards are unrelated to their core activities. Additionally, some certifications may be obtained without rigorous verification processes, leading to inflated claims.

Implication: Irrelevant or exaggerated certifications can mislead consumers into thinking that a product or service is more sustainable than it actually is. This can create a false sense of trust and discourage consumers from seeking out genuinely sustainable alternatives.

Tokenism and minimal efforts

Tokenism refers to the practice of making minimal efforts towards sustainability without any substantial changes to an organization's overall practices. An organization may engage in a single sustainable initiative or publicize a small aspect of their operations, while ignoring larger, more impactful opportunities for improvement.

Implication: Tokenism can create the illusion of sustainability without actually addressing the underlying environmental issues. This can lead to complacency and hinder meaningful progress towards a more sustainable future.

Green imagery and aesthetics

Some organizations employ green imagery and aesthetics to create the perception of environmental consciousness. This can include the use of natural landscapes, wildlife, or other symbols of nature in marketing materials, regardless of the actual impact of their products or services.

Implication: Green imagery and aesthetics can evoke positive emotions and associations with nature, leading consumers to assume that a company is environmentally friendly. However, this can divert attention from the actual environmental impact of their operations and products.

Lack of transparency and accountability

A lack of transparency and accountability is another common greenwashing technique. Some organizations may withhold or manipulate data related to their environmental performance, making it difficult for stakeholders to assess their true sustainability efforts.

Implication: Without transparency and accountability, it becomes challenging for consumers, investors, and the public to hold organizations accountable for their claims and actions. This lack of accountability undermines trust and hinders progress towards genuine sustainability.

Implications and consequences

The implications of greenwashing are far-reaching and have significant consequences for both the environment and society. Some of these implications include:

- Undermining consumer trust: Greenwashing erodes consumer trust in environmental claims and can lead to skepticism about the authenticity of sustainable practices.

- Detrimental environmental impact: By diverting attention and resources away from genuine sustainability initiatives, greenwashing may contribute to continued environmental degradation.

- Stifling innovation and progress: Greenwashing can discourage organizations from investing in truly sustainable practices, as they rely on superficial or irrelevant gestures instead.

- Missed opportunities for positive impact: By focusing on deceptive marketing tactics, organizations miss the opportunity to make meaningful contributions to environmental preservation and societal well-being.

It is crucial for individuals, organizations, and regulatory bodies to be aware of and actively counter greenwashing practices. This can be achieved through increased transparency, standardized certifications, robust verification processes, and consumer education.

By promoting genuine sustainability and challenging greenwashing tactics, we can foster a more honest and responsible approach to environmental conservation and create a future that truly embraces sustainable media practices.

How to identify and combat greenwashing in media

Greenwashing is a deceptive marketing practice employed by companies to create a false impression of environmental responsibility. It involves the use of misleading claims or actions that make a product or organization appear more environmentally friendly than it actually is. In the context of media, greenwashing can occur through advertisements, press releases, or sponsored content that promotes an environmentally conscious image without genuinely committing to sustainable practices. This section will explore various methods to identify and combat greenwashing in media.

Understanding the signs of greenwashing

To effectively tackle greenwashing, it is essential to be able to identify the signs of deceptive environmental claims. While each case may vary, there are some common indicators to be aware of:

- **Vague language:** Greenwashing often involves using terms like "eco-friendly," "sustainable," or "natural" without providing specific details or evidence.

- **Irrelevant claims:** Some companies may make environmental claims that are unrelated to their primary product or service. For example, a company manufacturing disposable plastic bottles might highlight its efforts to protect wildlife.

- **Lack of third-party verification:** Greenwashing claims should ideally be supported by credible certifications or independent assessments. Without external verification, there is a higher chance of deceptive advertising.

- **Claims of being the "greenest":** Companies claiming to be the most environmentally friendly in their industry should be scrutinized, as it is often unlikely for a single entity to have achieved such a significant lead.

- **Exaggerated or unrealistic claims:** Beware of exaggerated statements that cannot be substantiated or promises that seem too good to be true.

- **Focus on a single environmental attribute:** Companies may highlight one aspect of their operations that appears environmentally friendly while neglecting other significant impacts.

- **Lack of transparency:** Companies that avoid disclosing comprehensive environmental data or fail to respond to inquiries about their practices may be attempting to hide less sustainable aspects of their operations.

It is essential to approach claims of sustainability with a critical mindset and not simply accept them at face value.

Research and fact-checking

The next step in combating greenwashing in media is conducting thorough research and fact-checking. Several resources and tools can help in this process:

- **Certification and labeling schemes:** Look for recognized certifications such as ENERGY STAR, Fairtrade, Forest Stewardship Council (FSC), or Cradle to Cradle Certified™ to validate environmental claims. Research the credibility and rigor of these certifications to ensure they align with your values.

- **Independent organizations and reports:** Consult trustworthy organizations like Greenpeace, World Wildlife Fund (WWF), or Environmental Working Group (EWG) to access reliable information about a company's environmental practices. These organizations often publish reports and guides that expose greenwashing tactics.

- **Company sustainability reports:** Many companies release annual or biennial sustainability reports that disclose their environmental goals, achievements, and ongoing initiatives. These reports provide valuable insights into a company's commitment to sustainability and can help verify environmental claims.

- **Investigative journalism:** Investigative journalism exposes greenwashing practices, holding companies accountable for their misleading claims. Stay updated on investigative reports that uncover deceptive tactics employed by corporations.

By conducting thorough research and fact-checking, it becomes easier to separate genuine sustainability efforts from mere greenwashing.

Consumer empowerment and responsible purchasing

Individual consumers have the power to encourage genuine sustainability and discourage greenwashing by making informed purchasing decisions. Here are some steps consumers can take:

- **Research products and brands:** Before making a purchase, research the company's environmental practices, certifications, and sustainability initiatives. Support companies that demonstrate a genuine commitment to sustainability.

- **Consider the entire product life cycle:** Evaluate a product's environmental impact throughout its entire life cycle, including its raw materials, production processes, packaging, use, and disposal. This holistic approach helps uncover any greenwashing attempts.

- **Support third-party verified products:** Look for products that have been independently certified by recognized organizations. Trustworthy certifications provide confidence in the authenticity of environmental claims.

- **Engage with companies:** Contact companies directly to seek clarification or inquire about their sustainability practices. Their willingness to engage and provide transparent information can be an indication of their commitment to sustainability.

- **Support transparent reporting:** Encourage companies to publish comprehensive sustainability reports that include measurable goals, progress updates, and environmental impact data. Transparency is crucial in holding companies accountable for their claims.

- **Spread awareness:** Educate friends, family, and colleagues about greenwashing, its implications, and how to identify it. By raising awareness, more people can make informed decisions and collectively combat greenwashing.

Consumer activism and responsible purchasing can create a demand for genuine sustainability, pushing companies to be transparent and accountable for their environmental claims.

Media literacy and critical thinking

Media literacy plays a crucial role in combating greenwashing. By empowering individuals to think critically about media messages, they can better discern greenwashing tactics. Here are some strategies to enhance media literacy:

- **Promote critical thinking skills:** Educate individuals on the principles of critical thinking, including the ability to question, analyze, and evaluate information. This equips them with the tools to identify greenwashing attempts.

- **Encourage media literacy education:** Schools, colleges, and community organizations should incorporate media literacy education into their curriculum. This education should include understanding marketing strategies, recognizing bias, and evaluating environmental claims.

- **Diversify media sources:** Encourage individuals to seek information from a variety of sources to gain a broader perspective. This helps avoid relying solely on corporate media that may be susceptible to greenwashing.

- **Monitor social media discussions:** Monitor social media platforms for discussions and debates on greenwashing. Engage in these conversations and share accurate information to counter misleading claims.

- **Support investigative journalism:** Investigative journalism plays a pivotal role in uncovering greenwashing practices. Become a patron of independent journalism or support platforms that prioritize investigative reporting.

By fostering media literacy and critical thinking skills, individuals can become active agents in identifying and combating greenwashing practices.

Government regulations and industry standards

Government regulations and industry standards are necessary to deter greenwashing and enforce transparency. Here are some ways governments and industries can combat greenwashing:

- **Strengthening regulations:** Governments can enact stricter regulations regarding environmental claims in advertising and packaging. These regulations can include penalties for companies found guilty of greenwashing.

- **Establishing independent certification bodies:** Governments can support the establishment and recognition of reliable third-party certification bodies. These bodies would ensure that certifications are credible and trustworthy.

- **Encouraging reporting standards:** Governments can set reporting standards that require companies to disclose comprehensive environmental data, making it easier to assess the authenticity of their claims.

- **Collaboration between industries:** Industries can collectively establish industry-wide standards for environmental sustainability and promote responsible marketing practices. This collaboration ensures a level playing field and discourages greenwashing across the board.

Government regulations and industry standards are instrumental in creating an environment where greenwashing becomes less appealing and riskier for companies.

Case Study: The Volkswagen emission scandal

The Volkswagen emission scandal serves as a cautionary tale and an example of how greenwashing can have severe consequences. In 2015, it was revealed that Volkswagen had intentionally manipulated emissions tests in their diesel vehicles to comply with environmental regulations falsely. This scandal demonstrated the significance of independent regulatory bodies and the need for robust mechanisms to detect and prevent greenwashing.

The incident spurred increased scrutiny of the automotive industry's environmental claims and resulted in stricter regulations and greater transparency. It also highlighted the importance of media and investigative journalism in exposing greenwashing practices, holding corporations accountable, and driving change.

Conclusion

Identifying and combatting greenwashing in media requires a critical mindset, thorough research, informed consumer choices, media literacy, and regulatory measures. By staying vigilant and demanding transparency, individuals and society can ensure that sustainability claims are genuine and that companies are held accountable for their environmental impact.

The role of media in promoting genuine sustainability

In today's digital age, media plays a critical role in shaping public opinion and behavior. With its widespread reach and influence, media has the power to educate, inspire, and mobilize individuals towards sustainable practices. This section explores the important role that media can play in promoting genuine sustainability.

Understanding the concept of genuine sustainability

Genuine sustainability goes beyond mere lip service or greenwashing. It involves a deep commitment to long-term environmental, social, and economic well-being. Genuine sustainability requires a holistic approach that considers the interconnectedness of various systems and strives for solutions that are equitable, inclusive, and regenerative.

Media has the ability to influence public perception of sustainability, and therefore it is crucial for media organizations to uphold the principles of genuine sustainability. This involves promoting truthful, evidence-based information, avoiding sensationalism, and showcasing real-world examples of sustainable practices.

The power of storytelling and media narratives

One of the most effective ways media can promote genuine sustainability is through storytelling. Humans are wired to connect with narratives, and stories have the power to evoke emotions, provoke critical thinking, and inspire action.

By highlighting stories of individuals, communities, and organizations that are leading the way in sustainable practices, media can create a sense of hope and empowerment. These stories can demonstrate the positive impact of sustainable choices and solutions, making them more accessible and relatable to a wider audience.

Additionally, media narratives can challenge the status quo and question unsustainable practices. By exposing the environmental and social consequences of unsustainable actions, media can raise awareness and encourage individuals to reconsider their own behaviors.

Countering misinformation and greenwashing

One of the key roles of media in promoting genuine sustainability is countering misinformation and greenwashing. Greenwashing refers to misleading or deceptive practices used by companies or organizations to create a false impression of environmental responsibility.

Media organizations have a responsibility to fact-check and critically evaluate sustainability claims made by companies, politicians, or other influential figures. By providing accurate information and exposing greenwashing tactics, media can empower the public to make informed decisions and support genuinely sustainable practices.

Collaboration with sustainability experts and organizations

To promote genuine sustainability, media organizations should collaborate with sustainability experts and organizations. These partnerships can provide valuable insights, research, and expert opinions, ensuring that media coverage is grounded in credible information.

Additionally, collaborating with sustainability organizations can foster a sense of collective responsibility and encourage dialogue around sustainability issues. By giving voice to diverse perspectives and facilitating discussions, media can amplify the conversation and contribute to the development of sustainable solutions.

Promoting actionable steps and behavior change

While raising awareness is important, media should also focus on promoting actionable steps and behavior change. People often feel overwhelmed by the scale of global challenges and may believe that their individual actions are insignificant. Media can play a crucial role in breaking down complex issues and showcasing practical ways in which individuals can contribute to sustainability.

Through informative articles, videos, and interactive content, media can educate the public about sustainable practices and provide resources for further action. This can include tips for reducing carbon footprint, guidance on sustainable consumption, and information on local sustainability initiatives.

Engaging the audience through interactive media

To effectively promote genuine sustainability, media should embrace interactive formats that engage the audience. This can include interactive websites, online forums, social media, and immersive experiences such as virtual reality.

Through interactive media, individuals can actively participate in the sustainability conversation, ask questions, share their experiences, and learn from each other. This can help create a sense of community and empower individuals to take ownership of their role in promoting genuine sustainability.

Conclusion

The media has an immense role to play in promoting genuine sustainability. By embracing storytelling, countering misinformation, collaborating with experts, and engaging the audience, media organizations can inspire, educate, and empower individuals towards sustainable practices.

It is important for media professionals to recognize their ethical responsibility in shaping public opinion and prioritize genuine sustainability over greenwashing or profit-driven agendas. By doing so, media can contribute to a more sustainable future for generations to come.

Let us now move on to the next section, which explores the concept of media bias and its impact on sustainability discourse.

Media Bias and Agenda-Setting

The influence of media on public opinion

The media plays a crucial role in shaping public opinion on various issues, including sustainability. Through its ability to disseminate information, convey emotions, and present different perspectives, the media has the power to influence how people perceive and interpret the world around them. In this section, we will explore the ways in which media influences public opinion and the implications it has for sustainability discourse.

The power of media narratives

One of the primary mechanisms through which media influences public opinion is through storytelling and narrative construction. Media outlets have the ability to shape the narrative surrounding a particular topic, framing it in a way that appeals to their target audience and aligns with their own interests or ideologies. Through the use of language, imagery, and selective reporting, media organizations can manipulate public perception and opinion.

For example, in the context of sustainability, media narratives can either emphasize the urgent need for environmental action or downplay the significance of sustainability issues. By framing environmental problems as distant or disconnected from everyday life, the media may foster a sense of complacency or apathy among the public. Conversely, by presenting relatable stories of individuals and communities affected by environmental degradation, the media can elicit empathy and inspire action.

Agenda-setting and media bias

Another way in which media influences public opinion is through agenda-setting. This theory suggests that the media not only influences what people think about but also what they think is important. By giving certain issues more coverage and attention, the media can shape public perception and priorities.

Media bias is an inherent challenge in this process. Bias can occur in various forms, including political, corporate, ideological, or cultural biases. Media outlets may have their own agendas or interests that influence how they report on sustainability issues. For example, a media organization funded by fossil fuel companies may downplay the urgency of climate change or promote alternative explanations for environmental degradation.

To address media bias and ensure a more balanced representation of sustainability issues, it is essential for media consumers to engage in critical thinking and media literacy. By seeking out diverse perspectives, fact-checking information, and being aware of potential biases, individuals can make more informed judgments and decisions related to sustainability.

The role of social media

In recent years, the rise of social media platforms has further amplified the influence of media on public opinion. Social media allows for the rapid dissemination of information and facilitates the formation of online communities around specific issues. However, it also poses challenges in terms of filtering out misinformation and promoting civil discourse.

Social media algorithms prioritize content based on user preferences, which can create echo chambers and reinforce existing beliefs. This can lead to the polarization of public opinion, making it difficult to have productive discussions on complex issues like sustainability.

To leverage the power of social media for positive change, it is crucial for individuals to critically evaluate the information they encounter and engage in respectful and evidence-based dialogue. By sharing accurate and reliable information, individuals can contribute to the dissemination of sustainable narratives and counteract misinformation.

Examples and case studies

To illustrate the influence of media on public opinion, let's consider a couple of examples:

1. Climate change coverage: Media outlets have a significant impact on the public's perception of climate change. Studies have shown that media coverage can affect the salience of climate change as an issue and influence public attitudes and behaviors. For instance, media coverage that emphasizes scientific consensus and highlights the potential consequences of climate change can increase public concern and support for climate action.

2. Environmental activism and media representation: Media plays a crucial role in amplifying the voices of environmental activists and marginalized communities. By providing a platform for their stories and struggles, media can bring attention to environmental justice issues and inspire collective action.

Promoting media literacy and responsible consumption

To counteract the influence of media on public opinion, it is essential to promote media literacy and responsible consumption. Here are some strategies:

1. Critical thinking skills: Educating individuals about media literacy and critical thinking can help them identify bias, misinformation, and manipulation techniques.

2. Diverse sources of information: Encouraging media consumers to seek out diverse sources of information, including independent journalism and scientific literature, can provide a more comprehensive understanding of sustainability issues.

3. Fact-checking and verification: Encouraging individuals to fact-check information before sharing it can help prevent the spread of misinformation and ensure the accuracy of shared content.
4. Engaging in constructive dialogue: Encouraging respectful and evidence-based discussions on social media platforms can foster understanding and facilitate the exchange of different viewpoints.

By promoting media literacy and responsible consumption, individuals can become active participants in shaping public opinion and contribute to sustainable discourse.

In conclusion, the media has a significant influence on public opinion, including perceptions of sustainability. Understanding the power of media narratives, agenda-setting, and media bias is crucial for engaging with sustainability issues in a critical and informed manner. By promoting media literacy and responsible consumption, individuals can play an active role in shaping public opinion and contributing to a more sustainable future.

The role of media in shaping social justice narratives

Media plays a crucial role in shaping social justice narratives and influencing public opinion on various social issues. It has the power to highlight societal inequalities, challenge systemic oppression, and promote positive change. In this section, we will explore the different ways in which media shapes social justice narratives and the impact it has on sustainable media.

Media as an agenda-setter

One of the primary roles of media is to set the agenda for public discourse. Media outlets have the power to decide which issues receive attention and coverage, thus shaping the public's perception of what is important. When it comes to social justice narratives, media plays a pivotal role in amplifying marginalized voices and shedding light on injustices.

For example, consider the Black Lives Matter movement. Media coverage of police brutality against Black individuals and systemic racism has brought these issues to the forefront of public consciousness. The extensive media coverage has helped raise awareness and mobilize people to take action, leading to widespread protests and demands for change.

By highlighting social justice issues, media can influence public opinion, shape attitudes, and inspire collective action. This, in turn, contributes to the broader discourse on sustainability and the need for a more just and equitable society.

Framing social justice narratives

Media has the power to frame social justice narratives by presenting stories and information in a particular way. The framing of an issue can influence how it is perceived and understood by the audience. Therefore, media professionals have a responsibility to be mindful of the frames they use when addressing social justice issues.

For instance, media coverage of environmental activism can shape public attitudes towards sustainability. If the media frames environmental activists as radical troublemakers, it can undermine the legitimacy of their cause. On the other hand, framing activists as concerned citizens working towards a better future can generate empathy and support for their efforts.

Moreover, media can play a role in challenging stereotypes and promoting inclusivity. By showcasing diverse voices and experiences, media can break down barriers and promote a more inclusive society. For example, the representation of LGBTQ+ individuals in the media has played a significant role in challenging societal prejudices and promoting equal rights.

Media as a platform for social change

In addition to framing social justice narratives, media can act as a powerful platform for social change. It provides a space for marginalized communities to share their stories and experiences, amplifying their voices and empowering them to demand justice.

Documentaries, films, and television shows have the potential to spark conversations, raise awareness, and change societal attitudes. For instance, the documentary "13th" directed by Ava DuVernay shed light on systemic racism in the criminal justice system, leading to a broader discourse on racial inequality and mass incarceration.

Furthermore, social media platforms have democratized the ability to share information and mobilize communities. Hashtags such as #MeToo and #BlackLivesMatter have created online movements that have translated into real-world action.

Media's responsibility in promoting social justice

While media plays a crucial role in shaping social justice narratives, it also carries a responsibility to ensure accuracy, fairness, and inclusivity in its coverage. Media professionals must strive for balanced reporting, avoiding biases that perpetuate systemic inequalities or misrepresent marginalized communities.

To promote social justice, media organizations should prioritize diverse representation in their stories, newsrooms, and decision-making processes. This means actively seeking out and amplifying the voices of underrepresented communities. Additionally, media outlets should collaborate with community organizations and experts to ensure accurate and nuanced coverage of social justice issues.

It is also essential for media consumers to be critical and discerning of the information they consume. Media literacy and critical thinking skills play a vital role in understanding the complexities of social justice narratives and identifying biased or misleading content.

In conclusion, media is a potent tool in shaping social justice narratives and influencing public opinion. By setting the agenda, framing the discourse, providing a platform for marginalized voices, and promoting social change, media can contribute to a more equitable and sustainable society. However, media professionals and consumers alike must exercise responsibility and ensure that social justice narratives are accurate, fair, and inclusive. Only through a collective effort can media be a force for positive social change.

Media bias and its impact on sustainability discourse

Media bias refers to the tendency of journalists and news organizations to favor certain perspectives or present information in a way that aligns with their own beliefs or interests. This bias can have a significant impact on the sustainability discourse as it affects how environmental issues are reported, discussed, and understood by the public. In this section, we will explore the different types of media bias, its consequences, and strategies for promoting unbiased and balanced media coverage.

Types of media bias

Media bias can manifest in various forms, and it is important to recognize and understand these biases in order to critically assess media content. Some common types of media bias include:

- **Political bias:** This bias occurs when media organizations favor a particular political ideology or party in their reporting. Political bias can influence how environmental issues are framed and discussed, leading to skewed or incomplete information being presented to the public.

- **Sensationalism and conflict bias:** Media outlets often prioritize sensational or controversial stories, as they generate higher ratings and increase profits. This bias can distort the coverage of sustainability issues, focusing on conflict rather than presenting a nuanced understanding of the complexities involved.

- **Corporate bias:** Media organizations may have financial ties to industries that contribute to environmental degradation. This bias can result in the under-reporting or misrepresentation of environmental issues to protect corporate interests.

- **Selective reporting bias:** Journalists may selectively report information that supports their pre-existing beliefs or biases, leading to a distorted view of sustainability problems and potential solutions.

Consequences of media bias in sustainability discourse

Media bias can have far-reaching consequences for the sustainability discourse. Some of these consequences include:

- **Distorted public understanding:** Media bias can shape public perceptions of environmental issues, leading to a misunderstanding of the challenges at hand. When certain perspectives are consistently favored or ignored, it becomes difficult for the public to make informed decisions and participate in meaningful conversations about sustainability.

- **Polarization of opinions:** When media coverage is biased, it can fuel polarization among different interest groups, hindering collaboration and cooperation on environmental issues. Biased reporting may amplify existing divisions and prevent the emergence of common ground and shared solutions.

- **Undermining trust in media:** Media bias erodes the trust that people have in journalistic institutions. When media outlets are perceived as pushing an agenda or being influenced by political or corporate interests, the public may become skeptical of the information presented, making it difficult to disseminate accurate and reliable information about sustainability.

- **Obstacles to policy-making:** Biased media coverage can hinder the development and implementation of effective environmental policies. When policy-makers are influenced by skewed information, it becomes challenging to create evidence-based policies that address the root causes of sustainability issues.

Strategies for promoting unbiased and balanced media coverage

Promoting unbiased and balanced media coverage is crucial for fostering a well-informed and engaged public. Here, we present some strategies that can help mitigate media bias in the sustainability discourse:

- **Encouraging diverse voices:** Media organizations should prioritize including diverse perspectives in their reporting. This means ensuring that a wide range of stakeholders, including marginalized communities and environmental experts, are given a platform to share their insights and experiences.

- **Fact-checking and verification:** Journalists and news organizations should prioritize fact-checking and verification of information before publishing. This can help counteract the spread of misinformation and ensure that environmental issues are accurately reported.

- **Transparency and accountability:** Media outlets should be transparent about their funding sources, potential conflicts of interest, and ideological leanings. By holding themselves accountable and being open about their biases, media organizations can build trust with their audience.

- **Media literacy education:** Promoting media literacy among the general public is essential for enabling critical analysis of news content. By equipping individuals with the skills to identify and evaluate biased reporting, they can make more informed decisions and become active participants in the sustainability discourse.

- **Support for independent journalism:** Encouraging the growth of independent and non-profit media organizations can help counteract the influence of biased reporting. These organizations often have a greater capacity to pursue investigative journalism and provide a more nuanced and balanced view of environmental issues.

It is important to recognize that total objectivity in media reporting may be challenging to achieve, as biases can be ingrained in various ways. However, by adopting these strategies, we can strive for a more accurate, balanced, and inclusive sustainability discourse that empowers individuals to take informed action towards a sustainable future.

Example: Shifting the narrative on renewable energy

In recent years, media bias has influenced the public perception of renewable energy. Some media outlets, driven by political or corporate interests, have portrayed renewable energy as unreliable, expensive, or even harmful to the economy. This biased reporting has hindered the widespread adoption of renewable energy technologies and policies.

To counteract this bias, organizations like the Renewable Energy Association have partnered with independent journalists and media outlets to produce balanced and evidence-based reports on renewable energy. By providing accurate information and highlighting the benefits of clean energy, they have successfully shifted the narrative and increased public support for renewable energy initiatives.

By challenging media bias and promoting unbiased reporting, we can empower individuals to make informed choices, participate in the sustainability discourse, and collectively work towards a more environmentally sustainable future.

Additional Resources:

- Bagdikian, B. H. (2004). The new media monopoly. Beacon Press.

- Boykoff, M. T. (2011). Who speaks for the climate? Making sense of media reporting on climate change. Cambridge University Press.

- Entman, R. M. (2012). Scandal and silence: Media responses to presidential misconduct. John Hopkins University Press.

- McChesney, R. W. (1999). Rich media, poor democracy: Communication politics in dubious times. University of Illinois Press.

- Stromer-Galley, J. (2007). Presidential campaigning in the internet age. Oxford University Press.

Exercises:

1. Choose a recent environmental issue and analyze the media coverage surrounding it. Identify any biases or skewed perspectives present in the reporting and discuss the potential impact of this bias on public understanding and engagement with the issue.

2. Conduct a media analysis of a sustainability-related topic by comparing coverage from different news outlets. Identify any differences in bias, framing, or agenda-setting and consider how these variations might shape public perception.

3. Engage in a media literacy exercise by critically analyzing a news article or video related to sustainability. Identify any potential biases, misconceptions, or factual inaccuracies, and present alternative perspectives or additional information to provide a more balanced view.

In conclusion, media bias can have a significant impact on the sustainability discourse by shaping public understanding, fueling polarization, and hindering the development of effective policies. However, by promoting diverse voices, fact-checking information, fostering transparency, and promoting media literacy, we can mitigate bias and foster a more informed and engaged public. Striving for unbiased and balanced reporting is crucial in empowering individuals to make sustainable choices and driving positive environmental change.

Strategies for promoting unbiased and balanced media coverage

Unbiased and balanced media coverage is essential for fostering a well-informed society and promoting a healthy public discourse. In order to achieve this, media organizations need to implement various strategies to ensure that their reporting is objective, fair, and unbiased. Here, we will discuss some effective strategies for promoting unbiased and balanced media coverage.

1. Diversify newsroom composition

One key strategy to promote unbiased and balanced media coverage is to establish a diverse and inclusive newsroom composition. By bringing together journalists from different backgrounds, experiences, and perspectives, media organizations can reduce biases and ensure a more comprehensive understanding of the issues at hand. This diversity should include not only racial and ethnic backgrounds but also gender, age, and socioeconomic diversity. When journalists with diverse perspectives collaborate, they can challenge each other's viewpoints and provide a more nuanced and balanced perspective on the news.

Media organizations can implement programs to actively recruit and retain journalists from underrepresented communities. Additionally, they should create an inclusive and supportive work environment that encourages open dialogue and the sharing of different viewpoints.

2. Provide comprehensive training for journalists

Journalistic training plays a crucial role in promoting unbiased and balanced media coverage. It is essential that media organizations invest in comprehensive training programs for their journalists to ensure they have the necessary skills and knowledge to report objectively and ethically.

Training programs should focus on critical thinking, fact-checking, and avoiding personal biases. Journalists should be equipped with the tools to critically analyze information, verify sources, and cross-reference different perspectives. They should also be trained to recognize their own biases and consciously strive for balanced reporting. Media organizations can invite experts from various fields to conduct workshops and seminars, offering practical guidelines and case studies on ethical journalism.

3. Implement fact-checking and editorial review processes

Fact-checking and editorial review processes are essential to ensure the accuracy and reliability of news reporting. Media organizations should establish robust fact-checking departments or collaborate with independent fact-checking organizations. This will help in verifying the accuracy of information before it is presented to the public.

Editorial review processes should involve multiple levels of scrutiny and editing. Senior editors should review reporters' work to ensure it meets the organization's standards of objectivity, fairness, and balance. Additionally, media organizations should have mechanisms in place to address complaints and corrections from readers or viewers.

4. Encourage diverse perspectives in reporting

Promoting unbiased and balanced media coverage requires providing space for diverse perspectives in reporting. Journalists should make a conscious effort to seek out and include a range of viewpoints in their stories. This not only helps to present a more comprehensive picture but also fosters a culture of inclusion and respect for different opinions.

Media organizations can establish partnerships with diverse communities and organizations to ensure the inclusion of underrepresented voices in their reporting. They can also create platforms for public participation, such as opinion sections, where members of the community can share their views on various issues.

5. Avoid sensationalism and clickbait

Sensationalism and clickbait have become pervasive in modern media, often compromising the integrity of news reporting. Media organizations need to prioritize substance over sensationalism and clickbait headlines.

Journalists should focus on telling stories that are important and impactful, rather than simply chasing ratings or clicks. By reporting on substantive issues with thorough research and analysis, media organizations can regain public trust and promote unbiased and balanced coverage.

6. Foster transparency and accountability

Transparency and accountability are essential to promote unbiased and balanced media coverage. Media organizations should be transparent about their editorial policies, ownership, and funding sources. This helps to build trust with the audience and ensures that reporting is not influenced by hidden agendas.

Additionally, media organizations should hold themselves accountable for any reporting errors or biases. Publicly acknowledging mistakes and taking steps to correct and learn from them is crucial in maintaining credibility and public trust.

By implementing these strategies, media organizations can promote unbiased and balanced media coverage. It is important for journalists and media organizations to recognize their role as information gatekeepers and strive to deliver accurate, fair, and balanced reporting to the public. Ultimately, an informed society depends on responsible journalism that promotes diverse perspectives and upholds the principles of objective and ethical reporting.

The ethical responsibility of media in reporting unbiased news

In today's fast-paced and interconnected world, the media has a significant impact on shaping public opinion and influencing societal discourse. With this influence comes a great ethical responsibility for media organizations to report news in an unbiased and objective manner. The media's role is not only to inform the public but also to hold the powerful accountable and provide a fair and balanced representation of events and issues.

Understanding media bias

Media bias refers to the systematic favoritism or prejudice towards particular ideologies, political parties, or interest groups in the presentation of news and information. It can manifest in various forms, such as the selection and framing of stories, use of language and rhetorical devices, and the omission or underreporting of certain perspectives.

There are different types of bias, including partisan bias, ideological bias, and sensationalism. Partisan bias occurs when media outlets favor one political party or ideology over another, leading to a skewed representation of events. Ideological

MEDIA BIAS AND AGENDA-SETTING

bias refers to the tendency of media organizations to promote a particular set of beliefs or values. Sensationalism, on the other hand, involves the exaggeration or dramatization of news stories to attract attention and increase viewership or readership.

The impact of media bias on sustainability discourse

Media bias can have a profound impact on the way sustainability issues are addressed and discussed in society. When media organizations are biased in their reporting, they may prioritize certain environmental concerns over others, leading to a distortion of the public's understanding of sustainability problems.

For example, if a media outlet has a bias towards the fossil fuel industry, it may downplay the urgency of transitioning to renewable energy sources and promote skepticism towards climate change. This biased reporting can hinder public support for sustainable initiatives and impede progress towards a greener and more sustainable future.

Furthermore, media bias can undermine public trust in the media and lead to a polarized society. When individuals are exposed to biased news sources that align with their preexisting beliefs, it can reinforce echo chambers and contribute to a deepening divide in public opinion.

Strategies for promoting unbiased and balanced media coverage

Promoting unbiased and balanced media coverage is crucial for fostering a well-informed society and ensuring the ethical responsibility of media outlets. Here are some strategies that can help achieve this goal:

1. **Transparency and accountability:** Media organizations should be transparent about their editorial processes, including how stories are selected, fact-checked, and edited. They should also have mechanisms in place to address and rectify any instances of bias or unethical reporting.

2. **Diverse newsroom representation:** Encouraging diversity in newsrooms is essential to ensuring a range of perspectives that can contribute to unbiased reporting. Media organizations should strive to have diverse teams that reflect the demographics and experiences of society.

3. **Fact-checking and verification:** Journalists have a responsibility to verify information before reporting it. Fact-checking is crucial in combating the spread of misinformation and maintaining credibility. Media organizations

should invest in training journalists in fact-checking techniques and provide resources for effective verification.

4. **Balanced reporting:** Media outlets should make a conscious effort to present multiple viewpoints on contentious issues to provide a balanced representation. This includes seeking input from experts, incorporating diverse voices, and avoiding the practice of false equivalency by giving equal weight to unfounded claims.

5. **Promoting critical thinking and media literacy:** Educating the public on how to critically evaluate news sources, discern reliable information, and identify bias is essential in combating the influence of biased reporting. Media literacy programs should be integrated into educational curricula to equip individuals with the skills to navigate the media landscape effectively.

The ethical responsibility of journalists

Journalists play a crucial role in upholding the ethical standards of reporting unbiased news. They have a responsibility to the public, their sources, and their profession. Here are some ethical principles that should guide journalists in their reporting:

- **Objectivity:** Journalists should strive to present the facts impartially, avoiding personal opinions and biases. They should differentiate between reporting and commentary and clearly label opinion pieces to distinguish them from news articles.

- **Independence:** Journalists should resist any external pressures, whether from advertisers, governments, or interest groups, that may compromise their independence and integrity. They should prioritize the public interest over any personal or organizational agenda.

- **Accuracy and fairness:** Journalists should diligently gather and verify information before publishing or broadcasting a story. They should provide context and strive for accuracy, ensuring that all relevant perspectives are represented fairly.

- **Accountability:** Journalists should be accountable for their work and willing to correct any errors promptly. They should respond to public feedback and concerns constructively and transparently.

- Ethical decision-making: Journalists should adhere to ethical principles and professional codes of conduct. They should evaluate the potential impact of their reporting on individuals and society, ensuring that their work respects privacy, avoids harm, and promotes justice and truth.

Case study: Unbiased reporting on climate change

One notable case study that demonstrates the ethical responsibility of media in reporting unbiased news is the coverage of climate change. Given the global implications of climate change and the urgent need for action, accurate and unbiased reporting on this issue is crucial.

News organizations have a responsibility to accurately communicate the scientific consensus on climate change and avoid false balance by presenting fringe views as equivalent to mainstream scientific understanding. By doing so, they can provide the public with a clear understanding of the risks and solutions associated with climate change.

Additionally, media outlets should prioritize long-term coverage of climate change, highlighting the connections between environmental sustainability, social justice, and economic development. By contextualizing climate change within broader societal issues, journalists can foster a more comprehensive understanding of the challenges and opportunities for sustainability.

Conclusion

The ethical responsibility of media in reporting unbiased news is paramount to the functioning of a democratic society. By adhering to principles of objectivity, fairness, accuracy, independence, and accountability, media organizations and journalists can contribute to a more informed and engaged public. Upholding these ethical standards is crucial to ensure the media's positive role in addressing sustainability challenges and promoting a just and sustainable future.

Social Justice Warrior (SJW) Agendas in Media

Understanding Social Justice Warrior (SJW) Movement

Definition and Origins of the SJW Movement

The term "Social Justice Warrior" (SJW) has become a popular and often controversial label in recent years. It refers to individuals who actively advocate for social justice causes, often through online activism and public demonstrations. The SJW movement emerged as a response to various social and political issues, aiming to address systemic inequalities and promote inclusivity in society.

The origins of the SJW movement can be traced back to the early 2000s, primarily within online communities and social media platforms. It gained momentum as individuals started using these platforms to voice their concerns about social inequality and injustice. With the increasing accessibility of the internet and the rise of social media, these conversations spread rapidly, bringing together people from diverse backgrounds who shared common goals of promoting social justice.

The core values of the SJW movement center around advocating for marginalized groups, promoting equality, and challenging oppressive structures that perpetuate social injustice. This includes fighting against racism, sexism, homophobia, transphobia, ableism, and other forms of discrimination. SJWs often call attention to, and work to dismantle, systems of power and privilege that disadvantage certain groups in society.

The movement has its roots in various social justice movements that have been active for decades, including civil rights, feminism, LGBTQ+ rights, and disability activism. It draws inspiration from the works of activists and scholars who have laid the foundation for challenging systemic oppression and promoting equality.

One key aspect of the SJW movement is its emphasis on amplifying marginalized voices and experiences. It seeks to create spaces where individuals who are often silenced or underrepresented can be heard and supported. This involves elevating the stories and perspectives of marginalized communities, as well as promoting dialogue and education around issues of social justice.

Like any movement, the SJW movement is not without its critics and controversies. Some argue that certain individuals within the movement employ aggressive tactics, engage in online harassment, or prioritize identity politics over substantive debate. However, it is important to note that the actions of a few individuals should not overshadow the broader goals and intentions of the movement.

In conclusion, the SJW movement emerged as a response to social injustices and inequalities, with the aim of promoting social justice and equality for all people. While it has faced criticism and controversy, it plays a vital role in challenging oppressive systems and amplifying the voices of marginalized communities. Understanding the definition and origins of the SJW movement is essential for engaging in constructive dialogue and working towards a more inclusive and just society.

The influence of SJWs in media production

Defining the SJW Movement

To understand the influence of Social Justice Warriors (SJWs) in media production, we need to first define the movement. SJWs are individuals who advocate for social justice causes, often through online activism and public advocacy. They seek to address various forms of social inequality, including gender, race, sexuality, and more. The SJW movement emerged primarily in the late 2000s and gained prominence through social media platforms.

Promoting Social Justice in Media

SJWs have significantly influenced media production by pushing for greater representation and inclusivity. They highlight the underrepresentation of marginalized groups in media, such as people of color, LGBTQ+ individuals, and individuals with disabilities. In response to these calls for representation, media producers have started incorporating more diverse characters and storylines into their content.

For example, television shows like "Orange is the New Black" and "Pose" feature diverse casts and explore issues related to race, gender, and sexuality. Films like

"Moonlight" and "Black Panther" have brought underrepresented voices and stories to the forefront, receiving critical acclaim and commercial success.

The influence of SJWs can also be seen in the advertising industry. Brands are now actively engaging in socially conscious advertising campaigns that address issues such as body positivity, gender stereotypes, and environmental sustainability. This shift is a direct result of the pressure exerted by SJWs, who have raised awareness about the importance of responsible advertising practices.

Challenges and Criticisms

While the SJW movement has made positive contributions to media production, it has also faced criticism and generated controversy. Some argue that the movement has led to a "cancel culture" where individuals or institutions are publicly criticized or boycotted for perceived violations of social justice principles.

Critics of SJWs claim that their influence has stifled freedom of speech and artistic expression, fearing that controversial or provocative content may be censored or shelved due to potential backlash. Additionally, some argue that the focus on social justice issues detracts from other important concerns, such as economic inequality or environmental sustainability.

Navigating the Balance

Navigating the balance between social justice concerns and media production is a complex task. It requires careful consideration of diverse perspectives and an ongoing dialogue between content creators, audiences, and social justice advocates.

Media producers need to strike a balance by promoting inclusivity and representation without compromising artistic freedom. This can be achieved by engaging in diverse hiring practices, involving underrepresented groups in the creative process, and actively listening to feedback from marginalized communities.

Additionally, media organizations should invest in diversity training and education to ensure the fair and accurate representation of various identities and social justice issues. By incorporating diverse voices and perspectives, media producers can create content that resonates with a wider audience and contributes to a more inclusive society.

It is important to acknowledge that progress in social justice representation is an ongoing journey. Media production must continue to evolve, adapt, and address the systemic barriers that prevent equal representation and fair treatment for all individuals.

Real-World Example: "Crazy Rich Asians"

One example that showcases the influence of SJWs in media production is the film "Crazy Rich Asians." This romantic comedy-drama, released in 2018, became a global phenomenon and a milestone in Asian representation in Hollywood.

Driven by the demand for more diverse and inclusive stories, "Crazy Rich Asians" featured an all-Asian cast and portrayed a modern Asian culture outside of stereotypes. The film's success demonstrated the economic viability of diverse storytelling and paved the way for more Asian-led film projects.

The impact of "Crazy Rich Asians" extended beyond box office success. It ignited conversations regarding representation and provided a platform for Asian actors, directors, and writers to share their stories authentically. This illustrates how the influence of SJWs can lead to significant positive change in media production.

Resources and Further Reading

For further exploration of the influence of SJWs in media production and the broader social justice movement, the following resources are recommended:

- "*So You Want to Talk About Race*" by Ijeoma Oluo provides an accessible guide to understanding and discussing racial injustice, including its portrayal in media.

- "*Reel Inequality: Hollywood Actors and Racism*" by Nancy Wang Yuen examines racial disparities in the entertainment industry and offers insights into the struggles faced by minority actors.

- "*Exposure: A Sociologist Explores Sex, Society, and Adult Entertainment*" by Chauntelle Tibbals explores the intersection of sex, media, and social justice through a sociological lens.

- The websites and social media accounts of prominent social justice organizations, such as Color of Change, GLAAD, and the National Association for the Advancement of Colored People (NAACP), provide valuable information and updates on social justice issues.

By engaging with these resources, individuals can gain a deeper understanding of the influence of SJWs in media production and contribute to the ongoing conversation surrounding social justice in media.

UNDERSTANDING SOCIAL JUSTICE WARRIOR (SJW) MOVEMENT

SJW Agendas and Their Impact on Sustainability Discourse

The influence of Social Justice Warrior (SJW) agendas on sustainability discourse cannot be ignored. SJWs are individuals who actively advocate for social justice causes and aim to create inclusive and equitable societies. While their intentions may be noble, the impact of their agendas on sustainability discourse is both positive and negative. In this section, we will delve into the different aspects of SJW agendas and examine their implications on the broader sustainability movement.

Defining SJW Agendas

SJW agendas refer to the social justice causes and concerns that individuals and groups promote within various sectors of society, including media. These agendas often focus on issues related to race, gender, sexuality, and other aspects of identity. Advocates of SJW agendas believe that these issues are integral to creating a fair and just society.

It is important to note that the term "SJW" is sometimes used derogatorily to dismiss or diminish the concerns raised by individuals fighting for social justice. However, for the purposes of this discussion, we will use the term to refer to individuals who actively engage in promoting social justice causes.

The Influence of SJW Agendas

The impact of SJW agendas on sustainability discourse is multifaceted. On one hand, SJWs bring attention to systemic inequalities and power structures that are often at the root of environmental and social problems. They emphasize the importance of addressing social justice issues in conjunction with environmental sustainability.

SJWs also play a crucial role in amplifying the voices of marginalized communities that have been disproportionately affected by environmental degradation. By highlighting the experiences of these communities, SJWs shed light on the intersectionality between social and environmental justice.

Moreover, SJWs have been instrumental in challenging traditional power structures and advocating for inclusivity and diversity in media. This includes representation of diverse voices, experiences, and perspectives in sustainability discussions. By doing so, they aim to ensure that sustainability discourse is inclusive and equitable.

Challenges and Criticisms

However, SJW agendas within sustainability discourse also face challenges and criticisms. Some argue that focusing on social justice causes detracts from the core goal of environmental sustainability. They believe that the emphasis on social issues diverts attention and resources away from environmental issues, hindering progress in areas such as climate change mitigation and biodiversity conservation.

Another criticism leveled against SJW agendas is the potential for the co-optation and dilution of important sustainability messages. Critics argue that the focus on identity politics within sustainability discourse can overshadow the urgent need for collective action to address global environmental challenges.

Balancing Social Justice and Environmental Sustainability

Finding a balance between social justice concerns and environmental sustainability is crucial for a holistic approach to sustainability discourse. It is essential to recognize the interconnectedness of social and environmental issues and work towards solutions that address both.

By acknowledging the importance of inclusivity and diversity, sustainability discourse can become more comprehensive and reflect the experiences of marginalized communities. This requires listening to and elevating the voices of those affected by environmental degradation and amplifying their perspectives.

Additionally, collaboration between different stakeholders is key to reconciling the potential conflicts between social justice and environmental sustainability. Engaging in dialogue and finding common ground allows for the development of shared goals and strategies that incorporate both social justice and environmental considerations.

Media's Role

The media plays a pivotal role in shaping the narrative around SJW agendas and their impact on sustainability discourse. It is important for the media to provide accurate and unbiased coverage of social justice and sustainability issues, avoiding sensationalism or trivialization.

Media outlets have the responsibility to ensure that diverse voices and perspectives are represented, promoting a well-rounded understanding of the complexities of sustainability. By giving space to underrepresented communities and highlighting their experiences, the media can foster dialogue and bridge divides within sustainability discourse.

Furthermore, the media can play a crucial role in educating the public about the importance of intersectionality in sustainability. Through documentaries, news articles, and social media campaigns, the media can raise awareness about the interconnections between social justice and environmental issues, encouraging individuals to take action.

Conclusion

SJW agendas have both positive and negative implications for sustainability discourse. While they bring attention to social justice issues and amplify marginalized voices, they can also face criticisms for detracting from environmental priorities. Finding a balance between social justice concerns and environmental sustainability is necessary to create an inclusive and equitable approach to sustainability. The media has a significant role to play in shaping the narrative around SJW agendas and fostering a comprehensive understanding of sustainability discourse.

Balancing social justice concerns with environmental sustainability

In the pursuit of sustainability, it is essential to consider not only the environmental aspects but also the social justice concerns that arise in the media industry. Balancing these concerns can be a complex task, as they often intersect and impact one another. In this section, we will explore the challenges and strategies involved in addressing both social justice and environmental sustainability in the media.

Understanding social justice concerns

To effectively address social justice concerns, it is important to have a clear understanding of what they entail. Social justice refers to the fair and equitable distribution of opportunities, privileges, and resources in a society. It involves addressing issues of inequality, discrimination, and marginalization based on factors such as race, gender, socioeconomic status, and more.

In the context of media, social justice concerns can manifest in various ways. This includes representation and diversity, cultural appropriation, and the amplification of marginalized voices. The media has a significant influence on shaping public opinion and perpetuating societal norms. Therefore, it plays a crucial role in both promoting and challenging social justice issues.

Environmental sustainability and social justice

While environmental sustainability focuses on reducing harm to the planet and future generations, it is essential to recognize that marginalized communities often bear a disproportionate burden of environmental degradation and climate change. These communities may experience higher levels of pollution, limited access to resources, and increased vulnerability to environmental hazards.

Striving for environmental sustainability without addressing social justice concerns may exacerbate existing inequalities. For example, policies promoting renewable energy may lead to the displacement of marginalized communities or result in unjust economic impacts. Therefore, it is crucial to consider the ways in which environmental actions can intersect with social justice concerns.

Promoting inclusivity and diversity in media

One way to balance social justice concerns with environmental sustainability is by promoting inclusivity and diversity in media production. This involves ensuring representation and accurate portrayal of diverse identities, perspectives, and experiences.

By incorporating diverse voices and stories into media content, it becomes possible to challenge stereotypes, combat discrimination, and foster empathy among audiences. It is important for media producers to work towards creating content that reflects the richness and diversity of our society.

Cultural sensitivity and environmental sustainability

Cultural appropriation is a social justice concern that is closely related to media representation. It refers to the borrowing, adoption, or imitation of elements from another culture without proper understanding, respect, or acknowledgment.

In the context of environmental sustainability, cultural sensitivity is crucial to ensure that practices and solutions are respectful and inclusive. It involves recognizing and valuing indigenous knowledge and perspectives regarding the environment. By engaging in inclusive dialogue and collaboration, it becomes possible to develop sustainable practices that are rooted in cultural wisdom and sensitivity.

Strategies for balancing social justice and environmental sustainability

Balancing social justice concerns with environmental sustainability requires a thoughtful and integrated approach. Here are some strategies that can help achieve this balance:

1. Intersectionality: Recognize the interconnected nature of social justice and environmental issues. Understand that different forms of inequality and oppression intersect and influence one another. Consider the multiple dimensions of identity and how they intersect with sustainability concerns.

2. Collaborative approaches: Foster collaborations between environmental organizations and social justice advocates. By working together, it becomes possible to address the interrelated challenges and identify solutions that promote both environmental sustainability and social justice.

3. Community engagement: Involve communities directly affected by environmental issues in decision-making processes. Engage in meaningful dialogue, listen to their concerns, and incorporate their perspectives into sustainable practices.

4. Education and awareness: Raise awareness about the intersection of social justice and environmental sustainability within the media industry. Educate media professionals and consumers about the importance of balancing these concerns and the potential impacts of their choices.

5. Ethical guidelines: Develop ethical guidelines for media production that encompass both social justice and environmental sustainability concerns. Encourage transparency, accountability, and responsible practices in the industry.

Example: Representation in sustainable fashion

To illustrate the balancing of social justice concerns with environmental sustainability, let's consider the example of sustainable fashion. The fashion industry has a significant impact on the environment, from resource-intensive production processes to the generation of textile waste. Addressing this environmental impact is crucial for sustainability.

However, sustainable fashion also raises social justice concerns related to labor rights, fair wages, and the treatment of garment workers. It is important to ensure that the push for sustainability does not come at the expense of workers' rights and well-being.

To strike a balance, sustainable fashion initiatives can prioritize fair trade practices, promote transparency in the supply chain, and empower workers through education and capacity-building programs. By incorporating social justice principles into sustainable fashion practices, it becomes possible to achieve a more holistic and equitable approach to sustainability.

Conclusion

Balancing social justice concerns with environmental sustainability requires an integrated and inclusive approach. By recognizing the interconnected nature of these issues and promoting inclusivity, diversity, and cultural sensitivity in media, it becomes possible to advance both social justice and environmental goals.

The media industry has a unique opportunity to shape narratives, challenge norms, and drive positive change. By leveraging this power responsibly and ethically, media can play a vital role in promoting a more just and sustainable society.

The need for inclusivity and diversity in media

In today's rapidly changing world, the media plays a vital role in shaping public opinion and influencing societal behaviors. As such, it is crucial for the media industry to embrace inclusivity and diversity to accurately represent the diverse perspectives and experiences of the global population. This section focuses on the importance of inclusivity and diversity in media, the benefits it brings, and strategies for promoting representation and equality.

Understanding Inclusivity and Diversity

Inclusivity in media refers to the representation and acknowledgement of individuals from all backgrounds, including race, ethnicity, gender, sexual orientation, age, abilities, and socio-economic status. Diversity, on the other hand, recognizes the existence of differences among people and aims to incorporate and celebrate these differences in media content.

Inclusivity and diversity in media are crucial for several reasons. Firstly, they reflect the reality of our diverse society, allowing individuals from different backgrounds to see themselves represented and validated. This representation enhances social cohesion and fosters empathy and understanding between different communities.

Furthermore, inclusivity and diversity in media have a positive impact on marginalized groups, providing them with a platform to share their experiences and perspectives. It helps to challenge stereotypes, break down barriers, and promote social justice.

The Benefits of Inclusivity and Diversity in Media

Promoting inclusivity and diversity in media offers numerous benefits. Firstly, it allows for a more accurate portrayal of society, ensuring that different voices and stories are heard and acknowledged. This helps to prevent the perpetuation of harmful stereotypes and biases.

Inclusivity and diversity also contribute to creativity and innovation in media content. When diverse perspectives and experiences are represented, new narratives, ideas, and approaches emerge, enriching the overall quality and relevance of media products.

Moreover, diverse representation in media has economic benefits. In an increasingly globalized world, diverse audiences seek content that resonates with their experiences and perspectives. By catering to diverse audiences, media organizations can tap into new markets, increase viewership, and foster brand loyalty.

Strategies for Promoting Inclusivity and Diversity

To promote inclusivity and diversity effectively, media organizations need to adopt intentional strategies and practices. Here are five key strategies for promoting inclusivity and diversity in media:

1. Embrace a diverse workforce: Media organizations should prioritize diversity in their hiring practices, ensuring that their workforce reflects the broader society. This can help create an inclusive workplace culture that encourages diverse perspectives and voices to be heard.

2. Conduct diversity audits: Media organizations should regularly assess their content and analyze representation across various dimensions of diversity. This includes examining the presence and portrayal of different racial and ethnic groups, genders, sexual orientations, and abilities. The findings from these audits can inform the development of strategies to address any gaps or biases in representation.

3. Collaborate with diverse communities: Media organizations should actively seek input from diverse communities when developing content. Engaging in meaningful collaborations with individuals from different backgrounds ensures that their stories and experiences are accurately represented. This collaborative approach fosters trust, promotes authenticity, and avoids misrepresentation or cultural appropriation.

4. Provide training and resources: Media organizations should invest in training programs and resources to educate their staff about the importance of inclusivity and diversity. This can include workshops on unconscious bias, cultural sensitivity, and responsible storytelling. Having a well-informed workforce is crucial for creating content that respects and includes all individuals.

5. Champion inclusive storytelling: Media organizations should actively promote inclusive storytelling by commissioning and highlighting diverse content. This includes prioritizing stories that challenge stereotypes, feature underrepresented communities, and amplify diverse voices. By showcasing the richness of human experiences, media can inspire empathy, foster understanding, and promote social change.

Inclusivity and Diversity in Action

Several media organizations have embraced inclusivity and diversity, leading the way for positive change. For example, the film industry has seen increased representation of marginalized groups in recent years, demonstrated by films like "Black Panther" and "Crazy Rich Asians" that showcased black and Asian communities respectively.

In television, shows like "Pose" and "Orange is the New Black" have provided platforms for LGBTQ+ and incarcerated individuals to share their stories authentically. These examples highlight how diverse storytelling not only promotes inclusivity but also leads to commercial success and critical acclaim.

Conclusion

Inclusivity and diversity are not mere buzzwords but essential components of responsible and impactful media. By representing the voices and stories of all individuals, media organizations can promote social justice, foster understanding, and contribute to a more inclusive society. Embracing and championing inclusivity and diversity ultimately enhances the credibility, relevance, and sustainability of the media industry as a whole.

Cultural Appropriation and Media Representation

Defining cultural appropriation and its portrayal in media

Cultural appropriation is a term that often sparks controversy and debate. In the context of media, it refers to the adoption or use of elements from a culture that is not one's own, without proper understanding, respect, or consent. It is important to recognize that cultural exchange and appreciation are not the same as cultural appropriation. Cultural exchange involves a respectful and mutually beneficial sharing of ideas, traditions, and practices between different cultures. Cultural appreciation involves acknowledging and honoring the contributions and significance of another culture.

Media plays a crucial role in shaping public perceptions and attitudes towards different cultures. However, cultural appropriation in media can perpetuate harmful stereotypes, reinforce power imbalances, and disrespect marginalized communities. It often occurs when elements of a particular culture are taken out of their original context and used in a superficial or harmful manner.

One common portrayal of cultural appropriation in media is the misrepresentation or caricaturization of cultural traditions and practices. This can involve stereotypes that reduce a culture to clichés or exaggerate certain aspects for entertainment purposes. For example, the depiction of Native American headdresses as fashionable accessories in music videos without regard for their sacred meaning is a form of cultural appropriation.

Another aspect of cultural appropriation in media is the lack of proper credit or recognition given to the originating culture. When elements of a culture are taken and presented as original or trendy without acknowledging their source, it erases the cultural heritage and contributions of marginalized communities.

Cultural appropriation in media can also lead to the commodification of traditions or symbols that hold deep cultural or religious significance. This can exploit and commercialize aspects of a culture, turning them into mere commodities for profit without giving back to the community from which they were taken.

Addressing cultural appropriation in media requires a combination of education, awareness, and respectful representation. Media creators need to cultivate a deep understanding of the cultures they draw inspiration from and approach their work with sensitivity and respect. This includes consulting with members of the culture being portrayed, giving credit where it is due, and avoiding harmful stereotypes.

Media organizations should also prioritize diverse hiring practices, ensuring that individuals from a variety of cultural backgrounds are involved in the creation and decision-making processes. This can provide a more accurate and nuanced perspective and help prevent cultural appropriation.

Furthermore, engaging in open dialogue and critical discussions about cultural appropriation in media can contribute to raising awareness and fostering change. By encouraging audiences to think critically about the media they consume, we can promote a more inclusive and respectful representation of cultures.

It is important to note that cultural appropriation is a complex and nuanced issue that can vary depending on the specific context and individuals involved. It requires ongoing reflection, sensitivity, and active efforts to dismantle harmful practices and promote a more inclusive and respectful media landscape.

To further explore the topic of cultural appropriation in media, here are a few thought-provoking questions for reflection and discussion:

1. Can you think of any examples of cultural appropriation in popular films or television shows? How do these portrayals contribute to stereotypes or misrepresentation?

2. In what ways can media creators ensure that they are practicing cultural appreciation rather than cultural appropriation?

3. How can media consumers contribute to addressing cultural appropriation? What can individuals do to raise awareness and hold media organizations accountable?

4. Are there any existing guidelines or best practices that media organizations can adopt to prevent cultural appropriation?

5. Can you think of any successful instances where media has portrayed a culture in a respectful and authentic manner? What made these portrayals effective?

Resources for further exploration:

- "Towards a More Perfect Union of Cultures: The Challenges of Cultural Appropriation and Cultural Rights" by Rauno K. Parrila - "Cultural Appropriation: A Textual Analysis of Bollywood Movie Queen" by Neha Yadav - "The Difference Between Cultural Exchange and Cultural Appropriation" by Taji Ameen - "But Is It Ethical? Ethical Decisions in Cultural Appropriation in Media and Popular Culture" by Michelle Newton-Francis

The importance of accurate and respectful media representation

Accurate and respectful media representation plays a crucial role in promoting diversity, inclusivity, and social justice in society. In the realm of sustainable media, it is essential to ensure that media content accurately reflects the perspectives, experiences, and identities of diverse communities. This section explores the importance of accurate and respectful media representation, the challenges in achieving it, and strategies for promoting inclusive media content.

Media representation refers to the depiction of individuals or groups in media, including their appearance, personalities, behaviors, and narratives. Accurate representation means portraying people and communities authentically, reflecting their lived experiences, and avoiding stereotypes or caricatures. Respectful representation involves treating marginalized communities with dignity, avoiding harmful or offensive content, and recognizing their unique perspectives and contributions.

Why is accurate and respectful media representation important? First and foremost, it promotes social justice by challenging and dismantling stereotypes and biases. Media has a powerful influence on shaping public perceptions, attitudes, and behaviors. When media content perpetuates harmful stereotypes or misrepresents marginalized communities, it can reinforce systemic discrimination, prejudice, and exclusion. On the other hand, accurate and respectful representation allows for greater recognition, understanding, and empathy towards diverse groups, fostering social cohesion and equity.

Additionally, accurate and respectful media representation is crucial for promoting environmental sustainability. Sustainable development encompasses social, environmental, and economic dimensions. By accurately representing the perspectives of marginalized communities who are disproportionately affected by environmental issues, media can highlight the importance of addressing social justice and environmental concerns together. This intersectional approach helps create a more comprehensive understanding of sustainability and promotes inclusive and equitable solutions.

However, achieving accurate and respectful media representation is not without challenges. Media industries have historically been dominated by a limited range of voices, often excluding or marginalizing minorities and underrepresented groups. This lack of diversity in media production can lead to biased narratives, stereotypes, and misrepresentations. Breaking through these barriers requires systemic change, including diversifying media organizations, promoting inclusive hiring practices, and empowering marginalized communities to share their own stories.

One strategy for promoting accurate and respectful media representation is through authentic collaboration and consultation with communities that are being represented. Media creators should engage in meaningful and ongoing dialogue with diverse groups, seeking their input, feedback, and expertise. By giving marginalized communities the opportunity to shape their own narratives and contribute to media production, greater authenticity and representation can be achieved.

Furthermore, media literacy and critical thinking are essential in addressing misrepresentation and stereotypes. Educating audiences about media biases, stereotypes, and manipulation empowers them to critically analyze and question media content. By encouraging media literacy, individuals can better understand the importance of accurate representation and actively seek out diverse voices and perspectives in media consumption.

It is also important to recognize and celebrate media creators and organizations that prioritize accurate and respectful representation. By highlighting and supporting media content that promotes diversity and inclusivity, individuals can influence the industry to prioritize these values. This can be done through social media campaigns, awards, and recognizing and uplifting the work of diverse creators.

In conclusion, accurate and respectful media representation is vital for promoting social justice, inclusivity, and environmental sustainability. Media has the power to shape narratives, challenge biases, and amplify diverse voices. By ensuring that media content accurately reflects the perspectives and identities of marginalized communities, we can foster understanding, empathy, and equitable solutions. Achieving accurate and respectful media representation requires systemic changes in media industries, collaboration with marginalized communities, media literacy, and recognizing and supporting inclusive media content.

Challenges in navigating cultural sensitivity in media production

In today's increasingly diverse and interconnected world, media plays a crucial role in shaping public perceptions and promoting cultural understanding. However, navigating cultural sensitivity in media production can be quite challenging due to various factors. This section will discuss some of the key challenges faced in this area and highlight strategies to overcome them.

Understanding cultural sensitivity

Cultural sensitivity refers to the awareness and understanding of cultural differences and the ability to navigate them respectfully and appropriately. In the context of media production, cultural sensitivity entails accurately representing diverse cultures, avoiding stereotypes, and promoting inclusivity. However, achieving cultural sensitivity can be complicated due to several challenges.

Stereotyping and misrepresentation

One of the main challenges in navigating cultural sensitivity is the prevalence of stereotypes and misrepresentations in media. Stereotypes are oversimplified and generalized depictions of certain cultural groups, which can perpetuate biases and lead to misunderstandings. Inaccurate and misleading portrayals can reinforce existing prejudices and contribute to the marginalization of certain communities.

To address this challenge, media producers should invest in thorough research and consultation with individuals from the cultures they aim to represent. By involving diverse voices in all stages of production, including writing, casting, and directing, more authentic and nuanced portrayals can be achieved. Additionally, media organizations should prioritize diversity and inclusion in their workforce to ensure a broader range of perspectives and experiences.

Cultural appropriation

Cultural appropriation occurs when elements from one culture are adopted by another culture, often without proper understanding or respect for their significance. This appropriation can be particularly problematic in the context of media production, where cultural practices and symbols are often commercialized for entertainment purposes. It is crucial to approach cultural elements with sensitivity and avoid appropriating them for profit or superficial value.

To tackle this issue, media practitioners should engage in meaningful collaborations with individuals and communities whose cultures are being represented. This collaboration should involve obtaining informed consent, sharing profits equitably, and actively seeking input and feedback. By fostering respectful partnerships, media producers can ensure that cultural elements are portrayed with authenticity and dignity.

Navigating cultural sensitivities in storytelling

Storytelling is a powerful tool in media production, but it can also present challenges in terms of cultural sensitivity. Different cultures have unique narratives, symbolism, and cultural norms that require careful consideration. Failure to navigate these sensitivities can result in misinterpretation, offense, and cultural insensitivity.

To overcome this challenge, media producers should invest time and effort into studying and understanding the cultures they aim to represent. It is important to consult experts and individuals from the respective cultures to gain insights into their values, customs, and storytelling traditions. By incorporating this knowledge, media producers can create narratives that not only entertain but also educate and foster cross-cultural understanding.

Language and translation issues

Another challenge in navigating cultural sensitivity is language and translation. Language carries cultural nuances that can be easily lost or distorted in translation, leading to misunderstandings or misrepresentations. Media practitioners must be aware of these challenges and work diligently to maintain the integrity and accuracy of cultural messages during the translation process.

To overcome language barriers, media producers should employ professional translators who are not only fluent in the target language but also well-versed in the cultural context being portrayed. It is crucial to ensure that translations capture the intended meaning and cultural subtleties to avoid misinterpretations or offensive representations.

Lack of diversity in media production

A significant challenge in navigating cultural sensitivity is the lack of diversity in media production. When the majority of media creators come from homogenous backgrounds, it can lead to uninformed or biased portrayals of other cultures. Lack of diversity perpetuates stereotypes, reinforces power imbalances, and hinders the ability to navigate cultural sensitivity effectively.

To address this challenge, media organizations should actively promote diversity and inclusivity in their hiring practices. By incorporating a variety of voices and perspectives, media producers can foster an environment that is more sensitive and respectful towards different cultures. Additionally, providing training and resources to enhance cultural understanding among media professionals can further improve the quality of cultural representations.

In conclusion, navigating cultural sensitivity in media production is a complex and challenging task. It requires overcoming stereotypes and misrepresentations, avoiding cultural appropriation, understanding diverse storytelling traditions, addressing language and translation issues, and promoting diversity in media production. By recognizing and actively addressing these challenges, media producers can create content that promotes cultural understanding, inclusivity, and respect. Ultimately, incorporating cultural sensitivity in media production contributes to a more diverse and equitable media landscape.

Strategies for promoting inclusive and diverse media content

In order to promote inclusive and diverse media content, it is important for media producers to acknowledge the power and influence they have in shaping societal narratives. By taking proactive measures to ensure representation and inclusivity, media can contribute to a more equitable and tolerant society. This subsection discusses various strategies and approaches that can be employed to achieve this goal.

Identifying and addressing biases

The first step in promoting inclusive and diverse media content is to identify and address any biases that may exist within the production process. This requires a critical examination of both conscious and unconscious biases that may contribute to the underrepresentation or misrepresentation of certain groups. It is essential to be aware of the different dimensions of diversity, such as race, ethnicity, gender, sexual orientation, and ability, to ensure a comprehensive and accurate representation.

Media producers can take the following steps to address biases:

1. Conduct diversity audits: Regularly assess the diversity within the media organization and its content. Identify areas where representation is lacking or stereotypes are perpetuated.

2. Provide diversity training: Offer training sessions to staff members to raise awareness about unconscious biases and stereotypes. This can help foster a more inclusive and understanding work environment.

3. Diversify decision-making roles: Actively involve individuals from diverse backgrounds in decision-making positions, such as writers, directors, and producers, to ensure a multiplicity of perspectives.

Engaging with diverse communities

Inclusivity and diversity can be effectively promoted by actively engaging with diverse communities. Media organizations can develop partnerships and collaborations with community organizations that represent different cultural, ethnic, and social groups. This can provide valuable insights and ensure authentic representation in media content.

Some strategies to engage with diverse communities include:

1. Conduct focus groups and consultations: Seek input from diverse communities and involve them in the decision-making process. This can help ensure that their perspectives and experiences are accurately portrayed in media content.

2. Hire consultants and advisors: Bring in individuals who have expertise and lived experiences related to the communities being represented. Their guidance can help avoid stereotypes and promote accurate portrayals.

3. Foster community-driven storytelling: Facilitate platforms and initiatives that allow diverse communities to tell their own stories. This can include supporting independent filmmakers or creating digital spaces for self-representation.

Promoting diverse talent and behind-the-scenes representation

Another key aspect of promoting inclusive and diverse media content is ensuring representation and opportunities for diverse talent both in front of and behind the camera. This extends beyond on-screen diversity to encompass the diverse voices and perspectives involved in the production and decision-making processes.

Strategies to promote diverse talent and representation include:

1. Encourage diverse hiring practices: Actively seek out and hire individuals from underrepresented communities, including writers, directors, actors, and crew members. This can help create a more inclusive industry and open doors for diverse perspectives.

2. Provide mentorship and training programs: Offer mentorship programs specifically targeted towards individuals from underrepresented communities. This can help develop their skills and provide networking opportunities within the industry.

3. Increase visibility of diverse creators and content: Actively promote and elevate the work of diverse creators and content through marketing campaigns, awards, and festivals. This can help create awareness and generate support for underrepresented voices.

Authentic storytelling and cultural sensitivity

Promoting inclusive and diverse media content requires a commitment to authentic storytelling and cultural sensitivity. It is important to go beyond token representation and engage in responsible storytelling practices that accurately portray different cultures, identities, and experiences.

Strategies for authentic storytelling and cultural sensitivity include:

1. Conduct thorough research: Invest time and resources in understanding the cultural and historical context of the communities being represented. This can help avoid stereotypes and misrepresentations.

2. Consult with cultural experts: Involve individuals from the communities being portrayed as consultants or advisors to ensure cultural accuracy and provide a nuanced perspective.

3. Foster collaboration with diverse creators: Actively seek out and collaborate with diverse writers, directors, and producers who have firsthand experiences or deep knowledge of the communities being portrayed.

4. Actively listen and learn: Be open to feedback and criticism from individuals and communities when it comes to the portrayal of their cultures and experiences. Use feedback as an opportunity for growth and improvement.

Creating inclusive and diverse narratives

Inclusive and diverse media content goes beyond representation on a surface level. It involves creating narratives and storylines that challenge stereotypes, celebrate diversity, and promote social justice.

Strategies for creating inclusive and diverse narratives include:

1. Feature multi-dimensional characters: Develop characters that reflect the complexity and diversity of real-life experiences. Avoid tokenism and ensure that characters from diverse backgrounds have depth and agency.

2. Address social issues: Use storytelling as a medium to shed light on social issues and promote dialogue around important topics such as racism, sexism, LGBTQ+ rights, and ableism. This can help create a more inclusive and empathetic society.

3. Promote positive representation: Highlight stories of resilience, empowerment, and success from underrepresented communities. Showcase the achievements and contributions of diverse individuals to counter negative stereotypes.

By adopting these strategies and approaches, media producers can play an active role in promoting inclusive and diverse media content. This not only fosters a more inclusive society but also enables media to effectively reflect the diverse experiences and perspectives of its audience. It is a collective responsibility to dismantle barriers and promote a media landscape where all individuals feel seen and heard.

Media's role in promoting cultural understanding

Media plays a crucial role in promoting cultural understanding by providing a platform for diverse voices and perspectives to be heard and represented. By showcasing different cultures, traditions, and experiences, media content can foster empathy, break stereotypes, and bridge cultural gaps. This section will explore the various ways in which media can promote cultural understanding and the importance of accurate and respectful representation.

The Power of Media in Shaping Perceptions

The media has the power to shape how we perceive the world and the people around us. Through films, TV shows, documentaries, news articles, and social media, we are exposed to a wide range of cultural narratives and representations. These portrayals can significantly influence our understanding and attitude towards different cultures.

Unfortunately, media has often perpetuated stereotypes and reinforced biases. For example, certain groups may be consistently portrayed in a negative light or reduced to harmful stereotypes. This not only hinders cultural understanding but also perpetuates discrimination and prejudice.

Challenges in Navigating Cultural Sensitivity

Promoting cultural understanding through media is not without its challenges. Navigating cultural sensitivity requires a delicate balance between representing diverse cultures authentically while avoiding stereotypes or misinterpretations.

One challenge lies in the accurate portrayal of cultural practices and traditions. It is essential for media creators to research and consult individuals from those cultures to ensure the portrayal is respectful and avoids misrepresentation. This can involve collaborating with cultural consultants, experts, or community members who can provide valuable insights and guidance.

Context is another critical aspect to consider. Different cultural practices and norms may be misunderstood or misrepresented without proper context. Media should strive to provide sufficient background information and context to help the audience understand and appreciate cultural nuances.

Strategies for Promoting Inclusive and Diverse Media Content

Creating media content that promotes cultural understanding requires intentional efforts and a commitment to inclusivity. Here are some strategies that can be employed:

1. Diversity behind the scenes: Encouraging diversity within the media industry itself is crucial. This includes diverse representation among writers, producers, directors, and decision-makers who have the power to shape narratives.

2. Authentic storytelling: Media should prioritize authentic storytelling that accurately represents diverse cultures and experiences. This can involve collaborating with individuals from those cultures to ensure authentic representation and bringing their voices to the forefront.

3. Cross-cultural collaborations: Collaborations between media professionals from different cultural backgrounds can lead to richer and more nuanced content. This can help break down stereotypes and foster mutual understanding.

4. Sensitivity training: Media organizations should invest in sensitivity training to educate their staff about cultural differences and potential pitfalls in representation. This can help create a more inclusive and respectful media environment.

5. Audience engagement and feedback: Interactive platforms, such as social media, provide an opportunity for audiences to engage with media content and express their opinions. Media organizations should actively listen to audience feedback and be responsive to concerns related to cultural representation.

Media's Role in Promoting Cultural Understanding

By portraying diverse and accurate images of different cultures, media can play a significant role in promoting cultural understanding. It can challenge stereotypes, break down barriers, and foster empathy among people from different backgrounds. Media content that showcases the richness and diversity of cultures can inspire curiosity, appreciation, and respect for cultural differences.

For example, documentaries that highlight lesser-known cultures can create awareness and understanding among viewers. TV shows and films that authentically depict characters from diverse backgrounds can humanize and normalize cultural differences. News outlets that provide unbiased coverage of global events can help combat prejudice and cultivate a more informed and empathetic society.

Example: Disney's "Coco"

One example of media's powerful role in promoting cultural understanding is Disney's animated film "Coco." The film tells the story of Miguel, a young boy who embarks on a journey through the Land of the Dead to uncover his family's ancestral history and passion for music. By beautifully representing Mexican culture, traditions, and the importance of family, "Coco" provided a window into a rich and vibrant culture for audiences around the world. The film was not only critically acclaimed but also had a significant impact on cultural appreciation and understanding.

Conclusion

Media has the potential to be a force for positive change by promoting cultural understanding. By accurately and respectfully representing diverse cultures, media can challenge stereotypes, foster empathy, and bridge cultural gaps. It is crucial for media creators, organizations, and audiences to actively engage in promoting and consuming media content that promotes cultural understanding. Through these efforts, we can create a more inclusive and empathetic society.

Intersectionality and Environmental Justice

Understanding Intersectionality and its relevance in sustainability

Intersectionality is a concept that originated in the field of critical race theory, and it recognizes that intersecting social identities, such as race, gender, class, sexuality, and ability, create unique and overlapping experiences of discrimination and oppression. It emphasizes that individuals cannot be understood solely through the lens of a single identity, but rather as the intersection of multiple identities and the complex ways in which these identities interact.

In the context of sustainability, intersectionality is crucial in understanding the unequal distribution of environmental burdens and benefits among different communities. It highlights the interconnectedness between social justice and environmental issues, and recognizes that certain groups, especially marginalized communities, bear a disproportionate burden of environmental harm.

One of the key principles of sustainability is that it should be equitable and inclusive, ensuring that all individuals and communities have equal access to environmental resources and opportunities for a healthy and prosperous life. However, without considering intersectionality, sustainability efforts can inadvertently perpetuate existing power imbalances and reinforce social inequalities.

For example, a sustainability initiative that aims to promote renewable energy in a low-income neighborhood may inadvertently overlook the specific needs and concerns of marginalized groups within that community, such as racial or ethnic minorities, immigrants, or individuals with disabilities. By not considering their unique social and economic challenges, the initiative may further deepen existing disparities and fail to bring about meaningful change.

To address this, a more intersectional approach to sustainability requires recognizing and acknowledging the different experiences and needs of various communities. It involves actively involving and empowering marginalized groups in decision-making processes, ensuring their perspectives are heard and their concerns are addressed.

Furthermore, an intersectional perspective emphasizes the importance of addressing systemic inequalities and creating solutions that are tailored to the specific needs of different communities. It requires recognizing that issues of environmental justice are interconnected with issues of social justice, and that sustainable solutions must address both simultaneously. This approach can help in dismantling institutional barriers and creating more inclusive and equitable systems that benefit all.

One practical example of intersectional sustainability is the concept of food justice, which recognizes that access to healthy, affordable, and culturally appropriate food is a basic human right. It acknowledges that food systems are intricately linked to social and economic inequities, and seeks to address these issues through community-led initiatives, urban farming, and policy changes.

Another example is the movement for climate justice, which advocates for environmental policies that prioritize the needs and voices of marginalized communities who are most affected by climate change. This movement recognizes that the impacts of climate change, such as extreme weather events or the loss of natural resources, disproportionately affect low-income communities, indigenous peoples, and people of color.

In conclusion, understanding intersectionality is crucial for achieving sustainability goals in an equitable and inclusive manner. It helps us recognize the interconnectedness between social justice and environmental issues, and ensures that sustainability efforts address the specific needs and concerns of different communities. By embracing an intersectional perspective, we can work towards building a more just and sustainable future for all.

The connection between environmental justice and social justice

The connection between environmental justice and social justice is a crucial aspect of sustainable media. It is important to understand that environmental issues do not exist in isolation from societal and economic frameworks. They are deeply intertwined with social injustice, inequality, and systemic oppression. In this section, we will explore the relationship between environmental justice and social justice, highlighting the significant impact of one on the other.

Environmental justice is a concept rooted in the belief that all individuals, regardless of their race, ethnicity, socioeconomic status, or geographical location, have the right to a clean and healthy environment. It recognizes that marginalized communities often bear a disproportionate burden of environmental harm, such as pollution, waste disposal, and industrial hazards. This can result in a range of negative health impacts and reduced quality of life for these communities.

Social justice, on the other hand, focuses on the fair distribution of resources, opportunities, and rights within a society, aiming to address the systemic inequalities that exist. It encompasses issues such as poverty, discrimination, access to education and healthcare, and the protection of human rights.

The connection between environmental justice and social justice arises from the recognition that marginalized communities are more likely to bear the brunt of environmental degradation and are often excluded from decision-making processes that impact their environment. The same communities that experience social injustices, such as racial discrimination and economic inequality, also face the greatest environmental burdens.

For example, low-income neighborhoods and communities of color are often located in close proximity to industrial facilities, waste sites, and transportation corridors, leading to increased exposure to air and water pollution. These communities may lack access to green spaces, clean water, and quality healthcare, further exacerbating the negative impacts of environmental degradation.

Furthermore, the pursuit of social justice and environmental justice share common goals. Both advocate for equity, inclusivity, and the recognition of human rights. By addressing environmental issues through a social justice lens, we can more effectively tackle the root causes of environmental degradation and create sustainable solutions that benefit all members of society.

To promote environmental justice and social justice simultaneously, it is crucial to take an intersectional approach. Intersectionality acknowledges that individuals may experience multiple forms of oppression or discrimination simultaneously due to the intersection of their identities. This means considering the unique challenges faced by marginalized communities based on factors such as race, gender, disability, and socioeconomic status.

By applying an intersectional lens to environmental and social justice issues, we can better understand the specific needs and concerns of different communities. This approach helps to amplify the voices of marginalized groups, ensuring that their perspectives are included in decision-making processes and that they have equal access to resources and opportunities.

An example of the connection between environmental justice and social justice can be seen in the fight against climate change. While climate change affects everyone, its impacts are often disproportionately felt by marginalized communities. These communities, particularly those in developing countries, are more vulnerable to extreme weather events, food insecurity, and displacement.

Addressing climate change requires not only reducing greenhouse gas emissions and transitioning to renewable energy but also tackling social inequalities. This includes ensuring access to affordable clean energy, creating green jobs, and supporting the most vulnerable communities in adapting to the impacts of climate change.

In conclusion, the connection between environmental justice and social justice is undeniable. Both are essential for promoting sustainability and creating a more equitable society. By recognizing and addressing the interplay between environmental issues and social injustices, we can work towards a future where everyone has equal rights and access to a healthy environment. It is our collective responsibility to advocate for sustainable media practices that amplify the voices of marginalized communities, promote inclusivity, and drive positive change for the benefit of all.

Media's role in amplifying voices of marginalized communities

The media plays a crucial role in amplifying the voices of marginalized communities and bringing attention to their lived experiences, challenges, and aspirations. Through various channels, including news outlets, social media platforms, and entertainment media, the media has the power to give a platform to those who have been historically underrepresented and marginalized.

Media representation is essential for promoting diversity, inclusivity, and social justice. When marginalized communities see their stories, struggles, and achievements reflected in the media, it can have a profound impact on their self-esteem, sense of belonging, and societal recognition. Moreover, media representation creates empathy among the wider audience and helps dismantle stereotypes and prejudices.

One of the challenges in amplifying the voices of marginalized communities is the lack of representation and diversity within media organizations. Many media outlets struggle to reflect the diversity of the societies they serve, which leads to biased narratives and limited perspectives. To address this issue, media organizations should prioritize diversity in their staff, content creators, and decision-making positions. This will ensure a more inclusive and authentic representation of marginalized communities.

In addition to representation, the media must also provide a platform for marginalized voices to be heard. This can be achieved through various means, such as interviews, panel discussions, op-eds, and documentaries. By actively seeking out and featuring stories from marginalized communities, media outlets can bring attention to important issues, highlight systemic inequalities, and challenge the status quo.

However, it is crucial for the media to approach the amplification of marginalized voices with sensitivity, respect, and cultural competence. This means actively listening, understanding, and being mindful of the unique experiences and perspectives of different communities. It also requires avoiding tokenism and ensuring that the voices of marginalized communities are not exploited or sensationalized for profit or clickbait.

One way the media can foster the amplification of marginalized voices is by establishing partnerships and collaborations with community organizations, grassroots movements, and advocacy groups. By working closely with these organizations, media outlets can gain access to stories, insights, and expertise that would otherwise go unnoticed or unheard. This collaborative approach allows for a more authentic representation of marginalized communities and ensures that their voices are accurately portrayed.

Furthermore, media literacy and education are instrumental in promoting the amplification of marginalized voices. Media literacy programs should focus on teaching individuals to critically analyze and question the narratives presented in the media. By encouraging media consumers to seek out diverse sources of information and challenging media biases, individuals can actively contribute to amplifying marginalized voices and promoting social justice.

It is important to recognize that amplifying marginalized voices goes beyond representation, it also involves supporting and uplifting these communities. The media can help by promoting initiatives, organizations, and movements that aim to address the specific challenges faced by marginalized communities. By giving a platform to community leaders, activists, and change-makers, the media can raise awareness and inspire action towards building a more inclusive and equitable society.

One real-world example of media amplifying marginalized voices is the

#BlackLivesMatter movement. Through extensive media coverage, social media campaigns, and documentaries, the media has shed light on the systemic injustices faced by Black communities and amplified their demands for racial equality and justice. The coverage of the movement has sparked global conversations, policy changes, and increased public awareness on the urgent need for social change.

In conclusion, the media plays a critical role in amplifying the voices of marginalized communities. Through representation, partnerships, education, and thoughtful storytelling, the media can bring attention to the challenges, experiences, and aspirations of underrepresented groups. By doing so, the media contributes to a more inclusive and just society where all voices are heard, acknowledged, and valued. It is essential for media organizations, journalists, and media consumers to actively engage in the amplification of marginalized voices for a more equitable world.

Promoting Intersectional Environmentalism through Media

Intersectional environmentalism is a concept that recognizes the interconnectedness of social justice issues and environmental concerns. It emphasizes the need to address environmental issues through a lens of inclusivity, acknowledging that marginalized communities often bear the brunt of environmental degradation and climate change impacts. In order to promote intersectional environmentalism, media plays a crucial role in amplifying voices, raising awareness, and fostering social change.

Representation and Inclusion in Media

One essential aspect of promoting intersectional environmentalism through media is ensuring representation and inclusion. Media can give a platform to individuals from marginalized communities who are leading environmental initiatives or impacted by environmental injustices. By showcasing diverse perspectives, media can challenge stereotypes and foster an understanding of the intersectional nature of environmental challenges.

To achieve this, media creators should strive for inclusive and accurate representation of underrepresented communities. This involves avoiding tokenism or stereotyping and providing opportunities for diverse voices to shape the narrative. By including a range of perspectives, media can counteract the historically dominant narrative and promote a more nuanced understanding of environmental issues.

For example, a documentary series about climate change could highlight the experiences of indigenous communities who have deep knowledge of their ecosystems and have been practicing sustainable methods of resource management for generations. By centering their voices, media can provide an alternative perspective and promote a more holistic approach to environmental solutions.

Collaboration and Partnerships

Media can also promote intersectional environmentalism through collaboration and partnerships with environmental organizations and community groups. By working together, media and these organizations can create powerful content that educates and inspires viewers. This collaboration can involve joint initiatives in advocacy, awareness campaigns, and storytelling projects.

For instance, a media outlet could collaborate with an environmental justice organization to produce a series of short films that highlight the environmental challenges faced by low-income communities in urban areas. By sharing the stories and experiences of these communities, media can raise awareness, create empathy, and inspire action among viewers.

Collaboration can also extend to involving individuals from marginalized communities in the production process. This can include hiring diverse writers, directors, and crew members, as well as consulting with community leaders and activists to ensure that the content is respectful, accurate, and reflective of the community's concerns.

Media: Catalyst for Social Change

Media has the power to act as a catalyst for social change by shaping public perceptions, influencing policy discussions, and encouraging collective action. In promoting intersectional environmentalism, media can foster dialogue, challenge existing power structures, and support movements for environmental justice.

One effective strategy is to incorporate diverse perspectives into mainstream media narratives. This can be done by featuring stories of individuals from marginalized communities who are working towards sustainable solutions and advocating for environmental justice. By highlighting their efforts, media can inspire others to get involved and work towards a more inclusive and sustainable future.

Additionally, media can play a crucial role in educating the public about the connections between social justice and environmental sustainability. This can be achieved through documentaries, news articles, and opinion pieces that explore the intersectionality of these issues. By providing comprehensive and well-researched content, media can promote a deeper understanding of the complexities and interconnections between environmental and social justice.

Media Literacy for Intersectional Environmentalism

Promoting intersectional environmentalism through media also requires building media literacy skills among audiences. By developing critical thinking skills and media literacy, individuals can analyze and evaluate the messages portrayed in media content. This empowers them to identify biases, challenge stereotypes, and demand more inclusive and accurate representations.

Media literacy education should focus on teaching individuals how to critically consume and engage with media. This includes understanding the motives and perspectives of media producers, recognizing hidden agendas, and questioning dominant narratives. By equipping audiences with media literacy skills, media can become a tool for empowerment and change.

In conclusion, promoting intersectional environmentalism through media requires representation, collaboration, and media literacy. By amplifying the voices of marginalized communities, fostering partnerships with environmental organizations, and educating audiences, media can raise awareness, challenge narratives, and inspire action. With a more inclusive and intersectional approach, media can contribute to a more sustainable and just world.

The role of media in promoting social change

In today's interconnected and digital world, the media plays a powerful role in shaping public opinion and influencing social change. Media platforms, such as newspapers, television, radio, and the internet, have the ability to reach a vast audience and amplify social justice narratives. They have the power to expose social injustices, raise awareness about pressing issues, and mobilize communities towards collective action for positive change.

The Influence of Media on Public Opinion

Media has a significant influence on public opinion due to its ability to disseminate information widely and shape public discourse. News outlets, for example, play a crucial role in framing stories and shaping how people perceive societal issues. The way media presents stories and narratives can influence the public's understanding, attitudes, and beliefs about social issues.

Media can also influence public opinion through agenda-setting, which is the process by which media determines what issues and topics are important and deserve public attention. By highlighting certain topics and giving them extensive coverage, the media can shape public opinion and influence the public's priorities for social change.

For example, media coverage of the Black Lives Matter movement has helped raise awareness about systemic racism and police brutality. Through in-depth reporting and powerful images, media platforms have shed light on the experiences and struggles of marginalized communities, leading to increased public support for social justice reforms.

Media's Role in Shaping Social Justice Narratives

Media has the power to shape social justice narratives by giving a voice to marginalized communities, shedding light on social inequalities, and challenging the status quo. By amplifying the stories and experiences of underrepresented groups, the media can create awareness and empathy, ultimately leading to social change.

Through investigative journalism, documentaries, and storytelling, media platforms can expose social injustices that would otherwise go unnoticed. By highlighting the lived experiences of individuals and communities affected by discrimination, media can drive empathetic understanding and mobilize public support for social justice causes.

For instance, documentaries like Ava DuVernay's "13th" and the miniseries "When They See Us" have sparked conversations about racial inequality and the criminal justice system. These powerful media narratives have not only raised awareness but also brought about policy changes and reforms.

Media Bias and its Impact on Sustainability Discourse

It is important to recognize that media bias can affect the effectiveness of promoting social change. Biased reporting or skewed narratives can reinforce stereotypes, perpetuate discrimination, and hinder progress towards social justice.

Media bias can occur in various forms, including partisan bias, sensationalism, and omission of certain perspectives. Biased reporting may influence public opinion and prevent a balanced and nuanced understanding of social issues.

To promote social change effectively, it is crucial for media organizations to strive for unbiased and balanced reporting. Journalists and media professionals should prioritize responsible journalism, fact-checking, and providing diverse perspectives to ensure an accurate representation of social justice issues.

Strategies for Promoting Unbiased and Balanced Media Coverage

To foster unbiased and balanced media coverage, there are several strategies that media organizations can employ:

- **Diversify newsrooms:** Media organizations should prioritize diversity and inclusion in their teams to ensure a wide range of perspectives and minimize bias.

- **Objective reporting:** Journalists should strive for objectivity by presenting facts, providing context, and offering multiple viewpoints. Clear delineation between news and opinion sections is also essential to prevent the blurring of perspectives.

- **Fact-checking and verification:** Media organizations should prioritize fact-checking and verification to ensure the accuracy of information being presented. This helps to combat misinformation and disinformation.

- **Transparency and accountability:** Media organizations should ensure transparency by disclosing potential conflicts of interest and being accountable for their reporting. Public accountability can help maintain trust with the audience.

- **Promote media literacy:** Educating the public about media literacy is crucial. By teaching critical thinking skills and providing tools to identify biases, individuals can better navigate media content and avoid falling prey to misinformation.

These strategies can help media organizations reclaim public trust and foster an environment that promotes unbiased reporting and encourages social change.

The Ethical Responsibility of Media in Reporting Unbiased News

Media outlets have an ethical responsibility to report news in an unbiased and fair manner. Journalistic ethics require journalists to be accurate, fair, and impartial, and to provide a comprehensive and balanced view of events and issues.

Additionally, media organizations should adhere to professional codes of conduct and ethical guidelines. These guidelines promote transparency, accountability, and fairness in reporting, ensuring that the media fulfills its role as a catalyst for social change in an ethical manner.

It is important for media professionals to reflect on their own biases, continuously educate themselves, and be aware of the potential impact their reporting can have on society. By upholding journalistic integrity and ethics, the media can play a crucial role in promoting social change and fostering a more just and inclusive society.

Promoting Social Change through Media

Media has the potential to be a powerful tool for promoting social change. To effectively contribute to social change, media organizations can:

- **Amplify marginalized voices:** Media platforms should provide a platform for marginalized communities to share their stories and perspectives. By empowering these voices, media can challenge existing power structures and advocate for social justice.

- **Expose hidden injustices:** Investigative journalism and in-depth reporting can uncover hidden injustices and hold institutions accountable. By shedding light on social issues, media can spark public discourse and drive the need for change.

- **Encourage public dialogue:** Media can facilitate public dialogue by providing opportunities for informed and respectful discussions on social issues. By giving space for diverse perspectives, media can help bridge societal divides and foster understanding.

- **Collaborate with grassroots organizations:** Media organizations can collaborate with grassroots organizations to elevate their initiatives and causes. By providing media coverage, resources, and visibility, media can amplify their impact and help bring about social change.

- **Inspire collective action:** Media can mobilize communities to take collective action by raising awareness, providing information, and inspiring empathy. By showcasing stories of resilience, grassroots movements, and successful social change efforts, media can inspire others to join the cause.

By adopting these strategies, the media can harness its potential to promote social change, advance social justice agendas, and create a more equitable and sustainable future.

In conclusion, the media plays a crucial role in promoting social change. By amplifying marginalized voices, challenging existing power structures, and fostering informed public dialogue, media platforms can be a catalyst for positive social transformation. However, media organizations must also be mindful of media bias, strive for unbiased reporting, and adhere to ethical guidelines to ensure responsible and effective promotion of social change. Ultimately, the role of media in promoting social change is to inform, educate, and inspire individuals and communities towards building a more just and sustainable world.

Sustainable Media Practices and Solutions

Green Production Certifications and Standards

Overview of green production certifications

In today's world, where environmental sustainability is becoming increasingly important, the media industry has a vital role to play in reducing its environmental impact. Green production certifications provide a framework to assess and recognize the efforts made by media productions to operate in an environmentally responsible manner. These certifications serve as a mark of credibility and assurance for the industry, and they help promote sustainable practices throughout the entire media production process.

One prominent green production certification widely recognized in the media industry is the Leadership in Energy and Environmental Design (LEED) certification. LEED is a globally recognized program developed by the United States Green Building Council (USGBC) to encourage and acknowledge sustainable building and operating practices. While LEED certification primarily focuses on the construction industry, it has expanded its criteria to accommodate media production facilities and studios.

LEED certification evaluates various aspects of a media production project, including the design, construction, and operation of production facilities. It takes into account energy efficiency, water conservation, waste management, and the use of sustainable materials. Media productions seeking LEED certification must meet specific requirements in these areas and earn points to achieve different levels of certification, such as Certified, Silver, Gold, or Platinum.

Another notable green production certification is the Green Seal certification. Green Seal is an independent non-profit organization that offers certifications for a wide range of products and services, including media production. Their certification focuses on evaluating the sustainability of production practices, such as energy efficiency, waste management, and the use of environmentally friendly materials.

Media productions aiming for Green Seal certification must meet rigorous criteria, including compliance with environmental regulations, implementation of pollution prevention measures, reduction of energy and water consumption, and the adoption of environmentally responsible purchasing practices. Green Seal's certification process involves thorough documentation and on-site audits to ensure compliance with their standards.

In addition to LEED and Green Seal, there are other regional, national, and international green production certifications available, depending on the location and scope of the media production. Some examples include BREEAM (Building Research Establishment Environmental Assessment Method) in the United Kingdom, CASBEE (Comprehensive Assessment System for Built Environment Efficiency) in Japan, and Green Star in Australia.

It is worth noting that different green production certifications have different criteria and standards. This can create complexity for media productions looking to navigate the certification process. However, the ultimate goal of these certifications is the same: to promote sustainable practices and reduce environmental impact in the media industry.

By achieving green production certifications, media productions demonstrate their commitment to environmental sustainability, setting an example for the entire industry. These certifications not only enhance the reputation and marketability of productions but also contribute to broader environmental goals. Through adopting sustainable practices, media productions can significantly reduce their carbon footprint, conserve resources, and inspire change in both the industry and the audience.

It should be acknowledged that while green production certifications can be a valuable tool, they are not without limitations. Some media productions may find the certification process costly or time-consuming. Additionally, the focus of certifications on specific aspects of sustainability may not cover all environmental concerns. Therefore, it is essential for media productions to view certifications as part of a broader commitment to sustainability, continuously seeking improvements and exploring additional sustainable practices beyond certification requirements.

Overall, green production certifications provide a set of guidelines and benchmarks for media productions to follow, ensuring that their operations align with sustainability principles. As the media industry evolves, it is crucial for productions to consider these certifications as a means to reduce environmental impact, promote responsible practices, and contribute to a more sustainable future.

The benefits and limitations of green production standards

Green production standards play a vital role in promoting sustainability in the media industry. These standards provide a framework for reducing the environmental impact of media production, ensuring that it aligns with sustainable principles. In this section, we will explore the benefits and limitations of green production standards, shedding light on their significance and potential challenges.

Benefits of green production standards

Green production standards offer several key benefits to the media industry and the environment:

1. **Environmental Impact Reduction:** The primary benefit of green production standards is the significant reduction in environmental impact. These standards establish guidelines that encourage media producers to minimize energy consumption, reduce waste, and limit emissions. By adopting sustainable practices, media productions can decrease their carbon footprint and contribute to a healthier planet.

2. **Resource Conservation:** Green production standards promote the efficient use of resources. By optimizing energy consumption, media productions can lower their dependency on non-renewable resources. Moreover, these standards often encourage the use of recycled or reclaimed materials, reducing the demand for new resources. This focus on resource conservation helps preserve natural ecosystems and fosters a more sustainable media industry.

3. **Cost Savings:** While the initial implementation of green production standards may require an investment, they can lead to significant cost savings in the long run. By adopting energy-efficient technologies and practices, media productions can lower their utility bills and operational expenses. Additionally, reducing waste and implementing recycling initiatives can result in lower waste management costs. Green production standards, therefore, offer both environmental and financial benefits.

4. **Brand Reputation and Audience Engagement:** Embracing sustainability through green production standards can enhance a media production's brand reputation. Consumers are increasingly conscious of environmental issues and are more likely to support sustainable businesses. By demonstrating a commitment to green practices, media producers can attract and retain environmentally-conscious

audiences. This positive brand image can lead to increased audience engagement and loyalty.

Limitations of green production standards

While green production standards provide numerous benefits, there are also some limitations and challenges to consider:

1. **Complexity and Cost:** Implementing green production standards can be complex and costly, particularly for smaller production companies with limited resources. Adhering to sustainable practices may require significant infrastructure upgrades and additional training for staff. The initial investment can be a barrier for some media producers, preventing them from fully adopting green production standards.

2. **Balancing Sustainability and Creativity:** Green production standards aim to minimize the environmental impact of media production, but they may pose challenges to creativity and artistic expression. Certain sustainable practices, such as using energy-efficient lighting or limiting travel, may restrict the creative choices available to filmmakers and producers. Striking a balance between sustainability and artistic vision is necessary to ensure the success of green production standards.

3. **Compliance and Verification:** Ensuring compliance with green production standards can be a challenge in the media industry. Continuous monitoring and verification of sustainable practices are essential. However, it can be challenging to accurately measure and assess the environmental impact of complex media productions. Developing standardized metrics and verification processes is crucial for the effective implementation of green production standards.

4. **Industry-wide Adoption:** While many media productions are embracing green production standards, achieving industry-wide adoption can be a slow and incremental process. Encouraging all stakeholders in the media industry to align with sustainable practices requires collaboration and awareness. Media organizations, government bodies, and industry associations must work together to promote and incentivize the adoption of green production standards.

Case Study: Green Production Certification

To illustrate the benefits and limitations of green production standards, let's explore the case of green production certification in the film industry. One of the prominent examples of a certification program is the "Green Seal" offered by the Environmental Media Association (EMA).

The EMA Green Seal provides recognition to film and television productions that demonstrate exceptional efforts in reducing their environmental impact. Productions can earn the Green Seal by meeting specific criteria related to energy efficiency, waste reduction, and sustainable practices. The benefits of obtaining the Green Seal include enhanced brand reputation, access to resources and funding, and recognition from industry peers.

However, the certification process also comes with limitations. Achieving and maintaining the Green Seal requires rigorous documentation and reporting on sustainable actions taken during production. This process may pose additional administrative burdens and expenses for smaller productions with limited resources. Moreover, the Green Seal may not be universally recognized, limiting its impact beyond the communities already engaged in sustainable practices.

Despite these limitations, green production certification programs like the EMA Green Seal serve as valuable examples of the benefits that can arise from adopting green production standards. They motivate media producers to prioritize sustainability, pushing the industry towards a more environmentally-friendly future.

Summary

In this section, we explored the benefits and limitations of green production standards in the media industry. The benefits include reducing environmental impact, resource conservation, cost savings, and improved brand reputation. However, limitations such as complexity and cost, balancing sustainability and creativity, compliance and verification challenges, and industry-wide adoption are important considerations. By understanding these benefits and limitations, media producers can make informed decisions and contribute to a more sustainable and responsible media industry.

Case studies of successful sustainable media projects

In this section, we will explore some real-world examples of successful sustainable media projects that have made a positive impact on both the environment and society. These case studies demonstrate the practical implementation of sustainable practices and showcase the potential for the media industry to lead the way in promoting sustainability.

Case Study 1: Greening Television Production

One notable sustainable media project is the greening of television production, exemplified by the hit TV series "The Office." The production team of "The Office" took proactive steps to reduce their environmental impact throughout the show's nine seasons.

One significant change was the adoption of energy-efficient lighting solutions. By replacing traditional incandescent bulbs with LED lights, "The Office" production team was able to reduce energy consumption by 70

Furthermore, "The Office" implemented a comprehensive waste management plan. They established recycling stations on the set, promoting the separation and proper disposal of waste materials. Additionally, they encouraged the use of reusable water bottles and eliminated single-use plastic bottles on set, reducing plastic waste significantly.

"The Office" also prioritized sustainable transportation for their cast and crew. They encouraged carpooling and the use of fuel-efficient vehicles, reducing carbon emissions associated with commuting to and from the set.

Through these sustainable practices, "The Office" set an example for the television industry, proving that it is possible to produce high-quality content while minimizing environmental impact.

Case Study 2: Sustainable Film Production

Another inspiring example of sustainable media is the film production of "Mad Max: Fury Road." This post-apocalyptic action film pushed the boundaries of sustainability in the industry, implementing innovative practices that contributed to a more environmentally friendly production process.

To minimize energy consumption, the production team of "Mad Max: Fury Road" utilized renewable energy sources. They set up a solar farm on the film's set, which generated clean energy to power various equipment and lighting during the shoot. This initiative not only reduced the film's carbon footprint but also raised awareness about the potential of renewable energy in the entertainment industry.

Water conservation was another key focus of sustainability in the film's production. "Mad Max: Fury Road" implemented water-saving strategies such as using water-efficient fixtures, capturing rainwater for reuse, and employing waterless toilets. By minimizing water consumption, the production team demonstrated the importance of responsible resource management in an arid environment.

Furthermore, the film actively promoted sustainability to the local community by establishing a sustainability hub. This hub offered educational programs and workshops to engage and empower community members, fostering environmental stewardship beyond the film production itself.

The sustainable production practices of "Mad Max: Fury Road" received acclaim and recognition within the industry, proving that sustainability and blockbuster filmmaking can go hand in hand.

Case Study 3: Greening Digital Media

In the realm of digital media, the video-sharing platform YouTube stands out as a platform that actively promotes sustainable practices among content creators. YouTube implemented the YouTube Sustainability Initiative, aimed at encouraging creators to adopt sustainable approaches in their content production and promoting environmental awareness to a global audience.

As part of this initiative, YouTube introduced the Sustainable Creator Development Program, which provides resources and guidance to creators on incorporating sustainable practices into their content creation process. This program educates creators on energy-efficient equipment, sustainable filming techniques, and responsible waste management.

YouTube also launched the Playbook for Sustainable Production, a comprehensive guide for creators to produce sustainable videos. The playbook outlines strategies for reducing energy consumption, minimizing waste, and utilizing renewable energy sources. It emphasizes the importance of storytelling that promotes environmental consciousness and inspires positive change.

By empowering content creators to adopt sustainable practices, YouTube is leveraging its immense reach and influence to drive positive environmental impact. The platform encourages creators to integrate sustainability into their narratives, fostering a global movement towards a more sustainable future.

Conclusion

These case studies highlight the success of sustainable media projects in various areas of the industry, including television production, film, and digital media platforms. By implementing energy-efficient technologies, responsible waste management, and innovative sustainable practices, these projects demonstrate that sustainability is not only achievable but also economically and creatively viable.

The examples presented here serve as inspiration for the media industry as a whole to embrace sustainability and commit to positive change. By learning from these case studies, media professionals and content creators can become catalysts for environmental stewardship and societal progress.

The future of sustainable media lies in the collective efforts of individuals, organizations, and the audience. By continuing to implement and innovate sustainable practices, and by demanding and supporting environmentally conscious content, we can shape a media landscape that is not only entertaining and informative but also actively contributes to a more sustainable world.

Let us now explore the role of media consumption in sustainability and strategies for promoting sustainable media choices in section 6.2.

Implementing green practices in media production

Implementing green practices in media production is crucial for reducing the environmental impact of the industry. By adopting sustainable strategies, media producers can minimize energy and resource consumption, reduce waste generation, and contribute to a more eco-friendly future. In this section, we will explore various green practices that can be implemented in media production, including production design, equipment choices, waste management, and the use of renewable energy sources.

Production design

One of the key aspects of implementing green practices in media production is through sustainable production design. This involves creating sets, props, and costumes that are environmentally friendly and minimize waste generation. Here are some strategies for sustainable production design:

- **Reuse and repurpose materials:** Instead of constantly purchasing new materials, consider reusing and repurposing existing ones. This can include using salvaged or reclaimed materials for set construction or repurposing costumes and props from previous productions. By doing so, you can reduce the demand for new resources and minimize waste.

- **Choose eco-friendly materials:** When designing sets or creating props, opt for materials that are eco-friendly and have a low environmental impact. For example, consider using sustainable woods, water-based adhesives, and low-VOC (volatile organic compounds) paints. Avoid materials that are toxic or non-biodegradable, as these can have long-lasting negative effects on the environment.

- **Design for disassembly:** Design sets and props in a way that facilitates easy disassembly and separation of materials for recycling or reuse. By considering the end-of-life stage of the production elements, you can ensure that they are disposed of responsibly and avoid contributing to landfill waste.

By implementing these production design strategies, media producers can minimize waste, reduce resource consumption, and create more sustainable productions.

Equipment choices

Another important aspect of implementing green practices in media production is through conscious equipment choices. By selecting energy-efficient and environmentally friendly equipment, media producers can significantly reduce energy consumption and minimize their carbon footprint. Here are some strategies for sustainable equipment choices:

- **Energy-efficient lighting:** Lighting plays a crucial role in media production, and using energy-efficient lighting solutions can lead to significant energy savings. LED (light-emitting diode) lights are highly energy-efficient and have a longer lifespan compared to traditional incandescent or fluorescent lights. Additionally, consider using dimmers and sensors to optimize lighting usage and reduce unnecessary energy consumption.

- **Green cameras and equipment:** Choose cameras and other production equipment that are designed with energy efficiency in mind. Look for models that have low power consumption, power-saving features, and are made with recycled or sustainable materials. Additionally, consider renting or sharing equipment to minimize resource consumption and reduce the need for new purchases.

- **Battery management:** Proper management of batteries is crucial to minimize waste in media production. Opt for rechargeable batteries instead of disposable ones, and establish a system for proper battery disposal and recycling. Consider using battery chargers that are energy-efficient and have automatic shut-off features to avoid overcharging and unnecessary energy consumption.

By making sustainable equipment choices, media producers can significantly reduce energy consumption, lower greenhouse gas emissions, and contribute to a greener production process.

Waste management

Effective waste management is essential in implementing green practices in media production. By reducing waste generation, promoting recycling, and minimizing landfill disposal, media producers can minimize their environmental impact. Here are some strategies for sustainable waste management:

- **Waste reduction at the source:** Implement practices that reduce waste generation right from the start. This can include using digital technology to minimize paper usage, encouraging digital distribution of media content, and promoting electronic communication instead of printing. By reducing the amount of waste generated, producers can save resources and reduce their carbon footprint.

- **Recycling and proper disposal:** Establish a comprehensive recycling program on set and in production offices. Provide clearly labeled recycling bins for paper, plastic, glass, and other recyclable materials, and educate cast and crew members about proper recycling practices. Additionally, ensure that hazardous materials, such as batteries and electronics, are disposed of properly following local regulations.

- **Donation and repurposing:** Identify opportunities to donate or repurpose materials or equipment that are no longer needed. This can include donating costumes or props to local schools or theaters, or repurposing set materials for future productions. By extending the lifespan of materials and equipment, media producers can reduce waste and support the local community.

By implementing effective waste management practices, media producers can minimize waste, conserve resources, and contribute to a more sustainable industry.

Renewable energy sources

Utilizing renewable energy sources is a significant step towards implementing green practices in media production. By shifting towards clean energy sources, such as solar or wind power, media producers can reduce their dependence on fossil fuels and decrease greenhouse gas emissions. Here are some strategies for utilizing renewable energy sources:

- **On-site renewable energy generation:** Install solar panels or wind turbines on production facilities to generate clean energy. This can help offset the energy consumption of the production process and reduce reliance on the grid. Additionally, consider using energy storage systems, such as batteries, to store excess energy for use during non-peak times or when renewable energy generation is low.

- **Green energy procurement:** If on-site renewable energy generation is not feasible, consider procuring green energy from renewable sources through power purchase agreements or green energy certificates. This allows media producers to support renewable energy projects and reduce their carbon footprint.

- **Energy-efficient practices:** In addition to renewable energy sources, focus on implementing energy-efficient practices to further reduce energy consumption. This can include optimizing heating, ventilation, and air conditioning (HVAC) systems, using energy-efficient appliances, and encouraging energy-saving habits among cast and crew members.

By embracing renewable energy sources and adopting energy-efficient practices, media producers can significantly reduce their environmental impact and contribute to a more sustainable future.

In conclusion, implementing green practices in media production is crucial for minimizing the environmental impact of the industry. By adopting sustainable production design strategies, making conscious equipment choices, implementing effective waste management practices, and utilizing renewable energy sources, media producers can reduce energy consumption, minimize waste generation, and lower their carbon footprint. These green practices not only benefit the environment but also contribute to a more sustainable and responsible media industry. It is important for media producers to embrace these strategies and collaborate with all stakeholders to create a greener future for the media industry.

The importance of industry-wide adoption of sustainable practices

The adoption of sustainable practices in the media industry is crucial for mitigating the negative environmental impacts associated with media production and consumption. This section will discuss the importance of industry-wide adoption of sustainable practices, highlighting the benefits, challenges, and strategies for implementing sustainable initiatives.

Benefits of industry-wide adoption

Industry-wide adoption of sustainable practices brings several benefits, both for the environment and the media industry itself. Here are some key advantages:

1. Environmental preservation: Adopting sustainable practices helps reduce the carbon footprint, energy consumption, and water usage associated with media production. It also minimizes waste generation and promotes responsible disposal of electronic devices, reducing the e-waste problem.

2. Cost savings: While transitioning to sustainable practices may require upfront investments, it ultimately leads to long-term cost savings. Energy-efficient technologies, for example, can significantly reduce utility bills, and recycling and responsible disposal of electronic devices can avoid costly fines and penalties.

3. Reputation and brand image: Consumers are increasingly demanding eco-friendly products and services. By adopting sustainable practices, media companies can enhance their reputation and differentiate themselves in a competitive market. Green certifications and labels can further validate their commitment to sustainability.

4. Regulatory compliance: As environmental regulations become more stringent, media companies can stay ahead of compliance requirements by adopting sustainable practices. This helps avoid legal and reputational risks associated with non-compliance.

Challenges in industry-wide adoption

Despite the benefits, there are challenges that media companies may face when trying to achieve industry-wide adoption of sustainable practices. These challenges include:

1. Resistance to change: Implementing sustainable practices often requires changes to established workflows and processes. Resistance to change from employees, stakeholders, or even consumers can hinder progress.

2. Financial constraints: The initial investment needed to adopt sustainable technologies and practices can be a barrier for smaller media companies with limited financial resources. Finding cost-effective solutions and securing funding can be challenging.

3. Lack of awareness and knowledge: Many media professionals may not fully understand the environmental impacts of their industry or the potential benefits of sustainable practices. Education and awareness programs are essential for creating a culture of sustainability within the sector.

4. Limited industry-wide collaboration: Coordinating sustainability efforts across the entire media industry can be challenging. Collaboration and collective

action are necessary to create meaningful change and industry-wide adoption of sustainable practices.

Strategies for industry-wide adoption

To promote industry-wide adoption of sustainable practices, the following strategies should be considered:

1. Education and training: Media companies should invest in educational programs and training sessions to raise awareness about the environmental impacts of media production. This includes educating employees about sustainable practices and providing them with the necessary skills and knowledge to implement them.

2. Collaboration and partnerships: Media industry associations, organizations, and regulators can play a vital role in facilitating collaboration and partnerships among stakeholders. This includes sharing best practices, conducting joint research, and developing industry-wide sustainability standards and guidelines.

3. Incentives and rewards: Governments and regulatory bodies can provide incentives, such as tax breaks or grants, to encourage media companies to adopt sustainable practices. Additionally, recognition programs and awards can motivate companies to showcase their sustainability efforts and achievements.

4. Industry-wide benchmarks and reporting: Establishing industry-wide benchmarks and reporting frameworks can help measure and track sustainability performance. This enables companies to benchmark their progress against peers and identify areas for continuous improvement.

5. Consumer awareness and demand: Media companies should engage with consumers through transparent communication and marketing campaigns that promote sustainable content consumption. Educating audiences about the environmental impacts of media and highlighting sustainable alternatives can empower individuals to make more informed choices.

6. Continuous improvement and innovation: The media industry should prioritize ongoing research and innovation to develop new technologies, materials, and practices that further reduce environmental impacts. Embracing advancements in renewable energy, energy-efficient technologies, and sustainable production methods can drive industry-wide sustainability.

7. External partnerships: Collaborating with environmental organizations and NGOs can provide media companies with guidance and expertise in implementing sustainable practices. Joint initiatives and campaigns can amplify the industry's impact in driving positive environmental change.

Case study: The Green Production Guide

The Green Production Guide is an excellent example of industry-wide adoption of sustainable practices. This online resource provides media professionals with practical information, case studies, and resources for incorporating sustainability into their projects. It covers various aspects of sustainable production, including energy efficiency, waste reduction, and responsible sourcing. The Green Production Guide shows how collaboration between media companies, industry associations, and environmental organizations can propel industry-wide adoption of sustainable practices.

Summary

Industry-wide adoption of sustainable practices is vital for the media industry to address its environmental impacts and contribute to a more sustainable future. By embracing sustainable technologies, minimizing waste, reducing energy consumption, and engaging stakeholders, media companies can align their operations with sustainable principles, realize cost savings, enhance their reputation, and contribute to a greener media landscape. Collaboration, education, and innovation are key in achieving industry-wide adoption, and partnerships with environmental organizations can further leverage the industry's potential for positive change.

Sustainable Consumption of Media

The impact of media consumption on sustainability

In today's digital age, media consumption has become an integral part of our daily lives. From streaming movies and TV shows to browsing social media platforms, we are constantly engaging with various forms of media. However, the environmental impact of our media consumption is often overlooked. In this section, we will explore the significant ways in which media consumption affects sustainability and discuss strategies for promoting sustainable media consumption.

Energy consumption

One of the key impacts of media consumption on sustainability is energy consumption. The production, storage, and distribution of media content require a significant amount of energy, which primarily comes from non-renewable sources such as fossil fuels. Streaming services, for example, rely on massive data centers that consume vast amounts of electricity to store and deliver content to users.

To put this into perspective, let's consider the energy footprint of streaming a high-definition movie. According to estimates, streaming one hour of content can generate approximately 0.5 kilograms of carbon dioxide emissions. With the growing popularity of streaming platforms and the increasing demand for high-quality video content, the energy consumption associated with media consumption is steadily rising.

Example: Imagine a scenario where a popular TV show releases a new season, and millions of viewers around the world binge-watch all the episodes within a few days. The collective energy consumption from streaming and powering the devices used for watching would be significant, leading to a higher carbon footprint.

Solution: There are several strategies to mitigate the energy consumption associated with media consumption.

Firstly, individuals can choose to download content instead of streaming, as downloading consumes less energy than continuous streaming. Additionally, adjusting streaming quality settings to lower resolutions can significantly reduce energy consumption.

Secondly, media companies and streaming platforms can invest in renewable energy sources to power their data centers and infrastructure. Transitioning to renewable energy not only reduces carbon emissions but also encourages the expansion of renewable energy generation.

Lastly, there is a need for greater awareness among consumers regarding the energy consumption of different media platforms. By making informed choices and supporting platforms that prioritize sustainable practices, consumers can play a crucial role in encouraging media companies to adopt greener alternatives.

Electronic waste

Another aspect of media consumption that has a significant environmental impact is electronic waste, commonly known as e-waste. Consumer electronics, such as smartphones, laptops, and tablets, play a vital role in media consumption. However, our constant demand for the latest devices contributes to the growing problem of e-waste.

E-waste contains hazardous materials like lead, mercury, and cadmium, which can contaminate soil and water if not disposed of properly. Moreover, the production and disposal of electronic devices require the extraction and processing of valuable resources, contributing to resource depletion and environmental degradation.

Example: When a new smartphone model is released, many consumers feel compelled to replace their current devices, resulting in a large number of perfectly usable devices being discarded as e-waste. This not only increases the amount of waste that ends up in landfills but also perpetuates a cycle of constant production and consumption, depleting finite resources.

Solution: There are several strategies to address the e-waste problem associated with media consumption.

Firstly, individuals can extend the lifespan of their electronic devices by repairing and upgrading them instead of immediately replacing them. This reduces the demand for new devices and extends the useful life of existing ones.

Secondly, responsible disposal and recycling of electronic devices play a crucial role in reducing e-waste. Consumers should make an effort to recycle their old devices through certified e-waste recycling programs or donate them to organizations that can refurbish and redistribute them.

Thirdly, media companies can contribute to reducing e-waste by promoting content accessibility across various devices. By encouraging users to access media through existing devices rather than constantly upgrading to new ones, the demand for new electronic devices can be reduced.

Resource consumption

In addition to energy and e-waste, media consumption also contributes to the consumption of other resources. The production of media content, including physical media like DVDs and Blu-rays, involves the extraction of raw materials such as plastic, aluminum, and paper, along with the use of water and chemicals. This consumption of resources puts a strain on the environment and contributes to ecological degradation.

Example: Consider the production of DVDs for a highly anticipated movie release. The manufacturing process requires the extraction and processing of raw materials, including petroleum for plastic production and aluminum for disc manufacturing. Furthermore, the packaging of DVDs involves additional resource consumption, such as paper for covers and plastic for cases.

Solution: To promote sustainability in media consumption, various strategies can be employed to reduce resource consumption.

Firstly, the transition to digital media formats can significantly reduce resource consumption. Streaming platforms and online media distribution eliminate the need for physical production and distribution, thereby reducing the extraction of raw materials and minimizing packaging waste.

Secondly, media companies can encourage the use of sustainable materials in physical media production. This can involve using eco-friendly packaging materials or exploring innovative solutions like biodegradable discs.

Lastly, consumers can play an active role by choosing digital media options over physical copies and supporting media companies that prioritize sustainable practices. By reducing the demand for physical media, individuals contribute to conserving resources and minimizing waste generation.

Promoting sustainable media consumption

Promoting sustainable media consumption requires collective efforts from individuals, media companies, and policymakers. Here are some strategies to promote sustainable media consumption:

1. Raising awareness: Increasing awareness about the environmental impact of media consumption is essential. Media literacy programs and educational campaigns can help individuals make more conscious choices regarding their media consumption habits.

2. Encouraging energy-efficient devices: Governments and policymakers can incentivize the production and adoption of energy-efficient devices. This can include measures such as energy efficiency labeling, tax incentives, and research grants for developing sustainable technologies.

3. Supporting sustainable media platforms: Individuals can choose to support media platforms that prioritize sustainability. This can involve subscribing to green streaming services that utilize renewable energy or partnering with media outlets that actively promote sustainability and environmental awareness.

4. Advocating for policy changes: Citizens can engage in advocacy efforts to encourage policymakers to implement regulations that promote sustainable media practices. This can include lobbying for stricter e-waste recycling laws or supporting policies that incentivize sustainable production and distribution methods.

By implementing these strategies, we can collectively reduce the environmental impact of media consumption and pave the way for a more sustainable media industry.

Key Takeaways

- Media consumption has a significant impact on sustainability, primarily through energy consumption, e-waste generation, and resource consumption.

- Strategies such as downloading content instead of streaming, using energy-efficient devices, and supporting renewable energy sources can help mitigate the environmental impact of media consumption.
- Responsible e-waste disposal, extending the lifespan of electronic devices, and promoting digital media formats are effective ways to address the e-waste problem associated with media consumption.
- Transitioning to digital media, using sustainable materials, and supporting media companies that prioritize sustainability can reduce resource consumption in media production and distribution.
- Raising awareness, encouraging energy-efficient devices, supporting sustainable media platforms, and advocating for policy changes are strategies that can promote sustainable media consumption.

In conclusion, considering the environmental impact of our media consumption is crucial in achieving a more sustainable future. By making conscious choices and supporting sustainable practices in the media industry, we can contribute to the preservation of our natural resources and reduce carbon emissions. Let us embrace sustainable media consumption as a means to shape a more environmentally conscious society.

Strategies for promoting sustainable media consumption

Promoting sustainable media consumption entails encouraging individuals to make conscious choices that minimize their environmental impact while still enjoying the benefits of media. Here, we will discuss several strategies that can be employed to achieve this goal.

1. Reduce media consumption

One of the most effective strategies for promoting sustainable media consumption is to reduce overall media consumption. Encouraging individuals to be more mindful of the content they consume and limiting excessive screen time can have significant environmental benefits. This is because media production requires substantial energy, resources, and water, and reducing consumption directly reduces the environmental impact associated with media production.

2. Opt for digital media

Digital media consumption, such as streaming, downloading, or accessing content online, is generally more environmentally friendly compared to physical media formats. Traditional forms of media like DVDs, CDs, and printed books require raw materials, manufacturing processes, and transportation, resulting in a larger carbon footprint. By opting for digital media, individuals can significantly reduce waste and energy consumption.

3. Choose energy-efficient devices

The choice of electronic devices used for media consumption plays a crucial role in promoting sustainability. Encouraging individuals to choose energy-efficient devices, such as those with ENERGY STAR or other eco-label certifications, can significantly reduce energy consumption. These devices are designed to operate at lower power levels, thereby reducing both energy usage and greenhouse gas emissions.

4. Practice responsible device usage

Promoting sustainable media consumption also involves practicing responsible device usage. Encouraging individuals to turn off devices when not in use, utilize power-saving settings, and avoid unnecessary charging can lead to significant energy savings. Additionally, reminding users to recycle electronic devices properly and to dispose of them in designated e-waste recycling centers contributes to reducing environmental harm.

5. Support sustainable media platforms

Choosing media platforms that prioritize sustainability in their operations is another effective strategy. Look for platforms that have implemented measures to reduce their carbon footprint, such as using renewable energy sources to power their servers or implementing energy-efficient data centers. This way, individuals can support companies that align with their values and contribute to the overall promotion of sustainable media consumption.

6. Engage in media activism

Media activism involves using media platforms to raise awareness about sustainability issues and advocate for change. By actively participating in discussions, sharing sustainable content, and encouraging others to adopt eco-friendly media consumption practices, individuals can have a significant impact. Utilize social media platforms, create and share videos, podcasts, and articles that promote sustainable media consumption, and collaborate with like-minded individuals and organizations.

7. Foster media literacy

Enhancing media literacy is crucial to promoting sustainable media consumption. Educate individuals about the environmental impact of media production and consumption, as well as the efforts being made by the industry to improve sustainability. Encourage critical thinking and provide resources for fact-checking and evaluating the reliability and biases of media sources. Media literacy empowers individuals to make informed and environmentally conscious choices.

8. Support local and independent media

Supporting local and independent media outlets can contribute to promoting sustainability. Local media often have a smaller carbon footprint compared to larger, centralized media organizations. By subscribing to local newspapers, supporting independent filmmakers, and accessing locally produced media, individuals can contribute to the sustainability of the media industry while fostering diversity and community engagement.

9. Encourage collaboration and knowledge sharing

Promoting sustainable media consumption requires collective effort and knowledge sharing. Encourage individuals, communities, and organizations to collaborate and share best practices for sustainable media production and consumption. This can include sharing tips on energy-efficient media production techniques, recommending sustainable media content, and highlighting successful sustainability initiatives within the industry. Collaboration and knowledge sharing create a positive feedback loop, inspiring others to adopt sustainable practices.

Conclusion

Strategies for promoting sustainable media consumption include reducing overall consumption, opting for digital media, choosing energy-efficient devices, practicing responsible device usage, supporting sustainable media platforms, engaging in media activism, fostering media literacy, supporting local and independent media, and encouraging collaboration and knowledge sharing. By implementing these strategies, individuals can actively contribute to reducing the environmental impact of media production and consumption while still enjoying the benefits of media. Remember, the choices we make as media consumers can shape the future of the industry and contribute to a more sustainable world.

Alternative media platforms and their sustainable practices

As we navigate the challenges of sustainability in media consumption, it is essential to explore alternative media platforms that prioritize environmentally friendly practices. These platforms not only offer an array of content but also promote sustainable values and practices. In this section, we will delve into the sustainable practices adopted by alternative media platforms and their contribution to the overall goal of sustainable media.

Green Hosting and Data Centers

One of the primary sustainability concerns in the digital age is the energy consumption associated with data centers. Traditional media platforms rely heavily on energy-intensive servers and infrastructure. However, alternative media platforms are taking steps to address this issue by adopting sustainable hosting and data center practices.

These platforms engage in green hosting, which entails hosting websites and content on servers powered by renewable energy sources, such as solar or wind power. By harnessing clean energy, alternative media platforms significantly reduce their carbon footprint. Moreover, they often prioritize data centers that implement energy-efficient technologies and practices to minimize energy waste.

For example, the alternative media platform "EcoStream" partners with eco-friendly data centers that use energy-efficient cooling systems, virtualization techniques, and optimized infrastructure to reduce energy consumption. Through such initiatives, these platforms aim to demonstrate that the digital landscape can be sustainable and eco-friendly.

Content Curation and Minimization of Resource Consumption

Traditional media platforms often engage in excessive content production and distribution, leading to resource depletion and waste generation. In contrast, alternative media platforms focus on curated content that promotes sustainability and embodies environmental values.

These platforms adopt practices such as minimalism, where they prioritize quality over quantity and strive to deliver meaningful content to their audience. By doing so, they reduce the production and distribution of unnecessary content, thus minimizing resource consumption.

Furthermore, these platforms promote efficient use of resources by adopting responsible content creation and delivery methods. For instance, they may utilize cloud-based storage and delivery systems, which significantly reduce the need for physical media and minimize waste generation. By streamlining their operations, these platforms minimize their ecological impact.

Collaboration and Sharing Economy

Alternative media platforms often embrace collaboration and the sharing economy as core values. Collaborative media platforms provide tools and platforms for content creators to collaborate and share resources, reducing the need for individual production and wasteful duplication.

For example, the platform "ShareStream" allows content creators to share equipment, locations, and expertise, reducing the environmental impact associated with individual content production. By facilitating collaboration, these platforms not only reduce resource consumption but also promote community-building and knowledge-sharing.

Additionally, alternative media platforms actively support and promote the use of open-source technologies and licenses. Open-source software, for instance, enables greater access, transparency, and collaboration, leading to more sustainable and efficient media production processes.

Ethical Advertising and Revenue Generation

Advertising is a crucial revenue stream for many media platforms, but it often comes with sustainability concerns. Traditional media platforms tend to rely on unethical and unsustainable advertising practices that prioritize profit over environmental responsibility.

Alternative media platforms, however, strive to adopt ethical advertising practices that align with their core sustainability values. They prioritize advertising partnerships with environmentally responsible brands and organizations. This not only supports sustainability-focused businesses but also ensures that the advertising content aligns with the platform's values.

Furthermore, these platforms often implement advertising strategies that minimize the reliance on intrusive ad formats, such as pop-ups or autoplay videos. By prioritizing non-intrusive and targeted advertising, they create a more positive user experience and reduce unnecessary energy consumption associated with excessive ad loading.

User Empowerment and Education

Alternative media platforms focus on empowering their users and educating them about sustainable practices. These platforms often provide informative content, resources, and tools to help users make environmentally conscious decisions.

For instance, media platform "ConsciousStream" offers educational videos on sustainable lifestyle choices, highlighting the environmental impact of various consumer decisions. They provide viewers with practical tips and resources to adopt sustainable habits and reduce their ecological footprint.

Additionally, these platforms incorporate user feedback and suggestions into their content and operation strategies. By listening to their audience, they foster a sense of community and shared responsibility for sustainability.

Conclusion

Alternative media platforms play a significant role in promoting sustainable media practices. By adopting sustainable hosting and data centers, curating content, embracing collaboration, promoting ethical advertising, and empowering users, these platforms showcase the potential for sustainable media consumption.

As users, we can actively support these platforms and make conscious choices in our media consumption. By engaging with alternative media platforms and adopting sustainable media practices, we contribute to a more environmentally responsible and inclusive media landscape. Let us embrace these platforms and together create a future where sustainable media becomes the norm.

Educating audiences about sustainable media choices

In order to promote sustainable media choices, it is crucial to educate audiences about the environmental impacts of their media consumption and provide them with alternatives that align with sustainability principles. This section will explore the different strategies and approaches to effectively educate audiences about sustainable media choices.

The importance of media literacy

Media literacy plays a key role in educating audiences about sustainable media choices. By developing media literacy skills, individuals can critically evaluate the content they consume and understand its environmental implications. Media literacy empowers individuals to be conscious consumers and make informed decisions about the media they engage with.

To promote media literacy, educational initiatives can be implemented at various levels, from schools to community organizations. These initiatives can focus on teaching individuals how to analyze media messages, identify biased or misleading information, and understand the environmental impact of different forms of media production. Through media literacy education, audiences can gain a deeper understanding of sustainable media choices and their role in shaping a more environmentally responsible society.

Collaboration with media platforms and content creators

Another effective way to educate audiences about sustainable media choices is through collaboration with media platforms and content creators. Media platforms play a significant role in shaping public opinion and behavior, and they have the potential to influence audience preferences towards sustainable content.

Media platforms can promote sustainable media choices by featuring eco-friendly productions, highlighting sustainability initiatives in the media industry, and providing information about the environmental impact of different forms of media consumption. This can be done through dedicated sections on their websites or through partnerships with environmental organizations.

Content creators, on the other hand, can integrate sustainability themes and messages into their media projects. By incorporating environmentally conscious narratives, characters, and settings, content creators can raise awareness about sustainability issues and inspire audiences to make sustainable choices. For example, a television show could depict characters using public transportation or engaging in recycling practices, showcasing sustainable behaviors in a relatable and entertaining way.

Using social media and online campaigns

Social media platforms provide a powerful tool for educating audiences about sustainable media choices. With the widespread use of social media, campaigns can reach a large audience and create meaningful engagement. Online campaigns can use creative and interactive content to inform and inspire audiences to make sustainable media choices.

Social media influencers and environmental advocates can play a crucial role in disseminating information about sustainable media choices. By partnering with influencers who have a strong following and align with sustainability values, educational content can reach a broader audience and have a greater impact. These influencers can create videos, articles, or social media posts that provide tips, recommendations, and insights into sustainable media choices.

Additionally, online platforms can host discussions, webinars, or virtual events that focus on sustainable media consumption. These platforms can provide resources, share success stories, and facilitate conversations between audiences, content creators, and industry professionals. By fostering an online community centered around sustainable media choices, audiences can learn from each other and collectively strive for a more sustainable media landscape.

Measuring the impact

To assess the effectiveness of educational efforts in promoting sustainable media choices, it is important to measure the impact of these initiatives. Surveys, interviews, and online analytics can provide valuable insights into audience perceptions, behaviors, and knowledge about sustainable media options.

By collecting data on audience attitudes and behaviors before and after educational campaigns, it is possible to identify changes in behavior and awareness. This data can inform future strategies and help refine educational initiatives to better meet audience needs and interests.

Case study: The Green Media Education Initiative

The Green Media Education Initiative is an example of a comprehensive educational program aimed at promoting sustainable media choices. This initiative combines media literacy education, collaborations with media platforms, and online campaigns to raise awareness about the environmental impact of media consumption.

The initiative partners with schools, colleges, and community organizations to integrate media literacy education into existing curricula. It provides resources for educators to teach students about sustainable media choices, environmental impact assessment, and critical analysis of media content.

In collaboration with media platforms, the initiative curates a collection of sustainable media content, making it easily accessible for audiences. It also works with content creators to develop environmentally themed projects and supports sustainable practices in media production.

Online campaigns on social media platforms engage audiences through interactive quizzes, informative videos, and tips for sustainable media consumption. The initiative also tracks engagement metrics to measure the impact of their educational efforts.

Through the Green Media Education Initiative, audiences become more knowledgeable about sustainable media choices, leading to a shift in media consumption patterns and an overall increase in demand for sustainable media content.

Key takeaways

Educating audiences about sustainable media choices is essential in promoting a sustainable media landscape. Media literacy education, collaboration with media platforms and content creators, online campaigns, and measuring the impact are all important elements in this educational process.

By empowering audiences with knowledge and providing them with sustainable alternatives, individuals can make informed decisions that contribute to a more environmentally responsible media industry. Through collective efforts, we can create a media ecosystem that aligns sustainability principles with audience preferences and contribute to a greener future.

Resources:
- The Green Media Education Initiative website: www.greenmediaeducation.org. - Media Literacy Project: www.medialiteracyproject.org. - Sustainable Media Choices: A Guide for Audiences, by Jane Greenberg. - Sustainable Media Campaigns on Social Media: Best Practices and Case Studies, compiled by the Green Media Education Initiative.

Media literacy and critical thinking in media consumption

Media literacy and critical thinking are essential skills for navigating the vast amount of information and media content that we encounter on a daily basis. In an era where fake news, misinformation, and biased narratives are prevalent, it is imperative for individuals to develop the ability to critically analyze and evaluate media messages. In this section, we will explore the importance of media literacy and critical thinking in media consumption and provide strategies for developing these skills.

Understanding media literacy

Media literacy refers to the ability to access, analyze, evaluate, and create media content. It involves understanding how media messages are constructed, the techniques used to influence audiences, and the impact of media on society. Media literacy empowers individuals to become informed and active media consumers, rather than passive recipients of information.

To become media literate, it is crucial to develop the following key skills:

1. **Media analysis:** This involves critically examining media messages, identifying their intended purposes, and recognizing the techniques used to

manipulate or persuade audiences. By analyzing media content, individuals can uncover underlying biases, stereotypes, and hidden agendas.

2. **Evaluation of credibility**: Media literacy includes the ability to assess the credibility of sources and determine the reliability and accuracy of information presented. This involves fact-checking claims, verifying sources, and cross-referencing information from multiple sources.

3. **Understanding representation**: Media literacy requires understanding how different groups and identities are represented in media. This involves recognizing stereotypes, promoting diverse and inclusive representations, and challenging media narratives that perpetuate discrimination or exclusion.

4. **Awareness of media influence**: Media literacy involves recognizing the influence media has on public opinion, attitudes, and behaviors. By understanding the power dynamics within media industries, individuals can question and resist media messages that seek to shape their beliefs or behaviors.

Strategies for developing media literacy

Developing media literacy skills is an ongoing process that requires active engagement and practice. Here are some strategies to enhance media literacy and critical thinking in media consumption:

1. **Question everything**: Encourage a healthy skepticism towards media content. Don't take information at face value. Ask questions about the source, the evidence presented, and the potential biases involved. Develop a habit of seeking multiple perspectives and verifying claims before accepting them as true.

2. **Diversify media sources**: Avoid relying solely on one media outlet for information. Consume news and other media content from a variety of sources, including reputable mainstream sources, independent media, and alternative viewpoints. This helps to gain a more comprehensive understanding of different perspectives and avoid echo chambers.

3. **Fact-check and verify**: Take the time to fact-check information, especially before sharing it with others. Consult reliable fact-checking organizations or cross-reference information with reputable sources. Be cautious of viral social media posts or sensational headlines that may lack credibility.

4. **Consider the context:** When analyzing media messages, consider the context in which they are presented. Pay attention to the motivations behind the creation or dissemination of the content. Consider the social, political, and economic factors that may influence media narratives and agendas.

5. **Develop critical awareness:** Raise awareness about the techniques used in media to influence emotions and opinions. Be aware of common manipulative strategies such as emotional appeals, use of visuals, framing, and selective presentation of information. Apply critical thinking skills to recognize these techniques and separate facts from opinions.

6. **Engage in media creation:** Actively participate in creating media content to understand the process of media production. By creating content, individuals can gain insights into media construction, ethics, and responsible storytelling. This can also help to counterbalance the influence of mainstream media and amplify diverse voices.

7. **Educate others:** Share your knowledge and skills with others. Teach media literacy to friends, family, or community members. By spreading media literacy, you can empower others to critically engage with media and contribute to a more informed society.

Exercising critical thinking in media consumption

To exercise critical thinking in media consumption, it is essential to apply these strategies to real-world examples. Let's consider a hypothetical situation:

Suppose you come across an online article that claims a new technology can solve all environmental problems and reduce carbon emissions to zero. The article provides limited information about the technology and its source, and it is published on a website known for promoting pseudoscience. How would you approach this situation using media literacy and critical thinking?

First, question the credibility of the source and evaluate whether it aligns with reputable scientific sources. Verify the claims made in the article by seeking additional information from reliable sources or scientific studies. Look for potential conflicts of interest or financial motives behind the technology's promotion.

Consider the context in which the article is published. Are there other reputable sources reporting on this technology? Has it been peer-reviewed or tested by independent researchers? Assess whether the article presents a balanced view by looking for counterarguments or alternative perspectives.

By applying critical thinking skills and media literacy strategies, you can make an informed decision about the credibility and reliability of the information presented. In this case, you might conclude that the article lacks sufficient evidence or verification from reputable sources, and therefore, the claims made about the technology should be approached with caution.

Resources for further exploration

Enhancing media literacy and critical thinking skills requires ongoing learning and exploration. Here are some resources to delve deeper into this topic:

- **Media Education Foundation** - Provides educational films, documentaries, and teaching resources on media literacy: `https://www.mediaed.org/`

- **Center for Media Literacy** - Offers resources, research, and training programs on media literacy education: `https://www.medialit.org/`

- **FactCheck.org** - A nonpartisan, nonprofit organization that monitors the accuracy of claims made by politicians and media outlets: `https://www.factcheck.org/`

- **Snopes.com** - A fact-checking website that debunks urban legends, myths, and misinformation: `https://www.snopes.com/`

- **The News Literacy Project** - Provides resources and programs to teach students how to navigate the digital information landscape: `https://newslit.org/`

Remember, developing media literacy and critical thinking skills is an ongoing process. By incorporating these skills into your media consumption habits, you can become a more discerning and responsible consumer and contribute to a more informed and media-literate society.

Collaboration between Media Industry and Environmental Organizations

The importance of partnerships in promoting sustainable media

In order to effectively promote sustainable media, partnerships between various stakeholders are crucial. Collaboration between media industry players, environmental organizations, government agencies, and the public can lead to more impactful and widespread sustainability initiatives. These partnerships can bring together resources, expertise, and influence to drive positive change in the media landscape. In this section, we will explore the importance of such partnerships and discuss their potential benefits and challenges.

Benefits of partnerships

Partnerships offer several benefits in promoting sustainable media. Firstly, they allow for the sharing of knowledge and best practices. Media industry players can learn from environmental organizations about sustainable production and consumption methods, while environmental organizations can gain insights into the complexities of the media industry. This knowledge exchange can lead to improved strategies and approaches to sustainability.

Secondly, partnerships provide access to resources and funding. Environmental organizations often have access to grants, research funding, and networks of sustainability professionals. By collaborating with these organizations, media companies can access financial and technical resources to implement sustainable initiatives. This can include funding for energy-efficient equipment, training programs for employees, or research into sustainable media practices.

Furthermore, partnerships enhance credibility and legitimacy. When media companies join forces with reputable environmental organizations, it not only demonstrates a commitment to sustainability, but also helps to build trust with audiences. By showcasing partnerships and collaborative initiatives, media companies can position themselves as leaders in sustainable practices and increase their brand value.

Challenges in forming partnerships

While partnerships offer many benefits, there are also inherent challenges that need to be addressed. One of the main challenges is the difference in goals and priorities between media industry players and environmental organizations. Media companies are often driven by profit and audience engagement, while environmental organizations focus on conservation and sustainability. Balancing these differing objectives and finding common ground can be a complex task.

Another challenge is the potential power imbalances within partnerships. Media companies, particularly those that are larger and more influential, may dominate decision-making processes, restricting the input and influence of environmental organizations. It is important for partnerships to ensure equal representation and meaningful involvement of all stakeholders to foster a collaborative and inclusive approach.

Additionally, partnerships require significant coordination and communication among participating organizations. This can be challenging due to differences in organizational cultures, structures, and communication styles. Effective communication channels and clear roles and responsibilities should be established to streamline collaboration and ensure that goals are achieved.

Successful examples of partnerships

Despite the challenges, there have been successful examples of partnerships in promoting sustainable media. One notable example is the collaboration between the film industry and environmental organizations to promote eco-friendly practices in film production. Several environmental organizations provide resources and certifications, such as the Green Seal and Green Production Guide, to help productions minimize their environmental impact. These partnerships have resulted in the adoption of sustainable practices, such as reducing energy consumption, minimizing waste, and promoting environmentally friendly transport options.

Another successful partnership is the collaboration between media outlets and environmental organizations in raising awareness about climate change and environmental issues. Media companies have partnered with organizations like Greenpeace and WWF to produce documentaries and educational programs that highlight the importance of sustainability. These collaborations have reached a wide audience and sparked meaningful conversations about the environment.

Conclusion

Partnerships play a crucial role in promoting sustainable media by bringing together diverse expertise, resources, and influence. Collaboration between media industry players, environmental organizations, government agencies, and the public can lead to the adoption of sustainable practices, increased awareness of environmental issues, and the promotion of positive change. While challenges exist, successful examples demonstrate the potential impact of partnerships in shaping a more sustainable media landscape. It is imperative for stakeholders to work together to address these challenges and harness the power of partnerships in driving sustainability in the media industry.

Examples of successful collaborations between media and environmental organizations

Collaborations between media and environmental organizations have proven to be a powerful tool in promoting sustainable practices and raising awareness about environmental issues. Through joint initiatives, these partnerships have effectively captured the attention of the public and inspired action towards a greener and more sustainable world. In this section, we will highlight some notable examples of successful collaborations between media and environmental organizations.

Example 1: The Nature Conservancy and BBC's "Planet Earth" series

One of the most prominent collaborations between media and environmental organizations is the partnership between The Nature Conservancy and the BBC's "Planet Earth" series. This groundbreaking documentary series, narrated by Sir David Attenborough, captivated audiences worldwide with its stunning visuals and compelling storytelling.

The Nature Conservancy, a global environmental organization focused on conserving important natural habitats, joined forces with the BBC to create a multi-platform campaign that went beyond the TV screen. The campaign aimed to raise awareness about the importance of biodiversity and conservation while encouraging individuals to take action in their own communities.

The partnership leveraged the popularity of the "Planet Earth" series to engage viewers and provide them with tangible ways to get involved. Through online resources, educational materials, and community events, The Nature Conservancy and the BBC empowered individuals to make a difference by supporting conservation efforts and implementing sustainable practices in their daily lives.

Example 2: National Geographic and Leonardo DiCaprio Foundation's "Before the Flood"

Another impactful collaboration in the realm of sustainable media is the partnership between National Geographic and the Leonardo DiCaprio Foundation for the documentary film "Before the Flood". This thought-provoking film, featuring actor and environmental activist Leonardo DiCaprio, explores the causes and consequences of climate change and highlights potential solutions.

National Geographic, a leading media organization dedicated to exploring the world and protecting the planet, teamed up with the Leonardo DiCaprio Foundation to create a comprehensive outreach campaign alongside the film. The campaign aimed to raise awareness about climate change, empower individuals to take action, and drive policy changes on a global scale.

Through a combination of screenings, educational programs, and online engagement, this collaboration effectively reached millions of people around the world. The partnership utilized National Geographic's extensive media reach and the influence of Leonardo DiCaprio to amplify the film's message and mobilize individuals to support sustainable practices and advocate for climate action.

Example 3: Greenpeace and The Guardian's "Keep it in the Ground" campaign

Greenpeace, an international environmental organization known for its direct action and advocacy, partnered with The Guardian, a leading news organization, for the "Keep it in the Ground" campaign. This collaboration aimed to raise awareness about the environmental and social impacts of fossil fuel extraction and advocate for a transition to renewable energy sources.

The Guardian committed to divesting its own endowment fund from fossil fuels and launched a dedicated section on its website to cover the campaign. Through investigative journalism, opinion pieces, and multimedia content, this collaboration effectively highlighted the urgency and significance of keeping fossil fuels in the ground.

By joining forces, Greenpeace and The Guardian provided a platform for scientists, activists, and communities affected by fossil fuel extraction to share their stories and inform the public about the environmental harm caused by continued reliance on these finite resources. The collaboration facilitated a global conversation and prompted individuals and institutions to reconsider their relationship with fossil fuels and support renewable energy alternatives.

Example 4: World Wildlife Fund (WWF) and Google's "Street View" project

The World Wildlife Fund (WWF), a leading conservation organization, partnered with Google for the "Street View" project to bring virtual wildlife experiences to a global audience. This collaboration combined the technological capabilities of

Google's Street View platform with WWF's expertise in conservation to create immersive and educational virtual tours of some of the world's most diverse ecosystems.

Through this collaboration, individuals could explore breathtaking locations, such as the Amazon rainforest and the Great Barrier Reef, from the comfort of their homes. The virtual tours not only showcased the natural beauty of these habitats but also raised awareness about the threats they face and the importance of their preservation.

WWF and Google's collaboration enabled people from all over the world to connect with and develop a deep appreciation for nature. By providing a digital platform for immersive experiences, the partnership inspired individuals to support conservation efforts, donate to WWF's initiatives, and take action to protect biodiversity and combat climate change.

These examples of successful collaborations between media and environmental organizations demonstrate the power of partnerships in promoting sustainability and driving positive change. By combining their unique strengths and resources, media outlets and environmental organizations can leverage their influence to raise awareness, spark conversations, and inspire action for a greener and more sustainable future.

Note: The examples provided are for illustrative purposes only and do not represent an exhaustive list of successful collaborations between media and environmental organizations. There are numerous other notable collaborations that have made significant contributions to the field of sustainable media.

Opportunities for joint initiatives in advocacy and awareness

Advocacy and awareness play a crucial role in promoting sustainability and creating positive change. In the context of sustainable media, joint initiatives between the media industry and environmental organizations can have a significant impact in raising awareness, educating the public, and advocating for sustainable practices. This section explores some of the opportunities for collaboration between these two sectors in fostering advocacy and awareness.

Understanding the power of media in advocacy

Media has a unique ability to reach large audiences and influence public opinion. By leveraging their reach and influence, media organizations can effectively amplify sustainability messages and advocate for positive environmental change. They can use their platforms to educate the public, shed light on environmental issues, and inspire action. However, it is essential for media organizations to approach advocacy in a responsible and unbiased manner, ensuring accurate information and balanced coverage.

The importance of partnerships for advocacy

Collaboration between media organizations and environmental organizations can greatly enhance the effectiveness of advocacy efforts. By joining forces, these two sectors can combine their expertise, resources, and networks to create impactful initiatives. Partnerships allow for the sharing of knowledge and ideas, as well as the pooling of resources to reach a broader audience.

Examples of successful collaborations

Several successful collaborations between the media industry and environmental organizations serve as inspiring examples of joint initiatives in advocacy and awareness. One such example is the partnership between National Geographic and the World Wildlife Fund (WWF). Through joint documentaries and educational campaigns, they have raised awareness about critical environmental issues such as climate change, habitat loss, and wildlife conservation. This partnership not only educated millions of people but also mobilized them to take action.

Another notable collaboration is the Greenpeace and MTV partnership. By integrating environmental themes into music videos, concerts, and social media campaigns, this partnership effectively reached young audiences and empowered them to make sustainable choices. The power of celebrity endorsements and influencers was utilized to bring attention to environmental issues and engage the youth in advocacy.

Opportunities for joint initiatives

There are several opportunities for joint initiatives in advocacy and awareness between the media industry and environmental organizations. These include:

1. **Collaborative content creation:** Media organizations and environmental organizations can come together to produce content that promotes sustainability. This could involve creating documentaries, films, television shows, or online campaigns that raise awareness about environmental issues and advocate for sustainable practices. By combining their storytelling skills with environmental expertise, they can create compelling narratives that inspire action.

2. **Sponsorship and funding:** Environmental organizations can collaborate with media organizations to secure sponsorship and funding for sustainability-focused initiatives. By partnering with businesses or foundations, they can support the production of content that promotes sustainability and funds awareness campaigns. This collaboration can help ensure the financial sustainability of advocacy efforts.

3. **Information sharing and research:** Media organizations can work hand in hand with environmental organizations to gather and share accurate information about sustainability. This collaboration can involve conducting research, organizing forums and conferences, and disseminating knowledge to the public. By combining their research capabilities, these partnerships can contribute to evidence-based advocacy and awareness.

4. **Community engagement:** Joint initiatives can also focus on community engagement and grassroots advocacy. Media organizations can provide platforms for local communities to share their stories and experiences related to sustainability. By amplifying these voices, they can raise awareness about the impact of environmental issues on marginalized communities and advocate for their rights and well-being.

5. **Education and outreach:** Media organizations and environmental organizations can collaborate to develop educational materials and outreach programs that promote sustainable practices. This can involve creating curriculum resources for schools, organizing workshops and training sessions, and using digital platforms to reach a wider audience. By combining their expertise in media and environmental education, these partnerships can empower individuals with the knowledge and skills needed to make sustainable choices.

Challenges and considerations

While joint initiatives in advocacy and awareness offer great potential, there are also challenges and considerations that need to be addressed. These include:

- **Maintaining independence and integrity:** Media organizations must ensure their independence and journalistic integrity when collaborating with environmental organizations. It is important to maintain a balance between advocacy and unbiased reporting to avoid compromising credibility.

- **Balancing diverse perspectives:** Collaboration between media organizations and environmental organizations should strive to include diverse perspectives. It is important to ensure that different voices, including those of indigenous communities, marginalized groups, and local stakeholders, are represented in the advocacy and awareness initiatives.

- **Measuring impact:** Evaluating the impact of joint advocacy initiatives can be challenging. It is important to develop metrics and evaluation frameworks to assess the effectiveness of these collaborations. This will help determine the success of the initiatives and guide future efforts.

- **Long-term commitment:** Advocacy and awareness efforts require long-term commitment and sustained engagement. Joint initiatives should be designed to ensure ongoing collaboration and support, rather than short-term projects. This will help create lasting impact and foster a culture of sustainability in both the media industry and society as a whole.

Conclusion

Collaboration between the media industry and environmental organizations provides exciting opportunities for joint initiatives in advocacy and awareness. By leveraging their unique strengths and resources, these partnerships can amplify sustainability messages, educate the public, and advocate for positive change. By embracing these opportunities, we can create a more sustainable future and empower individuals to make informed choices. As we move forward, it is essential to address the challenges and considerations to ensure the integrity and effectiveness of these joint initiatives. Through ongoing collaboration and continuous innovation, we can harness the power of sustainable media to shape a better world.

Leveraging media for environmental activism

In today's digital age, media plays a crucial role in shaping public opinion and influencing social change. It has the power to raise awareness, inspire action, and mobilize individuals and communities towards meaningful causes. One such cause that requires urgent attention is environmental activism. This section explores the potential and impact of leveraging media for environmental activism, highlighting the ways in which media can be used as a tool for promoting environmental stewardship and facilitating positive change.

The power of media in environmental activism

Media, encompassing various platforms such as television, radio, print, and digital media, has the ability to inform, educate, and engage audiences on pressing environmental issues. It allows for the widespread dissemination of information, enabling people from different geographies and backgrounds to access crucial knowledge about environmental challenges and their potential solutions. This accessibility empowers individuals to take action, advocating for sustainable practices and influencing policy decisions.

By leveraging the power of storytelling, media has the ability to create emotional connections with audiences, evoking empathy and inspiring action. Documentaries, films, and news reports that shed light on the devastating effects of climate change, deforestation, or pollution can generate public outcry and support for environmental initiatives. Additionally, media can amplify the voices of environmental activists and experts, providing a platform for them to share their insights and recommendations.

Challenges in leveraging media for environmental activism

While media has immense potential in driving environmental activism, it is not without its challenges. One of the primary obstacles is the presence of corporate interests and political biases that can influence media coverage and narratives. In some cases, media outlets may prioritize profit over the accurate reporting of environmental issues, leading to misinformation, greenwashing, or the downplaying of urgent concerns.

Furthermore, the complex and scientific nature of many environmental issues poses a challenge in effectively communicating these topics to a wide audience. Simplifying complex concepts without losing their essence is a skill that environmental activists and media professionals must develop to engage and educate the public effectively.

In addition, the ever-evolving landscape of media platforms and technologies presents both opportunities and challenges. While social media and online platforms offer unprecedented reach and engagement, they also present risks of misinformation, echo chambers, and information overload. Striking a balance between captivating content and accurate information is paramount in leveraging media for environmental activism.

Strategies for effective environmental activism through media

To effectively leverage media for environmental activism, several strategies can be employed:

1. **Engaging storytelling:** Crafting compelling narratives that resonate with audiences is key to mobilizing support for environmental causes. By highlighting real-life stories and personal experiences, media can create an emotional connection and inspire action. Documentaries, short films, and interviews can be powerful tools for raising awareness and promoting environmental activism.

2. **Collaborating with influencers and celebrities:** Utilizing the reach and influence of social media influencers and celebrities can significantly amplify environmental messages. Engaging with influential figures who are passionate about environmental conservation can help raise awareness and mobilize their followers towards taking action.

3. **Utilizing social media platforms:** Social media platforms provide a unique opportunity to engage with a wide audience and facilitate dialogue. By sharing visually compelling content, infographics, and videos, environmental activists can effectively communicate complex issues in a digestible format, inspiring action and driving engagement.

4. **Promoting citizen journalism:** Encouraging citizen journalism empowers individuals to document and share local environmental issues. By providing platforms and resources for citizen journalists, media can amplify grassroots voices and bring attention to critical environmental challenges.

5. **Collaborating with environmental organizations:** Media can forge partnerships with environmental organizations to co-create content and leverage their expertise. This collaboration can ensure the accuracy and credibility of environmental messaging, further enhancing its impact.

Case study: "Planet Earth" documentary series

A notable example of leveraging media for environmental activism is the "Planet Earth" documentary series produced by the BBC. This groundbreaking series, narrated by David Attenborough, showcases the Earth's natural wonders and the challenges faced by various ecosystems and wildlife due to human activities.

Through breathtaking cinematography and storytelling, "Planet Earth" captivated global audiences and sparked conversations about environmental conservation. The series raised awareness about the impacts of climate change, habitat destruction, and pollution, inspiring viewers to take action and support related initiatives.

Moreover, the success of "Planet Earth" demonstrated the value of innovative filming techniques and technologies in capturing the beauty of nature and emphasizing the need for its protection. It showcased the power of media in highlighting environmental issues and provided a platform for environmental activists and scientists to advocate for change.

Conclusion

Leveraging media for environmental activism holds immense potential for raising awareness, inspiring action, and driving positive change. Through engaging storytelling, collaborations, and creative use of social media platforms, media can mobilize individuals and communities towards sustainable practices and environmental conservation.

However, it is crucial to navigate the challenges posed by corporate interests, political biases, and the evolving media landscape. By addressing these challenges and employing effective strategies, media can truly become a transformative force in the fight for environmental sustainability.

The role of media in promoting environmental stewardship

Environmental stewardship refers to the responsible and sustainable management of natural resources and the environment for future generations. It involves individuals and organizations taking active steps to minimize their impact on the environment and actively contribute to its conservation. Media plays a crucial role in promoting environmental stewardship by raising awareness, disseminating information, and influencing public opinion. In this section, we will explore the various ways in which media can contribute to environmental stewardship.

Informative and Educational Programs

One of the primary roles of media in promoting environmental stewardship is through informative and educational programs. Documentaries, news reports, and educational shows can highlight pressing environmental issues, provide insights into sustainable practices, and showcase successful environmental initiatives. These programs can help educate the public about the importance of environmental stewardship and empower them to take action.

For example, a documentary series on climate change can raise awareness about the urgency of addressing this global issue. By featuring scientific research, interviews with experts, and real-life examples, media can help individuals understand the impacts of climate change and the need for sustainable solutions.

Such programs can inspire individuals to make changes in their own lives and advocate for environmental policies.

Advocacy and Campaigns

Media can also play a significant role in advocating for environmental stewardship through targeted campaigns and advocacy efforts. By using their platforms to raise awareness and mobilize public support, media outlets can influence public opinion, shape policies, and drive positive change.

For instance, media organizations can collaborate with environmental NGOs to launch campaigns focused on specific environmental issues like plastic pollution or deforestation. Through compelling storytelling, factual reporting, and visual content, media can capture the attention of the audience and encourage them to take action. By highlighting the consequences of unsustainable practices and promoting sustainable alternatives, media can effectively promote environmental stewardship.

Responsible and Sustainable Media Production

In addition to promoting environmental stewardship through content, media organizations can also lead by example through responsible and sustainable production practices. The media industry, including film and television production, has a significant environmental footprint due to energy consumption, waste generation, and resource extraction. By adopting sustainable practices, media companies can reduce their own impact on the environment and inspire others to follow suit.

Some sustainable media production practices include using renewable energy sources, minimizing waste and recycling, embracing digital technologies to reduce paper usage, and implementing eco-friendly transportation options. Media organizations can also incorporate sustainability criteria when selecting filming locations and develop guidelines for sustainable set design and construction. By showcasing these practices, media can encourage other industries and individuals to adopt similar sustainable approaches.

Engaging the Audience

Media has the power to engage and mobilize large audiences, making it a valuable tool for promoting environmental stewardship. Through interactive formats such as games, quizzes, and social media campaigns, media can encourage individuals to actively participate in environmental activities and initiatives.

For example, a media campaign can encourage viewers to pledge to reduce their carbon footprint or participate in community clean-up events. By providing easy-to-understand information, practical tips, and resources, media can empower individuals to make sustainable choices in their daily lives. This engagement can extend beyond the passive consumption of media, creating a sense of ownership and responsibility among the audience.

Collaboration with Environmental Organizations

Media organizations can also collaborate with environmental organizations to amplify their efforts and promote environmental stewardship. By leveraging their reach and resources, media can help raise funds, increase awareness, and provide a platform for environmental organizations to communicate their messages effectively.

For instance, media outlets can host telethons or fundraising events to support environmental causes. They can also invite experts and activists to share their insights and experiences, shedding light on important environmental issues. By creating partnerships and showcasing the work of environmental organizations, media can inspire individuals to get involved and support environmental stewardship.

Promoting Environmental Tourism

Media can play a crucial role in promoting environmental tourism, which involves visiting natural areas in a manner that is sustainable and minimizes negative environmental impact. By showcasing the beauty and value of natural landscapes and biodiversity through photographs, videos, and articles, media can inspire individuals to appreciate and protect these fragile ecosystems.

Media can highlight sustainable travel options, eco-friendly accommodations, and responsible tourism practices. By promoting responsible travel behaviors such as minimizing waste, respecting local cultures, and supporting conservation efforts, media can contribute to the preservation of natural environments and promote environmental stewardship among tourists.

Conclusion

Media has a significant role to play in promoting environmental stewardship. By providing informative and educational content, advocating for environmental causes, adopting sustainable production practices, engaging audiences, collaborating with environmental organizations, and promoting responsible tourism, media can raise awareness, influence behavior, and drive positive change. It is essential for media organizations and individuals to recognize their influence and use it responsibly to promote a sustainable and environmentally conscious society. Let us all embrace the role of media in promoting environmental stewardship and work towards a greener future.

Conclusion

Recap of Sustainable Media Principles and Practices

Key takeaways from the book

In this final section of our book, we summarize the key takeaways from our exploration of sustainable media. Throughout the chapters, we have delved into the definition and importance of sustainable media, examined its historical perspective, and highlighted its environmental impacts. We have also discussed the concepts of greenwashing, media manipulation, and social justice warrior (SJW) agendas in media. Furthermore, we have explored sustainable media practices and solutions, as well as the collaboration between the media industry and environmental organizations.

Here are the main points to remember:

1. Sustainable media is crucial for shaping public opinion and behavior, as the media has a significant influence on society. It is important to understand the concept of sustainability and the role of media in promoting sustainable practices.

2. The evolution of the media industry has had profound environmental consequences, from the early days of media to the rise of mass media and the impact of technology. Media consolidation has also had an impact on sustainability.

3. Energy consumption in media production is a significant concern, with energy-intensive processes in film and television production. However, there are opportunities for energy-efficient technologies and practices to reduce the carbon footprint of digital media.

4. E-waste and consumer electronics pose challenges for sustainable media. Toxic materials in consumer electronics and planned obsolescence contribute to the environmental impact. We have discussed strategies for responsible disposal and sustainable alternatives.

5. Water consumption in media production is another important aspect, with strategies for reducing water consumption in film and television production. Water scarcity is a pressing issue that the media industry needs to address.

6. Greenwashing, the practice of misleading consumers about a company's environmental practices, is prevalent in media. We have discussed how to identify and combat greenwashing, emphasizing the importance of promoting genuine sustainability.

7. Media bias and agenda-setting play a significant role in shaping public opinion and influencing sustainability discourse. We have highlighted the need for unbiased and balanced media coverage and the ethical responsibility of the media.

8. The SJW movement and its influence in media production have implications for sustainability discourse. Balancing social justice concerns with environmental sustainability is essential, as is promoting inclusivity and diversity in media.

9. Cultural appropriation and media representation are important topics. Accurate and respectful media representation contributes to inclusivity, and media plays a crucial role in promoting cultural understanding.

10. Intersectionality and environmental justice highlight the connection between social justice and environmental sustainability. Amplifying the voices of marginalized communities through media is crucial for promoting social change.

11. Sustainable media practices and solutions encompass green production certifications and standards, sustainable consumption of media, and collaboration between the media industry and environmental organizations. Industry-wide adoption of sustainable practices is key.

12. Media literacy and critical thinking are vital for promoting sustainable media practices. Educating audiences about sustainable media choices is essential for making informed decisions.

In conclusion, sustainable media is a multifaceted field that requires collaboration, innovation, and responsible practices. We hope that this book has provided you with a comprehensive understanding of sustainable media and has inspired you to take action in promoting genuine sustainability in the media industry and beyond. Remember, the future of sustainable media lies in individual efforts, ongoing research, and innovative solutions. Let us all be stewards of our environment and contribute to a more sustainable future.

The future of sustainable media

As we look ahead to the future of sustainable media, it is clear that the continued growth and development of this field will play a crucial role in shaping a more environmentally conscious and socially responsible society. The need for sustainable practices in media production and consumption has become increasingly apparent, and there are several key areas that will drive the future of sustainable media.

One of the most important factors in the future of sustainable media is the continued development of green technologies and practices. As technology continues to advance, there will be more opportunities to reduce energy consumption, minimize waste, and create more environmentally friendly media production processes. Innovations such as energy-efficient equipment, renewable energy sources, and sustainable material choices will all play a significant role in reducing the carbon footprint of media production.

Furthermore, the future of sustainable media will also involve a shift in mindset and values within the industry. Media organizations and content creators will need to prioritize sustainability and social responsibility, making conscious choices about the messages they promote and the impact of their work on both the environment and society. This shift will require education and awareness campaigns to help individuals within the industry understand the importance of sustainable media practices and their role in creating positive change.

In addition, the role of media in promoting environmental and social issues will continue to grow in the future. Media has the power to shape public opinion, influence behavior, and drive social change. As the world becomes more aware of environmental challenges and social justice issues, sustainable media will play a critical role in raising awareness, promoting responsible behaviors, and advocating for necessary policy changes. The future of sustainable media will see an increased emphasis on reporting and storytelling that highlights the interconnectedness of environmental and social issues, inspiring audiences to take action.

The future of sustainable media will also involve the integration of technology and data-driven solutions. The use of artificial intelligence (AI) and machine learning algorithms can help media organizations measure and analyze their environmental and social impact, allowing for more informed decision-making and continuous improvement. Additionally, advancements in data-driven targeting and personalization can enable media organizations to deliver tailored messages to individuals and communities, furthering the reach and impact of sustainable media initiatives.

Furthermore, collaboration and partnerships between media organizations, environmental organizations, and other stakeholders will be crucial in the future of sustainable media. By working together, these entities can pool their resources, expertise, and influence to amplify the message of sustainability and drive collective action. Partnerships can take various forms, including joint initiatives, shared platforms, and collaborative storytelling projects, all aimed at promoting sustainable practices and driving positive change.

In conclusion, the future of sustainable media holds immense possibilities for creating a more environmentally conscious and socially responsible world. Through the continued development of green technologies, a shift in industry values, the promotion of environmental and social issues, the integration of technology and data-driven solutions, and collaboration between stakeholders, sustainable media will play a vital role in shaping a sustainable future. It is up to us as individuals, media professionals, and consumers to embrace these opportunities and contribute to a more sustainable media landscape.

The role of individuals in promoting sustainable media

Individuals play a crucial role in promoting sustainable media practices. While media companies, governments, and organizations have a significant impact on the industry, it is ultimately the actions and choices of individuals that can create lasting change. In this section, we will explore the different ways in which individuals can contribute to the promotion of sustainable media.

Raising Awareness

One of the most important roles individuals can play is raising awareness about sustainable media practices. By educating themselves and others, individuals can create a demand for media that is produced and consumed in an environmentally and socially responsible manner.

To promote sustainable media, individuals can:

- Stay informed about the environmental and social impacts of media production and consumption.

- Share information and resources on sustainable media practices with friends, family, and colleagues.

- Engage in conversations about sustainability and media, both online and offline.

- Use social media platforms to amplify messages about sustainable media and to hold media companies accountable for their practices.

By raising awareness, individuals can create a ripple effect that encourages others to make more sustainable choices in their media consumption.

Supporting Sustainable Media Projects

Another way individuals can promote sustainable media is by supporting projects and initiatives that prioritize sustainability. This can be done through financial support, volunteer work, or simply by being an engaged audience member.

Individuals can:

- Attend film screenings, festivals, and events that focus on sustainable media.
- Support crowdfunding campaigns for sustainable media projects.
- Contribute to sustainable media organizations and initiatives.
- Seek out and support media that aligns with sustainable values and practices.
- Provide feedback and positive reinforcement to media companies that are making efforts to be more sustainable.

By actively supporting sustainable media projects, individuals can help create a market for media that is both environmentally conscious and socially responsible.

Championing Individual Actions

Individuals can also lead by example and champion sustainable practices in their own media consumption habits. By making conscious choices, individuals can significantly reduce their environmental footprint.

Here are some actions individuals can take:

- Reduce media consumption by prioritizing quality over quantity.
- Opt for digital media formats whenever possible to reduce the demand for physical production and reduce waste.
- Support local and independent media producers who often have lower carbon footprints compared to larger industry players.
- Engage in media sharing and borrowing initiatives to reduce resource consumption.
- Advocate for energy-efficient media devices and practices, such as using energy-saving settings, charging devices with renewable energy, and properly disposing of e-waste.

By making sustainable choices in their own lives, individuals can inspire others to do the same and create a collective movement toward sustainable media consumption.

Promoting Media Literacy

Media literacy is an essential aspect of promoting sustainable media practices. Individuals need to develop critical thinking skills to navigate media landscapes, identify greenwashing, and understand the complex relationship between media and sustainability.

To promote media literacy, individuals can:

- Educate themselves about media biases and manipulation techniques.
- Question and verify information presented in media sources.
- Seek out diverse perspectives and voices in media consumption.
- Engage in open and respectful discussions about media and its societal impact.
- Support media literacy programs and initiatives in their communities.

By promoting media literacy, individuals can contribute to a more informed and empowered society that is capable of making sustainable media choices.

Engaging in Policy and Advocacy

Lastly, individuals can engage in policy and advocacy efforts to promote sustainable media practices. By voicing their concerns and demanding change, individuals can influence the development of regulations, industry standards, and corporate practices.

Here's how individuals can get involved:

- Stay informed about relevant policies and regulations pertaining to media and sustainability.
- Join or support organizations that advocate for sustainability in the media industry.
- Write letters to policymakers, media companies, and industry associations expressing the importance of sustainable media practices.

- Participate in public consultations and meetings to voice opinions on sustainability in media.
- Vote for political candidates who prioritize environmental and social sustainability.

By actively engaging in policy and advocacy, individuals can be a driving force for change and contribute to the development of a more sustainable media industry.

In conclusion, individuals have a crucial role in promoting sustainable media practices. By raising awareness, supporting sustainable projects, championing individual actions, promoting media literacy, and engaging in policy and advocacy, individuals can make a significant impact and help shape a more sustainable future for media production and consumption. Through collective action, individuals can drive industry-wide change and create a media landscape that aligns with environmental and social sustainability principles.

The importance of ongoing research and innovation in the field

Research and innovation play crucial roles in driving progress and advancements within the field of sustainable media. As the landscape of media production and consumption continues to evolve, it is essential to stay at the forefront of new technologies, techniques, and strategies that promote sustainability. In this section, we will explore the significance of ongoing research and innovation in ensuring the long-term viability and effectiveness of sustainable media practices.

Pushing the Boundaries of Sustainable Technologies

Advancements in technology have revolutionized the media industry, providing new tools and platforms for content creation and distribution. However, many of these technologies come with environmental implications, such as higher energy consumption or increased e-waste production. Ongoing research and innovation are vital in finding sustainable alternatives to mitigate these environmental impacts.

For example, researchers are actively developing energy-efficient technologies specifically tailored for media production. This includes the use of low-energy LED lighting systems and the incorporation of renewable energy sources, such as solar panels, to power film sets or studios. Through continuous research and technological innovation, the industry can reduce its carbon footprint while maintaining high production quality.

Additionally, academia and industry experts are exploring new ways to tackle the issue of e-waste generated by consumer electronics. Research efforts are focused on developing sustainable materials, extending product lifecycles through repairability and upgradability, and promoting responsible recycling and disposal practices. Innovation in packaging and design is also being explored to minimize waste generation and optimize resource utilization.

Addressing Emerging Challenges and Opportunities

Research and innovation within the field of sustainable media are essential in identifying and addressing emerging challenges and opportunities. As media consumption patterns shift and new technologies emerge, it is crucial to stay ahead of the curve to ensure a sustainable and responsible approach.

One emerging challenge is the rapid growth of streaming services and online media platforms. While these platforms have the potential to reduce carbon emissions associated with physical media, they also pose challenges related to increased data storage, energy consumption, and electronic waste. Ongoing research can help identify solutions such as more energy-efficient streaming algorithms, data center optimization, and the development of sustainable server infrastructure.

Furthermore, ongoing research can help identify new business models and revenue streams that align with sustainability goals. For example, exploring innovative ways to monetize sustainable media, such as through carbon offsetting sponsorships or partnerships with eco-conscious brands, can pave the way for a more sustainable media ecosystem.

Promoting Best Practices and Knowledge Sharing

Ongoing research and innovation facilitate the understanding and dissemination of best practices in sustainable media. By conducting studies, analyzing data, and sharing findings, researchers and industry professionals can collaborate to develop evidence-based guidelines and standards.

For instance, research can provide insights into the environmental impact of different media production techniques and help identify the most effective strategies for reducing energy consumption, minimizing water use, and promoting responsible waste management. These findings can then be shared with media producers, content creators, and consumers through industry conferences, workshops, and educational programs.

Additionally, ongoing research and innovation can foster cooperation between different stakeholders within the industry. By collaborating with environmental organizations, government agencies, and technology providers, the media industry can foster interdisciplinary approaches to sustainability. This can lead to the development of joint initiatives, shared resources, and innovative solutions that address sustainability challenges holistically.

Challenges and Future Directions

While ongoing research and innovation are paramount to the advancement of sustainable media, there are challenges that need to be addressed. Securing funding for research projects and ensuring their relevance to industry needs can be a hurdle. Collaboration between academia and industry is crucial to bridging this gap, as it allows researchers to align their work with practical applications.

Future research efforts should focus on integrating sustainable practices throughout the entire media value chain, from content creation to distribution and consumption. In addition, interdisciplinary research that explores the intersection of sustainability, media, and other fields like psychology, sociology, and design can provide valuable insights into human behavior and decision-making processes, leading to more effective sustainability interventions.

Finally, ongoing research and innovation should be complemented by continuous education and skill development within the industry. This includes providing training programs and resources that equip media professionals with the knowledge and tools to adopt sustainable practices. By fostering a culture of continuous learning and improvement, the media industry can actively contribute to the progress and adoption of sustainable media practices.

In conclusion, ongoing research and innovation are of utmost importance in the field of sustainable media. They drive advancements in technology, address emerging challenges and opportunities, promote best practices, and foster collaboration among stakeholders. By investing in research, industry collaboration, and education, we can ensure a sustainable and resilient future for the media industry.

Final thoughts and call to action

As we conclude our journey through the complex and interconnected world of sustainable media, it is important to reflect on the valuable lessons we have learned and consider the action steps we can take to drive positive change. In this final section, we will summarize the key takeaways from this book and provide a call to action for individuals, media professionals, and society as a whole.

Throughout this book, we have explored the definition and importance of sustainable media, acknowledging its role in shaping public opinion and behavior.

We have delved into the historical perspective of the media industry, examining its evolution, the impact of technology, and the rise of mass media. We have also examined the environmental impacts of media production, focusing on energy consumption, e-waste, water consumption, and the concept of greenwashing.

In addition, we have explored the role of media in promoting social justice narratives and examined the influence of the Social Justice Warrior (SJW) movement in media production. We have discussed cultural appropriation, media representation, and the importance of inclusivity and diversity. Furthermore, we have recognized the significance of intersectionality and environmental justice in the sustainability discourse.

Drawing from all the knowledge and insights gained, here are some final thoughts and a call to action:

1. Awareness is the first step: We must continue to educate ourselves and raise awareness about the environmental and social impacts of media production and consumption. This includes understanding the importance of sustainability, recognizing greenwashing, and challenging biased narratives.

2. Embrace sustainable practices: Media professionals should integrate sustainable practices into their workflows. This can involve adopting energy-efficient technologies, reducing water consumption, promoting responsible e-waste disposal, and engaging in green production certifications.

3. Foster media literacy and critical thinking: Individuals should develop media literacy skills to discern between genuine sustainability efforts and greenwashing. Critical thinking is crucial in analyzing media content and uncovering biased narratives and agendas.

4. Encourage responsible media consumption: As consumers, we have the power to shape the media landscape by supporting sustainable media platforms and content creators. We should also recognize the impact of our media consumption habits on energy consumption and strive towards more sustainable choices.

5. Promote diversity and inclusivity: Media should actively promote diversity and inclusivity, ensuring accurate and respectful representation of different cultures, perspectives, and communities. This can contribute to a more inclusive and sustainable society.

6. Advocate for collaboration and partnerships: The media industry should actively seek collaborations with environmental organizations and other stakeholders. Joint initiatives can drive advocacy, raise awareness, and foster positive change.

7. Empower communities: Media has the power to amplify the voices of marginalized communities and promote social and environmental justice. We need

to support and uplift these voices by providing platforms for their stories and concerns.

8. Drive innovation and research: Continued research and innovation are vital for the advancement of sustainable media practices and technologies. By supporting and participating in research efforts, we can contribute to the development of more sustainable solutions and practices.

9. Take personal responsibility: Every individual has a role to play in promoting sustainable media. From adopting sustainable consumption habits to reducing our carbon footprint, our collective actions can have a significant impact on the planet and society.

10. Engage in ongoing dialogue: Let us continue the conversation surrounding sustainable media, both within our personal circles and on a broader scale. By engaging in dialogue, sharing ideas, and learning from different perspectives, we can collectively drive meaningful change.

In conclusion, sustainable media is not just a theoretical concept, but a practical necessity. It requires a multidisciplinary approach, involving media professionals, consumers, policymakers, and researchers. By aligning our actions with the principles of sustainability, embracing diversity, and challenging the status quo, we can build a future where media plays a constructive role in shaping a sustainable and just society.

Let us embark on this journey together and be the agents of change that the world needs. The time for sustainable media and a better future is now.

Index

-effectiveness, 20

ability, 5, 26, 34, 91, 93, 94, 124, 126, 127, 132, 139, 170, 178, 182
ableism, 109
academia, 195, 197
access, 20, 23, 44, 58, 64, 68, 69, 116, 132–136, 149, 160, 166, 170, 174, 182
accessibility, 40, 109, 160, 182
acclaim, 111, 151
account, 22, 145
accountability, 3, 76, 85, 104, 107, 117, 142
accountable, 25, 27, 81, 83, 85, 89, 91, 104, 122
accumulation, 21, 53
accuracy, 96, 97, 103, 107, 126
achievement, 3
acknowledgement, 118
acknowledgment, 116
act, 5, 43, 81, 97, 138
action, 6, 7, 10, 14, 26, 27, 77, 91, 92, 94–96, 100, 107, 114, 115, 136, 138, 139, 150, 157, 176–179, 181–185, 190, 191, 195, 197, 198

activism, 7, 89, 95, 97, 163, 164, 181–184
ad, 166
addition, 6, 35, 37, 60, 66, 76, 97, 136, 160, 182, 185, 191, 197
address, 1, 4–6, 14, 17, 24–26, 35, 44, 46, 48, 49, 59, 61, 63, 69, 72, 73, 75, 83, 94, 103, 111, 114, 115, 117, 125–127, 133, 134, 136, 137, 158, 162, 165, 176, 181, 190, 197
adoption, 9, 57, 59, 73, 101, 116, 121, 146, 149, 155–158, 161, 175, 190, 197
advancement, 20, 197, 199
advantage, 82
advent, 15, 18, 20, 44
advertising, 5, 13, 80–83, 111, 166, 167
advice, 66
advocacy, 136, 138, 161, 177–181, 185, 194, 195, 198
advocate, 3, 7, 19, 73, 134, 135, 163, 177, 178, 181, 184, 185
age, 53, 91, 102, 118, 158, 165, 181
agenda, 6, 7, 40, 94, 96, 98, 140, 190

agriculture, 68
aim, 14, 46, 63, 110, 113, 125, 136, 165
air, 15, 16, 18, 19, 134
algorithm, 46
algorithms, 95, 196
alternative, 14, 36, 44, 57, 66, 69, 72, 94, 138, 165–167, 172
aluminum, 160
amount, 25, 31, 34, 35, 44, 46, 68, 158, 170
amplification, 115, 136, 137
analysis, 104, 169
apathy, 94
appearance, 123
appreciation, 121, 122, 131, 132, 178
approach, 2, 23, 45, 52, 53, 57, 61, 86, 87, 91, 114–118, 121, 123, 125, 133–136, 138, 139, 172, 175, 179, 196, 199
appropriation, 1, 115, 116, 121, 122, 125, 126, 190
area, 124
array, 165
article, 172, 173
aspect, 2, 51, 64, 73, 81, 83, 85, 110, 121, 128, 130, 134, 137, 153, 159, 190, 194
assessment, 72, 169
association, 80, 82
assurance, 145
atmosphere, 18
attempt, 81, 82
attention, 6, 7, 26, 28, 29, 81–83, 85, 94–96, 105, 109, 113–115, 135–137, 140, 176, 179, 181, 185

attitude, 130
audience, 4, 26, 36, 37, 73, 75, 76, 92–94, 97, 104, 111, 130, 131, 135, 139, 146, 151, 152, 165, 167–170, 175, 179, 182, 185, 186, 193
audit, 23, 67
audits, 83, 146
authenticity, 123, 125
Ava DuVernay, 97
Ava DuVernay's, 140
availability, 18, 58, 64, 68
awareness, 3, 5, 7, 9, 10, 12, 19, 20, 26, 28, 29, 36, 37, 40, 49, 56, 58–61, 64, 66, 68–71, 73–77, 83, 92, 96, 97, 111, 115, 117, 121, 122, 124, 131, 136–140, 150, 151, 156, 157, 159, 161–163, 168, 169, 175–181, 183–187, 191, 192, 195, 198

back, 56, 60, 109, 121
background, 130
backlash, 111
balance, 1, 2, 4, 9, 32, 67, 103, 107, 111, 114–117, 130, 182
balancing, 2, 117, 149
barrier, 156
basis, 170
battery, 53, 57
beauty, 178, 184, 186
behavior, 2, 4, 5, 7, 8, 10, 13, 16, 26, 53, 60, 73, 75–77, 82, 91, 92, 168, 169, 187, 189, 191, 197
being, 22, 23, 44, 70, 91, 94, 117, 121, 123, 125, 126, 136,

Index

164, 193, 196
belief, 134
benchmark, 157
benefit, 80, 133–135, 155
Bias, 94
bias, 14, 29, 93–96, 98–102, 104, 105, 140, 143, 190
biodiversity, 1, 114, 176, 178, 186
blockbuster, 151
body, 111
book, 13, 14, 190, 197
borrowing, 116
box, 112
boy, 132
brand, 43, 79, 119, 149, 156, 174
break, 118, 130, 131
bridge, 114, 130, 132
brightness, 45
broadcasting, 1, 16, 21, 44, 70
brunt, 134, 137
brutality, 96, 140
budget, 68
building, 117, 133, 136, 139, 143, 166
burden, 116, 132, 134
burning, 18
business, 2, 10, 50, 196

cadmium, 54, 59, 159
call, 14, 109, 197, 198
camera, 53, 57, 128
campaign, 74, 176, 177, 186
capacity, 117
car, 22
carbon, 1, 8, 9, 15, 16, 18, 21–23, 31–40, 43, 44, 93, 146, 150, 153, 155, 156, 159, 162–165, 172, 186, 189, 191, 195, 196, 199

caricaturization, 121
Carolyn S. Maher, 23
case, 8, 14, 22, 36, 37, 56, 70, 86, 103, 107, 149, 151, 152, 158, 173
cast, 66, 69, 112
casting, 125
catalyst, 138, 142, 143
catering, 4, 25, 64, 65, 119
cause, 27, 47, 97, 181
caution, 173
celebrity, 179
center, 109, 165, 196
centralization, 24
century, 50
certification, 66, 145, 146, 149
chain, 53, 58, 82, 83, 117, 197
challenge, 7, 24, 25, 53, 92, 94, 96, 102, 116, 118, 124–126, 129–132, 136–139, 175, 182, 196
champion, 193
change, 3–8, 10, 12, 19, 20, 26, 27, 29, 34, 40, 46, 61, 64, 68, 70, 75–77, 91, 92, 94–98, 102, 105, 107, 112, 114, 116, 118, 120, 122, 123, 132, 133, 135–143, 146, 151, 156–158, 163, 174–178, 181–185, 187, 190–192, 194, 195, 197–199
chapter, 13, 14
charging, 163
check, 7, 92, 96
checking, 61, 87, 88, 94, 96, 102, 103, 141, 164
choice, 6, 81, 163
choose, 82, 159, 161, 163

cinematography, 183
claim, 59, 79, 111
clarity, 81
class, 132
cleaning, 64–66, 68, 71
cleanup, 71
clichés, 121
clickbait, 103, 136
climate, 5–8, 10, 26, 34, 40, 68, 75, 81, 94, 95, 105, 107, 114, 116, 133, 135, 137, 138, 175, 177, 178, 182–184
clothing, 80, 82
cloud, 20, 33, 165
co, 114
coal, 18
code, 58
cohesion, 1, 118, 123
collaboration, 5, 12, 20, 58, 73, 114, 116, 123–125, 138, 139, 156–158, 164, 166–170, 175, 177–179, 181, 190–192, 197, 198
collection, 169
color, 133, 134
combat, 13, 25, 86, 90, 116, 131, 178, 190
combination, 121, 177
comedy, 112
comfort, 178
commitment, 33, 40, 42, 73, 80, 83, 91, 128, 131, 146, 156, 174
commodification, 121
communication, 18, 26, 27, 29, 72, 81, 157, 175
community, 25, 93, 98, 103, 121, 127, 130, 133, 136, 138, 151, 164, 166, 167, 169, 176, 186

company, 24, 36, 37, 46, 49, 74, 79–85, 190
competence, 136
competition, 19
complacency, 6, 85, 94
complexity, 32, 146, 149
compliance, 146, 149, 156
composition, 102
compression, 46
computer, 44, 56
computing, 33
concentration, 19, 24
concept, 1, 2, 4, 5, 13, 34, 50, 67, 80, 93, 132–134, 137, 189, 198, 199
concern, 21, 70, 72, 81, 95, 116, 189
conclusion, 26, 59, 73, 83, 96, 98, 102, 110, 124, 126, 133, 135, 137, 139, 143, 155, 162, 190, 192, 195, 197, 199
conduct, 67, 76, 103, 141
conjunction, 113
connection, 134, 135, 190
consciousness, 85, 96, 151
consensus, 95, 107
consent, 121, 125
consequence, 25
conservation, 10, 63, 64, 66, 67, 69–75, 77, 86, 114, 145, 149, 150, 175, 176, 178, 183, 184, 186
consideration, 69, 111, 125
consolidation, 13, 18, 19, 24–26, 189
construction, 16, 32, 64, 65, 68, 71, 94, 145, 185
consultation, 123, 125

Index 205

consumer, 4, 5, 8, 9, 12, 13, 47–51, 53, 54, 57–60, 82–84, 86, 91, 167, 173, 189, 195
consumption, 1–4, 6, 8–10, 13, 14, 16–24, 26, 31–38, 40, 43–47, 50, 53, 58–75, 93, 95, 96, 124, 146, 150–153, 155–175, 185, 186, 189–199
contamination, 16
content, 1, 4, 7–10, 20–26, 36, 44–46, 73, 75, 77, 86, 92, 95, 96, 98, 111, 116, 118, 119, 122–124, 126–132, 136, 138, 139, 150–152, 157–160, 162–170, 177, 182, 185, 186, 191, 195–198
context, 1, 2, 13, 20, 34, 53, 86, 94, 115, 116, 121, 122, 124–126, 130, 132, 172, 178
contrast, 165
contribution, 165
contributor, 21, 44
control, 19, 25, 35, 58
controversy, 110, 111, 121
convenience, 40, 53
conversation, 92, 93, 112, 177, 199
cooling, 22, 24, 31, 35–37, 71, 165
cooperation, 72, 196
coordination, 175
core, 82, 84, 109, 114, 166
corruption, 76
cost, 2, 20, 23, 56, 60, 149, 156, 158
couple, 95
cover, 146, 177
coverage, 6, 14, 19, 25, 28, 92, 94–98, 100, 102–105, 107, 114, 131, 140, 141, 179, 182, 190
creation, 20, 44, 68, 121, 151, 165, 195, 197
creativity, 9, 20, 119, 149
credibility, 79, 81, 83, 104, 120, 145, 172–174
credit, 121
crew, 32, 64–66, 69, 71, 138
crisis, 6, 75, 77
criticism, 82, 110, 111, 114
cross, 103, 126
culture, 58, 103, 111, 112, 116, 121, 122, 125, 132, 156, 197
curiosity, 131
curriculum, 61
curve, 196
cycle, 4, 32, 50

d. Green, 82
damage, 68, 72
data, 5, 8–10, 21, 22, 33, 45, 46, 73, 76, 85, 159, 163, 165, 167, 169, 192, 196
David Attenborough, 176, 183
David Leigey, 23
day, 71
debate, 110, 121
decision, 77, 98, 117, 122, 128, 131, 133–136, 173, 175, 197
decline, 25
deepening, 105
definition, 22, 44, 84, 110, 159, 197
deforestation, 5, 15, 18, 19, 182, 185
degradation, 19, 70, 94, 113, 114, 116, 134, 137, 159, 160
delivery, 45, 46, 165
demand, 4, 10, 12, 18, 19, 21, 23, 25, 31, 44, 45, 50, 58, 60, 68,

71, 83, 89, 97, 112, 139, 157, 159–161, 169, 192
democratization, 20
denial, 26
dependence, 58, 154
depiction, 121, 123
depletion, 4, 8, 16, 18, 19, 60, 68, 159, 165
depth, 26, 76, 140
desert, 63, 64, 69
design, 50, 53, 57, 59, 62, 64, 145, 152, 153, 155, 185, 196, 197
designing, 57
desire, 81, 82
destruction, 68, 183
detox, 24
development, 17, 18, 35, 37, 46, 92, 102, 107, 114, 123, 190–192, 194–197, 199
device, 22, 45, 46, 56, 163, 164
dialogue, 61, 92, 95, 96, 102, 110, 111, 114, 116, 117, 122, 123, 138, 143, 199
diesel, 90
difference, 9, 61, 174, 176
dignity, 123, 125
dilution, 114
dimming, 35
dioxide, 18, 159
director, 74
disability, 134
discourse, 14, 25, 26, 29, 93, 95–102, 104, 113–115, 139, 190
discrimination, 109, 115, 116, 123, 130, 132, 134, 140
discussion, 113, 122
disinformation, 79

displacement, 116, 135
display, 57, 84
disposal, 4, 13, 15, 47–50, 53–56, 59, 60, 134, 150, 154, 156, 159, 160, 162, 189, 196, 198
dissemination, 17, 18, 94, 95, 182, 196
distortion, 105
distribution, 4, 15, 17, 19, 21, 24, 44, 115, 132, 134, 158, 160–162, 165, 195, 197
diversity, 1, 7, 19, 21, 25, 26, 29, 102, 111, 113–116, 118–120, 122–129, 131, 135, 136, 164, 190, 198, 199
divide, 105
documentary, 6, 97, 138, 176, 183, 184
documentation, 146, 149
downplaying, 6, 182
drama, 112
dramatization, 105
drip, 65
driving, 4, 22, 43, 91, 102, 157, 176, 178, 182, 184, 192, 195
duplication, 166
dyeing, 82

e, 4, 13, 40, 50–54, 56, 57, 59, 60, 82, 83, 156, 159–163, 195, 198
Earth, 183, 184
echo, 21, 95, 105, 182
eco, 6, 9, 10, 25, 32, 36, 43, 49, 50, 60, 61, 66, 79–81, 83, 84, 152, 156, 161, 163, 165, 168, 175, 185, 186, 196
economy, 1, 3, 53, 56, 101, 166

Index

ecosystem, 46, 61, 68, 170, 196
edge, 82
editing, 1, 20, 31, 44, 103
education, 7, 36, 59, 83, 84, 86, 110, 111, 117, 121, 134, 136, 137, 139, 158, 168–170, 191, 197
effect, 18, 73, 192
effectiveness, 20, 34, 140, 169, 179, 181, 195
efficiency, 20, 22, 32, 34–37, 45, 46, 145, 146, 149, 158, 161
effort, 10, 25, 53, 98, 103, 125, 160, 164
electricity, 16, 22, 33, 36, 37, 44, 45, 60, 159
electronic, 4, 8, 9, 16, 21, 25, 48–51, 53–61, 156, 159, 160, 162, 163, 196
emergence, 18
emission, 18, 90
empathy, 1, 6, 27, 94, 97, 116, 118, 123, 124, 130–132, 135, 138, 140, 182
emphasis, 110, 114, 191
empower, 58, 75, 77, 83, 92, 93, 101, 117, 151, 157, 177, 181, 184, 186
empowerment, 91, 139
encoding, 46
end, 22, 45, 46, 51, 54
endowment, 177
energy, 1, 4, 6, 8–10, 13, 15, 16, 18, 21–24, 26, 31–37, 40–46, 58, 60, 71, 101, 105, 116, 133, 135, 145, 146, 149–166, 174, 175, 177, 185, 189, 191, 195, 196, 198
enforcement, 76, 83
engage, 9, 61, 73, 85, 93–95, 110, 113, 123, 125, 127, 129, 131, 132, 137, 139, 151, 157, 161, 165, 167, 169, 176, 179, 182, 185, 194
engagement, 7, 117, 131, 164, 168, 169, 171, 175, 177, 182, 186
enterprise, 53
entertainment, 16, 18, 53, 73, 121, 125, 135, 150
environment, 1, 3, 8, 13, 15, 24, 47, 48, 50, 54, 59, 61, 62, 64, 67, 68, 80, 81, 84, 85, 90, 102, 116, 117, 126, 131, 134, 135, 141, 147, 149, 150, 155, 156, 160, 175, 184, 185, 190, 191
environmentalism, 137–139
equality, 109, 110, 118
equipment, 8, 9, 20, 22, 24, 31–33, 35–37, 44, 64, 65, 71, 150–153, 155, 166, 174, 191
equity, 123, 134
equivalent, 22, 107
era, 170
erosion, 18
essence, 182
esteem, 135
ethnicity, 118, 127, 134
evidence, 5, 73, 79, 81, 84, 91, 95, 96, 101, 173, 196
evolution, 13, 15, 20, 189, 198
exaggeration, 105
examination, 127
example, 1, 4, 6, 7, 16, 19, 24, 26, 33, 46, 53, 57, 65, 66, 69–71,

79, 84, 90, 94, 96, 105,
110, 112, 116, 117, 120,
121, 130–135, 138–140,
146, 150, 156, 158, 159,
165, 166, 168, 169, 175,
183–186, 193, 195, 196
exchange, 96, 121, 174
exclusion, 123
execution, 62
exercise, 98, 172
existence, 118
expansion, 159
expense, 117
experience, 24, 116, 134, 166
expert, 5, 92
expertise, 20, 69, 123, 136, 157, 166, 174, 175, 179, 191
exploitation, 19
exploration, 112, 122, 173
exposure, 134
expression, 111
extraction, 15, 16, 60, 159, 160, 177, 185

face, 5, 8, 70, 75, 87, 114, 115, 134, 156, 178
fact, 7, 61, 80, 87, 88, 92, 94, 96, 102, 103, 141, 164
factor, 68
failure, 50
fairness, 97, 103, 107, 142
family, 132
farm, 150
farming, 133
fashion, 80, 117
favor, 98, 104
favoritism, 104
feasibility, 37
feature, 7, 60, 75, 81, 110

feedback, 111, 123, 125, 131, 164, 167
field, 14, 33, 132, 178, 190, 195–197
fight, 135, 184
fighting, 109, 113
film, 8, 9, 13, 16, 21, 31–37, 40, 43, 62–70, 74, 112, 120, 132, 149–151, 175, 177, 185, 189, 190, 195
filming, 1, 34, 64, 69, 151, 184, 185
filmmaking, 70, 151
filter, 21
finding, 3, 34, 114, 175, 195
flame, 54
flow, 65, 69, 71
focus, 9, 58, 61, 83, 92, 103, 104, 111, 113, 114, 136, 139, 146, 150, 165–168, 175, 197
following, 49, 72, 112, 127, 157, 168, 170
food, 19, 83, 133, 135
footage, 32
footprint, 1, 8, 9, 17, 22, 23, 31–35, 37–40, 43–46, 64, 70, 72, 73, 93, 146, 150, 153, 155, 156, 159, 163–165, 167, 185, 186, 189, 191, 193, 195, 199
force, 27, 98, 132, 184, 195
forefront, 3, 96, 111, 131, 195
form, 16, 79, 121
formation, 94
fossil, 32, 36, 37, 40, 94, 105, 154, 159, 177
Foster, 117, 198
foster, 58, 61, 86, 92, 94, 96, 102, 107, 114, 116, 119, 120, 124, 126, 130–132,

Index

136–138, 141, 167, 175, 196–198
foundation, 19
frame, 97
framework, 145, 147
framing, 6, 7, 94, 97, 98, 104, 139
freedom, 111
freshwater, 66
fringe, 107
front, 128
fuel, 32, 37, 94, 105, 177
fun, 61
functioning, 68, 107
fund, 177
funding, 72, 104, 149, 156, 174, 197
future, 1, 3, 5, 7, 10, 12, 14, 20, 37, 40, 43, 47, 50, 53, 56, 59–61, 64, 73, 77, 85, 86, 93, 96, 97, 100, 101, 105, 107, 116, 133, 135, 138, 142, 147, 149, 151, 152, 155, 158, 162, 164, 167, 169, 170, 178, 181, 184, 187, 190–192, 195, 197, 199

gain, 14, 69, 82, 112, 125, 136, 168, 174
gamification, 61
gap, 197
garment, 117
gas, 8, 15, 16, 34, 46, 60, 135, 153, 154, 163
gender, 102, 110, 111, 113, 115, 118, 127, 132, 134
generation, 18, 21, 25, 26, 50, 51, 53, 57, 117, 152, 154–156, 159, 161, 165, 166, 185, 196

George Miller, 69
goal, 1, 50, 67, 105, 114, 127, 146, 162, 165
government, 25, 174, 175, 196
gravity, 75
green, 14, 79–85, 134, 135, 145–149, 152–155, 161, 165, 190–192, 198
greenhouse, 8, 15, 16, 18, 34, 46, 60, 135, 153, 154, 163
greening, 150
greenwashing, 13, 59, 61, 79–93, 182, 190, 194, 198
Greta Thunberg, 7
grid, 32, 36, 44
ground, 114, 175, 177
growth, 2, 18, 190, 196
guidance, 69, 93, 130, 151, 157
guide, 2, 17, 59, 66, 106, 151

habitat, 15, 18, 183
hand, 22, 97, 102, 105, 113, 118, 123, 134, 151, 168
handling, 48
harassment, 110
hardware, 33, 57, 59
harm, 47, 76, 116, 132, 134, 163, 177
harvesting, 66, 72
health, 47–51, 53, 54, 56, 59, 134
healthcare, 134
heart, 1
heat, 31, 34
heating, 31, 36
heritage, 121
hiring, 111, 121, 123, 126, 138
history, 17, 19, 21, 132
Hollywood, 112
homogenization, 25

hope, 91, 190
hosting, 165, 167
hour, 22, 159
hub, 151
human, 26, 47, 48, 50, 54, 68, 133, 134, 183, 197
hurdle, 197

identification, 72
identity, 110, 113, 114, 117, 132
ideology, 104
illumination, 31
illusion, 82, 85
image, 43, 68, 79–83, 86, 156
imagery, 80, 82, 85, 94
imbalance, 68
imitation, 116
immediacy, 6
impact, 1, 3, 4, 6, 8, 9, 13–15, 17, 20–26, 35–38, 40, 43–47, 50, 52, 53, 56, 57, 59–61, 63, 68–75, 79–85, 91, 93, 95, 96, 98, 102, 104, 105, 112–115, 117, 118, 132, 134, 135, 142, 145–147, 149–152, 154, 155, 157–159, 161–164, 166–170, 175, 176, 178, 181, 184–186, 189, 191, 192, 195, 196, 198, 199
implement, 1, 3, 21, 35, 64, 72, 102, 152, 157, 161, 165, 166, 174
implementation, 36, 43, 59, 63, 71, 146, 149
importance, 5, 14, 19, 36, 37, 46, 47, 49, 50, 53, 54, 56, 58, 60, 64–66, 69–71, 73–75, 90, 111, 113–115, 117, 118, 123, 124, 130, 132, 133, 150, 151, 155, 170, 174–176, 178, 184, 190, 191, 197, 198
impression, 80, 86, 92
improvement, 3, 72, 85, 157, 197
incandescent, 31, 34, 36
incarceration, 97
incident, 90
inclusion, 29, 103, 125, 137
inclusivity, 1, 7, 29, 97, 111, 113, 114, 116, 118–120, 122, 124, 126, 127, 131, 134, 135, 137, 190, 198
income, 133, 134, 138
incorporation, 195
increase, 7, 24, 82, 95, 105, 119, 169, 174, 186
independence, 107
India, 66
individual, 3, 14, 21, 45, 53, 57, 92, 166, 190, 195, 199
industry, 1–5, 8, 10, 12–14, 18–20, 22–24, 29, 31–34, 36, 37, 40, 41, 43–46, 61–68, 70, 72–74, 90, 105, 111, 115, 117, 118, 120, 124, 131, 145–147, 149–152, 154–158, 161, 162, 164, 168–170, 174–176, 178, 179, 181, 185, 189–192, 194–198
inequality, 29, 97, 109, 111, 115, 117, 134, 140
influence, 2, 5–7, 13, 19, 25, 45, 60, 73, 75, 77, 82, 91, 93–97, 104, 111, 112, 115, 117, 123, 124, 127, 130, 139, 140, 151, 168, 170, 174,

Index

175, 177, 178, 182, 185, 187, 189–191, 194
information, 3, 5, 7, 18, 19, 26, 36, 57, 61, 75, 83, 91–98, 101–104, 130, 136, 139, 158, 167, 168, 170, 172, 173, 179, 182, 184, 186
infrastructure, 9, 21, 40, 44, 45, 72, 159, 165, 196
initiative, 56, 85, 133, 150, 151, 169
injustice, 27, 109, 134
ink, 15
innovation, 2, 5, 9, 12, 14, 33, 40, 58, 119, 157, 158, 181, 190, 195–197, 199
input, 123, 125, 175
insecurity, 135
insensitivity, 125
inspiration, 46, 70, 121, 151
instance, 1, 2, 44, 60, 80, 95, 97, 138, 140, 165–167, 185, 186, 196
integration, 9, 192
integrity, 9, 25, 26, 103, 126, 142, 181
interconnectedness, 5, 91, 114, 132, 133, 137, 191
interest, 26, 104, 172
intermittency, 43
internet, 8, 20, 22, 109, 139
interplay, 135
intersection, 19, 117, 132, 134, 197
intersectionality, 113, 115, 132, 133, 139
interview, 76
introduction, 13, 20
invention, 18
investment, 41, 156
involvement, 175

irrigation, 65, 68, 69, 71
isolation, 134
issue, 6, 13, 25, 49, 67–69, 75, 83, 95, 97, 107, 122, 125, 136, 165, 184, 190, 195

Jane Greenberg, 170
Janet Walker, 23
journalism, 6, 27, 76, 90, 95, 103, 104, 140, 141, 177
journey, 111, 132, 197, 199
justice, 1–3, 13, 14, 19, 20, 26, 27, 29, 95–98, 107, 109–118, 120, 122–124, 129, 132–142, 190, 191, 198

knowledge, 3, 14, 36, 58, 103, 116, 125, 138, 156, 157, 164, 166, 169, 170, 174, 179, 182, 197, 198

label, 163
labeling, 49, 161
labor, 19, 80, 82, 117
lack, 12, 53, 68, 81, 85, 121, 123, 126, 134, 136
landfill, 154
landscape, 5, 14, 17, 20, 40, 45, 46, 67, 122, 126, 130, 152, 158, 165, 167, 169, 170, 174, 176, 182, 184, 192, 195, 198
language, 81, 94, 104, 126
lead, 6, 25, 26, 34, 54, 59, 68, 72, 84, 85, 95, 105, 112, 116, 121, 123, 125, 126, 131, 149, 159, 163, 174, 175, 185, 193, 197
learning, 5, 67, 151, 173, 197, 199

led, 7, 17–21, 29, 35, 45, 111, 112, 133
legitimacy, 97, 174
leisure, 18
lens, 132, 134, 135, 137
Leonardo DiCaprio, 177
level, 129
leveraging, 29, 35, 118, 151, 178, 181–183, 186
life, 4, 75, 94, 132, 134, 160, 184
lifecycle, 45, 48
lifespan, 21, 50, 51, 57, 58, 60, 160, 162
lifestyle, 45, 167
light, 13, 26, 34, 51, 73, 76, 96, 97, 113, 130, 140, 147, 178, 182, 186
lighting, 9, 16, 24, 31–37, 44, 46, 150, 195
lip, 91
list, 178
literacy, 14, 59, 61, 83, 89–91, 94–96, 98, 102, 124, 136, 139, 161, 164, 167–173, 190, 194, 195, 198
literature, 95
loading, 166
location, 31, 32, 56, 62–64, 71, 134
longevity, 53, 57
look, 190
loop, 164
loss, 15, 18, 133
loyalty, 119

machinery, 18
mainstream, 107, 138
maintenance, 32, 65
majority, 25, 126
making, 14, 23, 50, 57, 59, 68, 75, 81–85, 88, 92, 95, 98, 117, 122, 128, 133–136, 153, 155, 159, 162, 169, 175, 185, 190, 191, 193, 194, 197
management, 9, 32, 35, 45, 46, 64, 65, 67–70, 72, 75, 77, 82, 138, 145, 146, 150–152, 154, 155, 184, 196
manipulation, 26, 95, 124
manner, 1, 22, 96, 104, 121, 122, 133, 141, 142, 145, 179, 186, 192
manual, 20
manufacturer, 56
manufacturing, 15–17, 60, 163
marginalization, 115, 125
mark, 145
market, 58, 80, 82, 156, 193
marketability, 146
marketing, 79, 84–86, 157
mass, 13, 17–20, 25, 50, 97, 189, 198
material, 18, 191
meaning, 121, 126
means, 1, 2, 18, 98, 123, 134, 136, 147, 162
measure, 83, 157, 169
measurement, 71
meat, 83
media, 1–10, 12–29, 31, 34–47, 59–64, 67–70, 72–77, 79–81, 83, 84, 86, 87, 89–98, 100–105, 107, 109, 111–132, 134–143, 145–147, 149–179, 181–187, 189–199
medium, 44

Index

meeting, 149
member, 193
mercury, 54, 59, 159
message, 177, 191
messaging, 79, 82
methane, 15
Michelle Newton-Francis, 122
Miguel, 132
milestone, 112
million, 22
mind, 67
mindset, 87, 91, 191
minimalism, 165
minority, 1
misinformation, 5, 26, 81, 92, 93, 95, 96, 170, 182
misinterpretation, 125
mismanagement, 68, 76
misrepresentation, 29, 121, 122, 124, 127, 130
mitigation, 10, 114
mode, 35, 37
model, 50
moisture, 65
momentum, 7, 17, 109
money, 57
monitoring, 71, 72
motion, 16
movement, 7, 29, 96, 109–112, 133, 140, 151, 190, 194
movie, 69, 159
mulch, 65
multimedia, 177
music, 18, 45, 121, 132, 179

Namibia, 69
narrative, 25, 94, 101, 114, 115, 137
nature, 38, 63, 80, 82, 85, 117, 118, 137, 178, 182, 184

necessity, 199
need, 3–5, 8, 10, 13, 17, 20, 21, 23, 28, 29, 35, 37, 40, 42, 57, 60, 66, 67, 77, 90, 94, 96, 102, 103, 107, 111, 114, 119, 121, 137, 159, 160, 165, 166, 174, 180, 184, 190, 191, 194, 197, 198
negligence, 25
Neha Yadav, 122
neighborhood, 133
network, 21, 22
news, 5, 6, 18, 26, 60, 73, 75, 98, 102–107, 115, 130, 135, 138, 141, 170, 177, 182, 184
newsroom, 102
Nicole Starosielski, 23
non, 1, 58, 66, 71, 145, 156, 158, 166
norm, 167
notion, 13
number, 19, 23

objective, 102, 104
objectivity, 100, 103, 107
obsolescence, 50–53, 189
offense, 125
offer, 40, 42, 43, 66, 147, 165, 174, 180, 182
office, 112
omission, 104, 140
one, 2, 3, 17, 22, 35, 46, 83, 104, 113, 115, 117, 121, 125, 134, 159
op, 136
operation, 16, 31, 33, 44, 81, 145, 167

opinion, 2, 5–8, 10, 13, 16, 19, 26, 27, 60, 73, 91, 93–96, 98, 103–105, 115, 118, 138–140, 168, 177, 178, 181, 184, 185, 189–191, 197
opportunity, 4, 8, 9, 118, 123, 131
oppression, 96, 117, 132, 134
optation, 114
optimization, 196
option, 40
order, 15, 71, 98, 102, 127, 137, 167, 174
organization, 85, 86, 94, 103, 138, 145, 176, 177
orientation, 118, 127
other, 2, 3, 18–20, 22, 25, 31, 33–36, 46, 50, 54, 56–58, 70, 76, 80, 81, 85, 92, 93, 97, 102, 105, 109, 111, 113, 118, 123, 126, 134, 160, 163, 168, 169, 172, 178, 185, 191, 197, 198
outcry, 182
outlet, 105, 138
output, 34
outreach, 177
overconsumption, 8
overload, 182
oversight, 83
overview, 13
ownership, 18, 19, 93, 104, 186

pace, 5
packaging, 9, 80, 82, 83, 160, 161, 196
panel, 136
paper, 15, 18, 19, 21, 25, 160, 185
part, 31, 44, 46, 53, 146, 151, 158

participate, 6, 93, 101, 185, 186
participation, 103
partner, 69
partnering, 25, 72, 161, 168
partnership, 64, 175–179
party, 83, 104
passage, 19
passion, 132
past, 16, 20
pathway, 43
peer, 172
people, 5, 6, 18, 57, 61, 75, 93, 94, 96, 109, 110, 118, 123, 130, 131, 133, 139, 177, 178, 182
perception, 80, 82, 85, 91, 94–96, 101
performance, 85, 157
period, 17–19, 23, 68
perpetuation, 26, 119
personalization, 21
perspective, 2, 19, 22, 102, 122, 133, 138, 159, 198
petroleum, 16
phase, 44, 46, 69
phenomenon, 81, 112
phone, 53, 57
picture, 103
pillar, 2
place, 17, 67, 103
plan, 67, 74, 150
planet, 1, 8, 50, 53, 56, 116, 177, 199
planning, 3, 41, 71
plastic, 6, 9, 25, 80, 83, 150, 160, 185
platform, 19, 24, 61, 95, 97, 98, 112, 118, 130, 135–137, 151, 165–167, 176–178, 182, 184, 186

Index

play, 4–6, 9, 10, 14, 27, 36, 37, 43, 58, 60, 64, 73, 75, 76, 81–83, 91–93, 96, 98, 106, 113, 115, 118, 130, 131, 138, 139, 142, 145, 147, 157, 159–161, 167, 168, 175, 178, 185, 186, 190–192, 195, 199
playback, 46
playbook, 151
point, 19
polarization, 95, 102
police, 28, 96, 140
policy, 5, 7, 12, 29, 53, 73, 133, 138, 140, 161, 162, 177, 182, 191, 194, 195
pollution, 1, 4–6, 8, 15, 16, 18, 19, 59, 68, 75, 76, 116, 134, 146, 182, 183, 185
pool, 3, 191
pooling, 179
pop, 166
popularity, 8, 57, 159, 176
population, 68, 118
portion, 22, 24, 37
portrayal, 5, 7, 116, 119, 121, 130
position, 73, 174
positivity, 111
post, 31, 33, 44, 62, 64, 150
potential, 7, 10, 17, 21, 26, 27, 29, 33, 37, 46, 60, 67, 74, 94, 95, 97, 111, 114, 117, 131, 132, 142, 147, 149, 150, 156, 158, 167, 168, 172, 174–176, 180–182, 184, 196
poverty, 134
power, 5–10, 13, 18, 19, 22, 24, 26, 27, 29, 31–33, 35–37, 40, 43–46, 71, 73, 88, 91, 93, 95–97, 109, 113, 118, 121, 124, 126, 127, 130, 131, 133, 135, 138–140, 143, 150, 154, 159, 163, 165, 175, 176, 178, 179, 181, 182, 184, 185, 191, 195, 198
practice, 13, 22, 45, 79–81, 85, 86, 171, 190
precipitation, 68
prejudice, 104, 123, 130, 131
presence, 47, 48, 50, 182
present, 5, 7, 20, 50, 93, 98, 100, 103, 125, 182
presentation, 34, 104
preservation, 1, 10, 156, 162, 178, 186
press, 17, 18, 86
pressure, 19, 76, 111
prevalence, 125
prevention, 146
preview, 13
print, 15, 19, 24, 25, 182
printing, 4, 15, 17–19, 25
privacy, 5
privilege, 109
problem, 6, 52, 75, 156, 159, 162
process, 3, 5, 15, 20–22, 24, 35, 37, 64, 67, 69, 72, 82, 87, 94, 111, 126, 127, 138, 140, 145, 146, 149–151, 153, 170, 171, 173
processing, 16, 33, 35, 37, 45, 159
procurement, 32
producer, 50
product, 51, 79–84, 86, 196
production, 1–4, 8–10, 13–21, 23–25, 31–38, 40, 42–44,

46–48, 50, 58–60, 62–74,
80, 82, 111, 112, 116, 117,
123–128, 138, 145–162,
164–166, 168, 169, 174,
175, 185, 186, 189–191,
195, 196, 198
profession, 106
professional, 20, 34, 126, 141
profit, 58, 93, 121, 125, 136, 145,
166, 175, 182
profitability, 82
program, 49, 50, 56, 151, 169
programming, 7, 25
progress, 64, 85, 105, 111, 114, 140,
152, 156, 157, 195, 197
project, 34, 67, 68, 145, 150
proliferation, 20, 21, 25, 45
promotion, 143, 163, 172, 176, 192
prop, 68
protection, 134, 184
proximity, 134
pseudoscience, 172
psychology, 197
public, 2, 3, 5–8, 10, 12, 13, 16, 18,
19, 26, 27, 29, 36, 57, 60,
61, 68, 73–76, 79, 81–83,
85, 91–98, 100–107, 115,
118, 121, 123, 124,
138–141, 143, 168,
174–178, 181, 182, 184,
185, 189–191, 197
pulp, 18
purchase, 50, 57
purchasing, 36, 45, 82, 88, 89, 146
pursuit, 115, 134
push, 117

quality, 9, 20, 22, 32, 34, 36, 45, 46,
65, 67, 119, 126, 134, 150,
159, 165, 195
quantity, 165
question, 92, 124, 136, 172
quo, 7, 92, 136, 140, 199

race, 110, 113, 115, 118, 127, 132,
134
racism, 96, 97, 109, 140
radio, 16, 24, 26, 75, 139, 182
rain, 66
rainforest, 178
rainwater, 66, 71, 72, 150
range, 20, 23, 44, 51, 76, 103, 123,
125, 130, 134, 137, 146
rationing, 68
Rauno K. Parrila, 122
reach, 26, 75, 91, 139, 151, 168,
177–179, 182, 186
readership, 105
reality, 4, 81, 84, 93, 118
realm, 57, 59, 122, 151
recap, 14
recognition, 121, 123, 134, 135, 149,
151, 157
recommendation, 21
recycle, 56, 67, 160, 163
recycling, 9, 21, 25, 49, 50, 53–56,
58, 60, 64, 69, 71, 80, 150,
154, 156, 160, 161, 163,
168, 185, 196
reduction, 9, 21, 58, 146, 149, 158
reflection, 122
reform, 28
refurbishing, 57
refurbishment, 57, 59
regard, 121
region, 68, 70
regulation, 4, 5, 83, 84
reinforcement, 21

Index 217

relation, 81
relationship, 134, 177, 194
release, 57
relevance, 119, 120, 197
reliability, 103, 164, 173
reliance, 21, 32, 36, 37, 44, 72, 166, 177
rendering, 33
repair, 57, 58, 60
repairability, 53, 58, 196
replacement, 21, 57
report, 94, 103, 104, 141
reporting, 26, 27, 29, 76, 81, 83, 94, 97, 100–107, 140–143, 149, 157, 172, 182, 185, 191
representation, 25, 26, 29, 94, 95, 98, 104, 111–113, 115, 116, 118–124, 127–131, 135–137, 139, 141, 175, 190, 198
reputation, 68, 72, 82, 146, 149, 156, 158
research, 14, 34, 40, 74, 76, 87, 88, 91, 92, 104, 125, 130, 157, 161, 174, 184, 190, 195–197, 199
resistance, 12
resolution, 22
resource, 4, 8–10, 19, 36, 62, 64, 70, 117, 138, 149, 150, 152, 153, 158–162, 165, 166, 185, 196
respect, 103, 116, 121, 125, 126, 131, 136
response, 110
responsibility, 1, 3, 6–8, 10, 34, 50, 56, 60, 64, 73, 75, 77, 82, 86, 92, 93, 97, 98, 104–107, 114, 130, 135, 141, 166, 167, 186, 190, 191, 199
restoration, 72
result, 2, 9, 21, 25, 68, 71, 72, 111, 116, 125, 134
return, 56
reusability, 9, 58
reuse, 67, 71, 150
revenue, 2, 166, 196
review, 103
revolution, 13
richness, 116, 131
right, 133, 134
rise, 8, 17–20, 35, 50, 94, 109, 189, 198
role, 2, 4–10, 13, 14, 18–20, 26, 27, 29, 34, 36, 37, 43, 58–62, 64, 73, 75–77, 81–83, 89, 91–93, 95–98, 102, 104, 106, 107, 110, 113–115, 118, 121, 122, 124, 130–132, 135, 137–139, 142, 143, 145, 147, 152, 157, 159–161, 163, 167, 168, 175, 178, 181, 184–187, 189–192, 195, 197, 199
root, 113, 134
run, 2, 31

salience, 95
sanitation, 64
saving, 9, 24, 32, 34–37, 45, 46, 64, 66, 67, 69, 72–75, 150, 163
scale, 17, 18, 37, 92, 177, 199
scandal, 90

scarcity, 13, 62, 67–70, 72, 73, 75, 190
scenario, 56
scheduling, 66, 71
scouting, 62, 64, 69
screen, 4, 22, 24, 45, 128, 162, 176
scrutiny, 68, 90, 103
section, 5, 8, 10, 17, 20, 24, 26, 31, 34, 37, 43, 47, 53, 62, 65, 67, 75, 84, 86, 91, 93, 96, 98, 115, 118, 122, 124, 130, 134, 147, 149, 152, 155, 158, 165, 167, 170, 174, 176–178, 181, 184, 192, 195, 197
sector, 67, 73, 156
selection, 104
self, 81, 83, 135
sensationalism, 7, 91, 103, 104, 114, 140
sense, 6, 77, 84, 91–94, 135, 167, 186
sensitivity, 116, 118, 121, 122, 124–126, 128–131, 136
separation, 150
series, 138, 150, 176, 183, 184
server, 22, 196
service, 81, 84, 91
set, 8, 10, 16, 32, 62–65, 68–71, 96, 105, 146, 150, 185
setting, 6, 7, 94, 96, 98, 140, 146, 190
setup, 66, 71
severity, 75
sexism, 109
sexuality, 110, 113, 132
shape, 5, 6, 10, 13, 60, 94, 96, 97, 118, 123, 124, 130, 131, 137, 139, 140, 152, 162, 164, 181, 185, 191, 195, 198
share, 3, 7, 20, 58, 82, 93, 97, 103, 112, 118, 123, 134, 163, 164, 166, 168, 177, 182, 186
sharing, 23, 36, 58, 73, 95, 96, 102, 121, 125, 138, 151, 157, 163, 164, 166, 174, 179, 196, 199
shift, 3, 4, 17, 21, 23, 31, 57, 111, 169, 191, 192, 196
shoot, 150
shooting, 31, 66, 68, 71
show, 150, 168
significance, 13, 14, 90, 94, 121, 125, 147, 177, 195
silver, 16
site, 32, 36, 37, 66, 146
situation, 172
size, 32
skepticism, 105
skill, 182, 197
sleep, 35, 37
smartphone, 20, 56
society, 1–3, 5, 17, 37, 61, 85, 91, 96, 98, 102, 104, 105, 107, 109–111, 113, 115, 116, 118–120, 122, 127, 130–132, 134–137, 142, 149, 162, 168, 170, 173, 187, 189–191, 194, 197–199
socio, 118
sociology, 197
software, 20, 33, 35, 44, 57–59, 166
soil, 18, 159
solar, 9, 32, 33, 36, 37, 40, 43, 44, 60, 150, 154, 165, 195

Index

solution, 8, 24, 72
sound, 9, 31
source, 36, 57–59, 71, 121, 166, 172
sourcing, 60, 72, 80, 83, 158
space, 43, 97, 103, 114
Spain, 22
spark, 26, 97, 178
speech, 111
spread, 58, 96, 109
stability, 2
staff, 37, 69, 131, 136
standpoint, 21
status, 7, 92, 115, 118, 134–136, 140, 199
steam, 18
step, 53, 87, 127, 154, 198
stewardship, 14, 25, 26, 151, 152, 181, 184–187
stock, 16
storage, 20, 35, 158, 165, 196
story, 6, 132
storyboard, 34
storytelling, 6, 7, 17, 91, 93, 94, 112, 125, 126, 128, 129, 131, 137, 138, 140, 151, 176, 182–185, 191
strain, 66, 72, 160
strategy, 50, 51, 84, 102, 123, 138, 163
stream, 166
streaming, 8, 9, 21–23, 43, 45, 46, 70, 158, 159, 161, 162, 196
strike, 2, 4, 9, 67, 111, 117
structure, 13
struggle, 136
studio, 32, 33
study, 36, 37, 70, 107
subsection, 127
substance, 103

success, 6, 60, 73, 111, 112, 151, 168, 184
suit, 58, 185
sulfur, 18
summary, 12, 46
sun, 37
supply, 10, 12, 53, 58, 68, 72, 82, 83, 117
support, 2, 6, 10, 12, 19, 27, 29, 58, 73, 79, 81, 84, 92, 95, 97, 101, 105, 138, 140, 161, 163, 166, 167, 177, 178, 182, 183, 185, 186, 193, 199
suppression, 25
surface, 129
surge, 18, 21
sustainability, 1–10, 13, 14, 19–26, 33, 34, 36, 37, 39, 40, 42, 45, 46, 50, 53, 58–61, 64, 70, 79–89, 91–102, 105, 107, 111, 113–118, 120, 123, 124, 132, 133, 135, 138, 145–147, 149–152, 156–158, 161–168, 170, 174–176, 178, 181, 184, 185, 189–191, 193–199
symbolism, 82, 125
system, 2, 46, 97, 140

tactic, 82
Taji Ameen, 122
tale, 90
talent, 128
tap, 82, 119
target, 94, 126
targeting, 51, 74
task, 34, 111, 115, 126, 175
tax, 4, 157, 161

team, 63, 64, 69, 150
tech, 20
technique, 84, 85
technology, 10, 13, 17, 19–24, 37, 40, 172, 173, 189, 191, 192, 195–198
telegraph, 17, 18
television, 5, 8, 9, 13, 16, 24, 26, 31–34, 40, 43, 44, 62, 64–68, 70, 74, 75, 97, 110, 122, 139, 149–151, 168, 182, 185, 189, 190
tendency, 98, 105
term, 1–3, 40, 60, 91, 107, 113, 121, 156, 195
textile, 117
the New Black", 110
the United States, 19
theater, 18
theory, 94, 132
thinking, 2, 3, 24, 59, 61, 84, 90, 91, 94, 95, 98, 103, 124, 139, 164, 170–173, 190, 194, 198
thought, 14, 122
Thunberg, 7
timber, 15
time, 2–4, 20, 22, 24, 45, 125, 146, 162, 199
today, 8, 13, 34, 53, 91, 104, 118, 124, 139, 145, 158, 181
Tokenism, 85
tokenism, 136, 137
tool, 7, 26, 98, 125, 139, 142, 146, 168, 176, 181, 185
topic, 24, 43, 94, 122, 173
tourism, 186
trade, 117
traffic, 22

training, 69, 71, 102, 111, 126, 131, 157, 174, 197
transformation, 143
transition, 37, 43, 160, 177
translation, 126
transmission, 18, 22, 24, 44, 45
transparency, 25, 61, 76, 83–86, 90, 91, 102, 117, 141, 166
transphobia, 109
transport, 175
transportation, 8, 9, 15, 17, 21, 32, 134, 163, 168, 185
travel, 186
treatment, 69, 111, 117
trend, 24
trivialization, 114
troubleshooting, 58
trust, 84, 85, 104, 105, 141, 174
turn, 71, 96, 163
turning, 19, 35, 65, 121

under, 68
underreporting, 25, 104
underrepresentation, 29, 127
understanding, 1, 2, 5, 14, 24, 26, 61, 67, 71, 95, 96, 98, 102, 105, 107, 112, 114–116, 118, 120, 121, 123–126, 130–133, 136, 137, 139, 140, 149, 168, 170, 190, 196, 198
unit, 57
up, 15, 20, 51, 54, 150, 177, 186, 192
upgradability, 196
upgrade, 36, 57, 60
upgrading, 21, 32, 57, 160
urgency, 5, 94, 105, 177, 184

Index 221

usage, 24, 25, 35, 45, 46, 64–67, 69, 71–73, 156, 163, 164, 185
use, 1, 4, 8, 15, 16, 18, 20–22, 32, 35, 37, 44, 45, 56, 62, 64, 65, 69, 74, 79–86, 94, 97, 104, 113, 121, 145, 146, 150, 152, 160, 161, 163, 165, 166, 168, 178, 184, 187, 195, 196
user, 20, 22, 95, 166, 167
utility, 156
utilization, 22, 196

vague, 81, 84
value, 87, 125, 174, 184, 186, 197
variation, 23
variety, 47, 121, 126
vegetation, 69
ventilation, 24, 32
verification, 81, 83, 84, 86, 96, 149, 173
viability, 1, 2, 40, 112, 195
video, 8, 22, 23, 25, 43, 45, 46, 151, 159
view, 141, 146, 172
viewership, 105, 119
viewing, 8, 21–23
virtualization, 165
vision, 67
visual, 34, 64, 82, 185
voice, 19, 25, 26, 92, 109, 140
volunteer, 193
vulnerability, 116

washing, 71
wastage, 68, 71
waste, 4, 8, 9, 13, 15, 21, 25, 26, 35, 40, 48–54, 56–60, 83, 117, 134, 145, 146, 149–156, 158–163, 165, 166, 175, 185, 186, 189, 191, 195, 196, 198
wastewater, 66, 71
watchdog, 83, 84
watching, 23
water, 13, 16, 62–77, 80, 134, 145, 146, 150, 156, 159, 160, 162, 190, 196, 198
way, 5, 6, 18, 20, 61, 65, 91, 94, 97, 98, 105, 112, 116, 120, 136, 139, 149, 161, 163, 168, 193, 196
weather, 68, 133, 135
website, 170, 172, 177
week, 23, 24
well, 3, 91, 100, 102, 105, 110, 114, 117, 126, 138, 139, 164, 179
whole, 120, 151, 197
wildlife, 68, 85, 183
wind, 9, 32, 36, 40, 43, 154, 165
window, 132
wire, 18
wisdom, 116
work, 7, 20, 22, 23, 53, 58, 59, 101–103, 109, 114, 116, 121, 124, 126, 133, 135, 138, 176, 186, 187, 191, 193, 197
workforce, 125
working, 3, 19, 46, 53, 72, 97, 110, 117, 136, 138, 191
world, 8, 13, 34, 40, 46, 67, 91, 93, 104, 118, 119, 124, 130, 132, 137, 139, 143, 145, 149, 152, 164, 172, 176–178, 181, 191, 192, 197, 199

youth, 7, 179

Milton Keynes UK
Ingram Content Group UK Ltd.
UKHW022349200824
447185UK00013B/509